Also by Natasha Frazier

The Life Your Spirit Craves

The Life Your Spirit Craves for Mommies

Not Without You Prayer Journal

How Long Are You Going to Wait?

Love, Lies & Consequences

Through Thick & Thin: Love, Lies & Consequences Book 2

Shattered Vows: Love, Lies & Consequences Book 3

Out of the Shadows: Love, Lies & Consequences Book 4

Kairos: The Perfect Time for Love

Thank you for your support!

Natasha

3/2023

Not Without You:
365 Days in the Lord's Presence

For Order Information, please visit: www.natashafrazier.com

From the author

This book was written during my personal prayer and study time. My prayer is that you will grow in God during the next year and become more of who He has called you to be. As you set out on this journey, there will be many obstacles along the way; however, rest assured that God is always with you and is the source for everything that you need to overcome those obstacles.

Before you begin reading this book, know that you may start on any day of the week in any month of the year. The seventh day of each week is a *Day of Reflection.* On this day, you should meditate on the scripture reading, make note of what the Holy Spirit is speaking to you and apply that lesson to your life.

Remember that above all, God desires you! Choose to submit to His perfect will, love Him and love others in the way that He desires. May this book encourage you and help guide you along your spiritual journey for the next 365 days.

Peace and blessings to you!

Not Without You

Strength and Courage

"Have I not commanded you? Be strong and courageous. Do not be afraid; do not be discouraged, for the LORD your God will be with you wherever you go." (Joshua 1:9 NIV)

If you read the entire chapter, you will find that Joshua was commanded to *"be strong and courageous"* four times! Because of the repetition, this command must have been very significant. The Lord knew that Joshua would face many obstacles when he succeeded Moses as leader of Israel to lead the Israelites into the Promised Land.

Just as the Lord knew what Joshua would experience, the Lord also knows what you will encounter throughout your life. His character has not changed. He promised that He would never leave nor forsake you. Through your life's journey, know that the Lord is right there with you and that He commands you to not be afraid but to be strong and courageous while trusting in Him.

Be encouraged to know that God loves you and His presence is always with you.

Prayer for Today: Lord, let me not forget that Your presence is always with me. Give me the strength to learn to trust and depend on Your promises and Your Word, for they are guidance for my life. In Jesus' name, Amen.

Additional Scripture reading: Joshua 1; Deuteronomy 31:6

Not Without You

In His Presence

Then Moses said, "If you don't personally go with us, don't make us leave this place. How will anyone know that you look favorably on me—on me and on your people—if you don't go with us? For your presence among us sets your people and me apart from all other people on the earth." (Exodus 33:15-16 NLT)

Oftentimes when we're given an assignment to complete, we become anxious and worry. We become concerned about who will support us, or distract us or about the many obstacles that will come our way. Not completing it in time. Lacking what we need. Many obstacles trip us into habitual worry rather than diligence and faith.

As you meditate on today's Scripture, focus on the fact that God planted the vision in you and He will see it through to completion. God is going with you! Don't focus on what people around you may be thinking about you but focus on what God thinks. He thought enough of you to choose you. Know that God has planted a seed within you and He wants to see the fruit.

Be sure to stay in His presence seeking His will and direction. His presence sets you apart from everyone else. Staying in His presence will bring about His purpose in you.

Prayer for Today: Lord, I don't want to be anywhere where Your presence is not! Help me to focus on You and what You have called me to do. Let me not be concerned about what others think but with what You think. I want to walk in Your will. In Jesus' name, Amen.

Additional Scripture reading: Exodus 33 and Psalm 32:8

Day 2

Not Without You

I'm Listening

And the LORD came and called as before, "Samuel! Samuel!"

And Samuel replied, "Speak, your servant is listening."

(1 Samuel 3:10 NLT)

If you read the previous verses, you will see that Samuel has just discerned God's voice. Once he did, he made himself available to God to receive the message that God was giving him.

Quite often in our lives, we're so busy with tons of things that we don't even set aside time to hear what God is saying to us. We often pray but we rarely make time to listen.

If you desire a more intimate and meaningful relationship with your Savior, I encourage you to set aside a specific time in your day where you can commune with God uninterrupted: no TV, no spouse, no kids, no cell phone, no Internet or anything else that will distract you. Spend time reading the Word of God; this is how you hear from Him - through His word. Make yourself available to Him. I often find that it is those times when I'm by myself that I receive all of the inspiration, direction and encouragement I need from God. It is in those quiet moments that I receive my fill of Him.

God is waiting for you to make yourself available and say, "Speak Lord, I'm listening."

Prayer for Today: Lord, help me to remove distractions to focus on You. I need to hear from You and spend time in Your presence. Let me not neglect this precious time with You. In Jesus' name, Amen.

Additional Scripture reading: 1 Samuel 3:1-14

Window to Your Soul

"Guard your heart above all else, for it determines the course of your life." (Proverbs 4:23 NLT)

It is important to monitor what you allow in your heart, because what is in your heart, determines what comes out of your mouth. Not only this, but what's in your heart also determines the direction of your life.

Be mindful of the things that you watch, read and listen to. These things manifest into thoughts and thoughts manifest into actions.

Focus on what is pure and holy. See Philippians 4:8-9.

Our eyes and ears are the windows to our soul, and what we allow in them determines what we allow into our hearts. Once these things are in our hearts, they become a part of us. Luke 6:45 confirms that out of the heart flows the issues of life. Proverbs 23:7 (NJKV) further confirms that as a man thinks in his heart, so is he.

Job spoke of making a covenant with his eyes (Job 31:1) to keep him from sinning. You too, can make a covenant with your eyes (and ears) so that you may be able to guard your heart from those things that are unlike Christ.

Prayer for Today: Lord, help me to focus on that which pleases You so that I may hear Your voice and continue to walk in Your will. Teach me to guard my heart by being selective about what I allow to come in through my eyes and ears. In Jesus' name, Amen.

Additional Scripture reading: Philippians 4:8-9 and Luke 6:45

Not Without You

Shift your thoughts

I will thank the Lord because he is just; I will sing praise to the name of the Lord Most High. (Psalm 7:17 NLT)

Regardless of how things are going in your life, it is always a good thing to have praise in your heart. Praising God often takes our minds off our circumstances and places our focus upon Him. God desires that we keep our focus on Him anyway.

Give thanks to God today just for being who He is. He is merciful, full of kindness, love and grace. Keep a song of praise on your heart for those times when life seems to be too heavy and you're overwhelmed with burdens.

I challenge you to shift your focus from your circumstances to your God -- who already knows what your circumstances are but desires more of you.

Prayer for Today: In the name of Jesus, Lord I come to You with praise on my lips and in my heart. Remind me daily to keep my focus on You and Your will for my life that I may walk along the path that You have predestined for me. May my praise be a sweet sound unto You. Amen.

Additional Scripture reading: Psalm 34 and Psalm 9.

Victory belongs to you

His companion answered, "Your dream can mean only one thing—God has given Gideon son of Joash, the Israelite, victory over Midian and all its allies!" (Judges 7:14 NLT)

Fact: God has a plan for you.

Fact: God will give you guidance regarding this plan.

Fact: You have been given the victory and the enemy knows that you have been given the victory!

When I studied this passage, I did a little dance afterwards. Why? I think there is something very important about this story. You see, even though God had already told Gideon that He would give him victory, He also allowed Gideon to receive confirmation. The awesome part is that the confirmation came from the enemy's camp. Wow! Life lesson: The enemy will fight you even though he knows that he will lose the battle. Therefore, you cannot become discouraged.

Although the voice of the enemy that you hear may not be as positive as Gideon's confirmation, it is confirmation nonetheless. The voices of negativity, discouragement and defeat are not from God and are simply designed to get you off track. Don't fall for it! Don't lose focus!

All you have to do is be obedient to what you have been called to do. Fight! You already have the victory and the enemy knows it. It's about time that you know it (and act like it) as well.

Prayer for Today: Lord, Thank You for the victory that You have given me. Thank You for giving me confirmation to keep me on track. Help me to always discern Your voice and follow it. In Jesus' name, Amen. *Additional Scripture reading*: Judges 7 and Romans 8.

~Day of Reflection~

Devoted to God

Read: 1 Chronicles 28:9 and Psalm 5

Meditate: Have I been devoted to God in prayer and deeds?

Apply: What will I do today that will help me become a more devoted follower of Christ?

In-Between

The Lord heard Elijah's prayer, and the life of the child returned, and he revived! (1 Kings 17:22 NLT)

In 1 Kings 17:8-24, the widow and her son had very little to eat and Elijah went to her asking for food. She explained to Elijah that she didn't have any food but only a little flour and oil to make the last meal for her and her son. Afterwards they were going to die for lack of food. Then Elijah gave her instructions from the Lord (v. 13-14) to not be afraid but to use what she had to prepare a meal for her and her son – but to feed him first! As a mother, my initial thought would have been "I have to feed my child first!" I don't know what her thoughts were but the Bible says that she did as she was told (v.15).

Because of her obedience, she was blessed!! She received exactly what was promised to her (v. 16). All was well until her son became sick and died (v.17). Lord, You have been faithful and have done just as You said. Now, You're taking my son away? Those were her thoughts. She questioned what Elijah did to her and why he came there (v.18).

But the Lord is faithful and gave restoration. Although her son died, Elijah took him upstairs to pray for him (v.21). The Lord heard his prayer and returned the child's life back to him (v. 22) Praise God!

While you're waiting on God to restore you, whether in this life or the next, just remember that He is faithful! Continue to seek Him in all that you do!

Prayer for Today: Lord, give me wisdom and understanding to trust You in the "in-between." Help me to remain faithful and steadfast to Your word regardless of what's going on in my life. In Jesus' name, Amen.

Additional Scripture reading: 1 Kings 17:8-24.

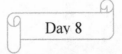

Priority

"You must worship no other gods, for the Lord, whose very name is Jealous, is a God who is jealous about his relationship with you." (Exodus 34:14 NLT)

As we enter into a New Year or any new beginning with resolutions, goals, plans, purpose and fresh desires, we must remember not to forsake our time alone with God. (Many people include rebuilding their relationship with God or growing closer to Him as part of their "change" for the New Year or other life goals) Although we attend church services, watch TV sermons, listen to gospel music in our homes, cars and cubicles, none of these things can take the place of genuine time spent alone with God.

While God wants us to have success and the desires of our hearts, He wants us to be in relationship with Him more than anything.

Think about your earthly relationships. How do you maintain them? By spending time with your loved ones, right? That is exactly what we must do with our Heavenly Father. Set aside time to pray each day. Set aside time to study God's Word. A friend recently mentioned to me that midnight was the best time for her to study. Each one of us must decide what is best for us and make spending time with God a priority. When are you least distracted?

So today, I encourage you to examine your *busy* schedule: Where are you spending your time? When are you spending meaningful time with God? Are you making your relationship with Him a priority?

Remember that God loves you and wants the best for you every year, not just this year! God's greatest desire is you getting to know Him. So as you chase after your dreams, be sure to always chase after the Dream Giver!

Prayer for Today: Lord, thank You for Your faithfulness. Give me the mindset to always chase after You. Help me clear my schedule to make time for You. Show me areas where I am wasting my time and can devote that time to You. In Jesus' name, Amen. *Additional Scripture reading*: Psalm 37:4 and Exodus 34

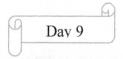

Day 9

The Company you keep

Do not be misled: "Bad company corrupts good character."
(1 Corinthians 15:33)

Have you ever found yourself saying a new word? It doesn't have to be a bad word but just a new word that you've picked up from someone else. You've heard the word so many times from this person that it has become a part of your speech.

Have you ever found yourself doing things you haven't done before? Have you found yourself in places you have never gone? Have places that once made you uncomfortable become comfortable? Have you really ever been in a place and thought, *"How did I get here?"*

Once you're around something or someone for a long time, you become like that thing or person. Whether good or bad, you're going to change. I would encourage you today to make sure that you're exposing your mind and spirit to the right things and people. . . people who are going to encourage you to grow and help you proceed in the right direction. Do not be fooled to think that the ways of those you are with most won't become a part of you, because they will. See our key verse.

Prayer for Today: Lord, give me wisdom in assessing the company that I keep. Let me not keep the company of those who will pull me away from You as I only desire to be more like You. In Jesus' name, Amen.

Additional Scripture reading: Proverbs 9:10-12 and Proverbs 11: 1-11.

Live in Expectancy

Finally the seventh time, his servant told him, "I saw a little cloud about the size of a man's hand rising from the sea."(1 Kings 18:44 NLT)

In the earlier verses, Elijah began to pray for rain. After he prayed, he sent his servant to look out toward the sea to see if he saw any rain coming. The Bible tells us that he did this seven times.

It is very important to be persistent and steadfast in our faith. When you have an unwavering mindset, it properly positions you to receive all that God has promised and helps build your faith. You may have to keep praying for what you desire; but remember that the Bible tells us in Matthew 7 to keep on praying, knocking and seeking God.

Keep an attitude of expectancy like Elijah when he prayed for rain. Although you may not see or receive it the first time, do not give up. Keep praying. Keep your vision sharp. Believe God. If He said it, it's going to happen.

Prayer for Today: In the name of Jesus, Lord I ask that You help me to remain steadfast in my faith even when it seems that it is taking much longer to receive that which I've been asking for. Strengthen me to trust in You without doubt. In Jesus' name, Amen.

Additional Scripture reading: 1 Kings 18:1 and 41-46; Matthew 7:7-8.

Predetermined Purpose

"And why have I called you for this work? Why did I call you by name when you did not know me? It is for the sake of Jacob my servant, Israel my chosen one." (Isaiah 45:4 NLT)

In Isaiah 45, the passage teaches us that Cyrus was chosen by the Lord to restore his city and free the Lord's people. Cyrus was chosen before he even knew the Lord (v.4). This confirms that our purpose –our destiny– is determined way before we meet the Lord, decide to follow Him and give our lives over to His purpose.

Verse 2 tells how the Lord will go before Cyrus to do His part in assisting Cyrus to accomplish the purpose God had predetermined. If you read further, the Bible teaches us that we should not question or argue with the Lord about why we have been given the assignments in which He purposed for us. The Lord himself will guide our actions (v. 12) and that is assurance enough. You should know that oftentimes, it may not be revealed to you as to why the Lord has chosen you for a specific task especially when the task doesn't line up with your background or education. When this is the case, you have to truly rely on God's power and guidance in order to accomplish what He has called you to accomplish. The scripture reveals that God will go before you; you just have to follow. Remember that your assignments are meant to give God glory and build up His people.

Prayer for Today: Lord, thank You for Your greatness and Your sovereignty. Thank You for Your purpose for my life. Even before I came to know You, You already had a plan for me. I seek You today so that You may speak to my heart. I want to know You more and what You have purposed for me. Thank You for choosing me. Help me to serve You with joy and boldness. In Jesus' name, Amen.

Additional Scripture reading: Isaiah 45:1-13

Getting to know God on another level

Then a certain prophet came to see King Ahab of Israel and told him, "This is what the LORD says: Do you see all these enemy forces? Today I will hand them all over to you. Then you will know that I am the LORD." (1 Kings 20:13 NLT)

Many times in life (as in our key verse), God does things or allows certain things to happen in our lives so that we will know who He is in all of His power. It is not to hurt or destroy our spirit or faith in Him. The victory isn't about us but about Him.

We may experience loss, (jobs, friends, finances, family, etc.) which oftentimes leaves heartache, pain and brokenness. However, there is always restoration; God heals the hurt caused by these experiences and our relationship with Him is strengthened. As a result of loss situations, we become better acquainted with God and develop a level of faith and intimacy like never before. I even went through a period where I was laid off and didn't find employment for six months. In the midst of that, I had to learn to trust God and what He was doing in me. It was during that time that my faith was strengthened and I came to know Him better.

Be confident in knowing that sometimes, things happen because God desires that you serve Him wholeheartedly. Sometimes things happen so that you will experience God in a fresh, new way. He desires that you praise Him. Most importantly, God desires you!

Prayer for Today: Lord God, I know that You desire more of me. Help me to cling to You and Your Word. I desire to be more like You so mold me into who You have called me to be. In Jesus' name, Amen.

Additional Scripture reading: 1 Kings 20:13-21 and 28-30.

~Day of Reflection~

Attitude

Read: Genesis 4:6-7; Numbers 14:1-4; Habakkuk 3:17-19

Meditate: Have I allowed my attitude to destroy relationships? Has my attitude led to poor decision making?

Apply: What can I do today that will help me maintain a positive attitude and loving spirit?

Not Without You

Excuses lead to destruction

The prophet said to him, "This is what the Lord says: Because you have spared the man I said must be destroyed, now you must die in his place, and your people will die instead of his people." (1 Kings 20:42 NLT)

When you do not destroy (get rid of) the sin in your life, the sin will destroy you.

You must be careful to do exactly what you have been called to do and not try to preserve your "favorite" sin(s). It is a lot easier to sin less in some areas as opposed to others. Sins that give you the greatest pleasure are the ones that you tend to try to rationalize why you still do them. You'll say things like, "God isn't through with me yet" or "I'm not perfect." Essentially these are excuses to make you feel better.

Consider what happened to Saul when he preserved the best of the cattle, sheep and goats when God commanded him to destroy everything. He lost his favor with God, and God then chose David to be king.

Don't miss out on the greater blessings that God has for you because you're holding on to something that is destroying you.

Prayer for Today: Lord, You know where I am weak. I thank You for being forgiving, merciful and kind. Thank you for not dealing with me as I deserve. Your grace and mercy are truly amazing! Thank You for loving me. Give me strength to get rid of those things in my life that do not please You. In Jesus' name, Amen.

Additional Scripture reading: Colossians 3: 5-10; 1 Samuel 15; 1 Kings 20:31-34

Not Without You

God answers prayers in His own way

But Naaman became angry and stalked away. "I thought he would certainly come out to meet me!" he said. "I expected him to wave his hand over the leprosy and call on the name of the LORD his God and heal me! Aren't the rivers of Damascus, the Abana and the Pharpar, better than any of the rivers of Israel? Why shouldn't I wash in them and be healed?" So Naaman turned and went away in a rage. (2 Kings 5:11-12 NLT)

Here's a little background: Naaman went to Elisha to be healed of his leprosy. He went to Elisha's house and waited at the door for him. Instead of coming out, Elisha sent a messenger giving him instructions on what he must do to be healed: wash seven times in the Jordan River. As you can see from today's meditational verses, Naaman became angry because he *thought* he would be healed in a different way. He thought that things would play out differently. Doesn't this same thing happen to us as well?

We seek God for a closer relationship with Him, new careers, new opportunities, financial stability, etc., and He answers us. But what happens? The answer comes in a way that we didn't expect. We've prayed about this thing for so long that we've already come up with *how* God is going to do it! Right? Then all of a sudden, we're in for a big surprise! We become frustrated, angry or even disappointed.

Just because things don't happen as we thought they would, we shouldn't get discouraged. God's thoughts are not our thoughts and His ways are not our ways. (Isaiah 55:8) I encourage you to be receptive to God's answers to your prayers even when they don't come in the way you expected. God knows what is best for you and His plan for your life is far greater than anything you can imagine.

Prayer for Today: Heavenly Father, in the name of Jesus, open my eyes and heart to Your blessings and Your answers to my prayers even when the answers aren't as I thought they would be. Help me find comfort in knowing that You have my best interest in mind and that Your plan for my life is far greater than any plans I could ever make. In Jesus' name, Amen.

Additional Scripture reading: 2 Kings 5 and Isaiah 55:8

Idols are forbidden and useless

"Their gods are like helpless scarecrows in a cucumber field! They cannot speak, and they need to be carried because they cannot walk. Do not be afraid of such gods, for they can neither harm you nor do you any good."(Jeremiah 10:5 NLT)

An idol is anything or anyone that you put before God. Throughout the Old Testament, God repeatedly speaks about the Israelites, His chosen people, who make their own gods by carving them out of wood, gold and other man-made items. These gods do not speak, do not walk; they do no harm nor do any good.

Who would want to serve a god that needed to be carried around and could not do anything for them, including saving them? These gods cannot make any promises; they cannot hear or answer prayers, neither can they provide protection and comfort in times of trouble.

The truth is that we often put many things and people before God, creating little gods. We often praise the things He has given us and not God Himself.

Spend more time getting to know the Lord because He is truly awesome. There is absolutely no one like Him. There is no need to carry Him around because He is the one carrying you.

Prayer for Today: Lord, please forgive me for putting things and people before You. Let me be mindful of my relationship with You and Your place in my life. Remove those things from my life that distract me and often try to take Your place. In Jesus' name, Amen.

Additional Scripture reading: Jeremiah 10: 1-16 and Exodus 20:3-7

Do the God thing

But Jonah got up and went in the opposite direction to get away from the LORD. He went down to the port of Joppa, where he found a ship leaving for Tarshish. He bought a ticket and went on board, hoping to escape from the LORD by sailing to Tarshish. (Jonah 1:3 NLT)

The Lord gave a message to Jonah and instructed him to go to Nineveh to give that message to the people there. Jonah heard the Lord but decided that he would attempt to hide from the Lord by going in the opposite direction and boarding a ship that would take him to a different place.

Jonah's actions had consequences. He was chosen by the Lord to carry out a specific task and he ran. Because of his disobedience, he caused the storm in the lives of those around him. When he revealed to the sailors aboard the ship that his disobedience caused the storm, they still tried other things to make it through the storm instead of getting rid of the problem (Jonah).

We can learn a few things from this situation: 1. It is likely that if there is a person in your life causing the storm, they already know it and they know what needs to be done for it to go away. They need to get off your boat! 2. Not only is it important that you are following God, but it is also important that those in your circle are doing what God is calling them to do as well. When those around you are running from God, their disobedience can cause storms in your life. 3. Don't be afraid to throw them off your boat if they reveal to you that they are running from the Lord. Do not attempt other methods to calm the storm in your life when you know who or what is causing it. Get rid of the culprit.

Prayer for Today: Lord, give me discernment so that I may know when there is someone in my life causing storms because they are running from You. Give me courage to not assist them in running from You but to push them back to You. Empower me to continuously walk in the path that You have set for me. In Jesus' name, Amen.

Additional Scripture reading: Jonah 1

Success and Faithfulness

Hezekiah trusted in the LORD, the God of Israel. There was no one like him among all the kings of Judah, either before or after his time. He remained faithful to the LORD in everything, and he carefully obeyed all the commands the LORD had given Moses. So the LORD was with him, and Hezekiah was successful in everything he did .(2 Kings 18:5-7a NLT)

This passage of Scripture mentions three important things about King Hezekiah's character that we can attribute to the Lord being with him and giving him success in everything that he did. King Hezekiah trusted the Lord, remained faithful to the Lord and carefully obeyed all the Lord's commandments.

Throughout life, you will encounter many situations that will test your faith and tempt you to stop trusting the Lord, lose faith or do things outside of God's will. However, if you want the Lord to be with you and grant you success in everything, you must do your part and remain steadfast in your faith.

Find strength in the power of God that has already been planted within you as King Hezekiah discovered. That is the key to experiencing the life that God has predestined for you to live.

Prayer for Today: Father in heaven, give me the strength to trust You, remain faithful and obey Your Word even when it's hard to do so. Let Your power rest within me so that I may live out my faith in You every day. In Jesus' name, Amen.

Additional Scripture reading: 2 Kings 18:1-8

Not Without You

Who do you trust?

"Then the Assyrian king's chief of staff told them to give this message to Hezekiah: "This is what the great king of Assyria says: What are you trusting in that makes you so confident? Do you think that mere words can substitute for military skill and strength? Who are you counting on, that you have rebelled against me?" (2 Kings 18:19-20 NLT)

When Assyria began to attack Judah, the Assyrian king sent a message to King Hezekiah of Judah. The Assyrian king was essentially taunting and talking trash to King Hezekiah. He told the people of Jerusalem to not be fooled into trusting in the Lord because none of the gods of the other nations could save their people; therefore, the people of Judah would be insane to think that the Lord could rescue Jerusalem from him!

This is just like the enemy. He knows that you are trusting in the Lord and will say and do anything to get you to doubt God's power. I encourage you to stand strong; trust in the Lord regardless of what's going on around you and regardless of what the enemy is whispering or shouting in your ear! Have faith that the Lord will take care of you, provide for you and sustain you regardless of the enemy's threats. Remember that the enemy can only do what the Lord allows him to do. He has to get permission from your Father to mess with you. Remember Job? Be confident and continue trusting that this is the Lord's battle and He already has the victory!

Prayer for Today: Oh how I love You and trust in Your faithfulness my Lord! Thank You for being in charge of my life. I thank You that the enemy cannot even come near me unless he gets permission from You. In knowing that, I trust that You will not put anything in my path that I cannot bear. Continue to strengthen me in Your Word. In Jesus' name, Amen.

Additional Scripture reading: 2 Kings 18:13-37 and Job 1

~Day of Reflection~

Trust

Read: Proverbs 3:4-7

Meditate: Do I have difficulty trusting God? Why? Am I holding on to past hurts?

Apply: What can I do to eliminate doubt and fully trust God?

Faith and Mercy

"Go back to Hezekiah, the leader of my people. Tell him, 'This is what the LORD, the God of your ancestor David, says: I have heard your prayer and seen your tears. I will heal you, and three days from now you will get out of bed and go to the Temple of the LORD. (2 Kings 20:5 NLT)

Earlier in this chapter, the Lord had just sent Isaiah to King Hezekiah to warn him to get his affairs in order because he was about to die. After hearing this, the king prayed to the Lord and reminded Him of how he had always been faithful in serving Him and always did what was pleasing in the Lord's sight.

As you can see from today's meditational Scripture, the Lord changed His mind! He gave Hezekiah fifteen more years of life!

There are two important things to learn here: Faithfulness has its advantages and God's mercy is everlasting. King Hezekiah's faithfulness before his sickness gave him favor with God. Faith activates favor! He didn't allow his circumstances to determine how or if he would continue to serve God. In addition, God is forever merciful. He answered Hezekiah's prayer with kindness and compassion.

Prayer for Today: Heavenly Father, forgive me for my unfaithfulness. Help me to live a life that is pleasing to You at all times, in deed and in spirit. In Jesus' name, Amen.

Additional Scripture reading: 2 Kings 20:1-10 and Hebrews 11

When you know more, become more

You were sorry and humbled yourself before the LORD when you heard what I said against this city and its people—that this land would be cursed and become desolate. You tore your clothing in despair and wept before me in repentance. And I have indeed heard you, says the LORD. (2 Kings 22: 19 NLT)

Earlier in this chapter, the court's secretary found the Book of the Law and read it to the king. When the king heard what was written in the Book of the Law, he humbled himself, repented and sought the Lord.

When we learn more about God and His Word, we are responsible for becoming better Christians. We must humble ourselves, repent and turn away from those things that do not please the Lord and seek Him.

First Peter 1 encourages us in the same way: we must live as God's obedient children and not live to satisfy our own desires. We did that when we did not know better but now that the Word of God is planted within us, we must adhere to it.

Prayer for Today: Heavenly Father, forgive me for living to please my fleshly desires. Help me to walk in Your ways at all times because You expect me to live a holy life. Let me not bring shame to Your holy name. In Jesus' name, Amen.

Additional Scripture reading: 2 Kings 22:8-20 and 1 Peter 1:14-16

Not Without You

Stand out

There was a man named Jabez who was more honorable than any of his brothers. His mother named him Jabez because his birth had been so painful. He was the one who prayed to the God of Israel, "Oh, that you would bless me and expand my territory! Please be with me in all that I do, and keep me from all trouble and pain!" And God granted him his request. (1 Chronicles 4:9-10 NLT)

It is quite interesting that as you read through this chapter, the writer abruptly stops giving the lineage to talk about Jabez. The writer of this book does not speak about the character of any other person but Jabez. What makes Jabez stand out? The Bible says that he was more honorable than any of his brothers and he was the *one* who prayed to God. The Bible does not tell us what makes him more honorable and why he had such favor with God.

Although there are a lot of unanswered questions about why Jabez was chosen, we do know that he was a praying man. This tells us that having communication with God (a prayer life) is very important. The book of Hebrews teaches that God rewards those who diligently seek Him! We can see that this is true because the Lord granted Jabez's request: to expand his territory, be with him in all that he does, keep him from trouble and pain.

Spend much time in prayer seeking God's face and His will. But equally important, spend time communing with Him - not because you want Him to move on your behalf but just because of who He is.

Prayer for Today: Lord I seek You because I want to be more like You and be all that You have created me to be. I want to be able to hear You clearly and walk according to your Will. You are so worthy of my praise and my time. Help me to focus on building a more meaningful prayer time with You. In Jesus' name, Amen.

Additional Scripture reading: Hebrews 11:6, Proverbs 15:29 and Matthew 21:22

Holy Invitation

So David did not move the Ark into the City of David. Instead, he took it to the house of Obed-edom of Gath. The Ark of God remained there in Obed-edom's house for three months, and the LORD blessed the household of Obed-edom and everything he owned. (1 Chronicles 13:13-14 NLT)

The Ark of God represents the presence of God. While the Ark of God was in Obed-edom's house, the Bible tells us that his household and everything he owned was blessed.

Although we do not have a physical Ark of God presence, the Lord's presence is always with us. We don't have the ark because we have something *better*. The sacrificial system is gone because of Jesus' once-for-all sacrifice (see Hebrews). It is through Christ that we no longer need such temporary elements as the temple furniture, because we have direct access to God Himself. It isn't our doing at all, but wholly God's grace. Welcome the presence of God into your home and receive the blessings of God.

How do you welcome the presence of God into your home? Set the atmosphere by living according to the Word of God and serving only Him; acknowledge Him in everything that you do. He promises to never leave nor forsake you.

Prayer for Today: Lord, I welcome Your Holy Spirit to dwell in my heart and in my house. I want to experience all of the blessings that You have for me and my family. Teach us to obey Your will and walk in Your ways. In Jesus' name, Amen.

Additional Scripture reading: Deuteronomy 31:8; Psalm 139:7 and Psalm 16

Proceed with prayer

"Because you Levites did not carry the Ark the first time, the anger of the Lord our God burst out against us. We failed to ask God how to move it properly."(1 Chronicles 15:13 NLT)

The first time David and his officials attempted to bring the Ark of God back to the City of David; Uzzah was killed because he reached out his hand to steady the Ark to keep it from falling to the ground. This angered the Lord and caused Him to kill Uzzah right there! All of this happened because David did not follow God's instructions on how to bring the Ark back safely.

We experience spiritual demise in many situations because we do not seek the Lord first to obtain guidance in how to proceed. When we fail to properly worship God and seek His face, we find ourselves struggling. Consider married people who are both selfish, they fight for their own way and end up in mutual pain rather than mutual blessing. The person who steals or lies is afraid he'll get caught; the person who gossips has a hard time trusting others. In each of these situations, no one is seeking or trusting God.

Whatever you have before you today, seek the Lord first. He desires to hear from you to guide you in the path that He has predestined for you. Proceed with prayer.

Prayer for Today: Heavenly Father, forgive me for not always proceeding with prayer. I want to experience the abundant life that You have prepared for me so let me not forget to acknowledge You in all things. In Jesus' name, Amen.

Additional Scripture reading: Psalm 34:10, Matthew 6:33 and Proverbs 3:5-6

The sin of friends

But Joab replied, "May the Lord increase the number of his people a hundred times over! But why, my lord the king, do you want to do this? Are they not all your servants? Why must you cause Israel to sin?" (1 Chronicles 21:3 NLT)

King David ordered Joab to take a census of all the people of Israel. This was counted as sin and both David and Joab knew this. However, in today's key verse, we find that Joab questioned David's decision but, David insisted that Joab proceed. David's sin brought consequences on the entire nation of Israel and not just David himself.

Likewise, the ramifications of the sins committed by those you are connected to will affect you as well. As a Christian, you have a responsibility to your brothers and sisters to warn them of the consequences of their sin (although they are likely already aware). You are the salt of the earth. Be bold and courageous to remind them of who they are in Christ!

Be mindful of who you are connected to and the type of lives they live because you are likely to reap the harvest (good or bad) of what they are sowing.

Prayer for Today: Father in Heaven, give me the spirit of discernment so that I may know who I am spending my time with. Allow me to be a light and encouragement to Your people. Let me be bold and steadfast in my faith so that I may please You. In Jesus' name, Amen.

Additional Scripture reading: 1 Chronicles 21:1-17; Matthew 5:13

~Day of Reflection~

Accountability

Read: Ezekiel 18:30; Matthew 12:36; 2 Corinthians 5:10; Luke 17:3

Meditate: Each of us will have to give an account to God for our words and actions. Am I mindful that God holds me accountable for what I know?

Apply: Choose a trustworthy friend that will support you and hold you accountable to living according to God's principles. This person should not have a problem telling you that you're wrong (in a loving manner) to help you get back on track.

Serve God willingly

"And Solomon, my son, learn to know the God of your ancestors intimately. Worship and serve him with your whole heart and a willing mind. For the Lord sees every heart and knows every plan and thought. If you seek him, you will find him. But if you forsake him, he will reject you forever." (1 Chronicles 28:9 NLT)

In this particular passage, King David began giving instructions to Solomon on the plans for building the temple. The instructions given to Solomon in the meditational Scripture are very powerful and can apply to our own lives.

Learn to know God intimately. In order to know God intimately, you must spend time with Him by praying and studying His Word. Worship and serve Him with your whole heart. The Word of God says that those who worship Him must worship Him in spirit and in truth. To worship and serve wholeheartedly, allow yourself to be led by Him and only Him.

Worship and serve Him with a willing mind! Make a decision to serve God. Serve Him because of who He is and His love for you. To get to this place, you need to know Him intimately and give the Lord your heart. If you seek Him, you will find Him. Hebrews 11:6 tells us that the Lord rewards those who diligently seek Him.

Prayer for Today: Heavenly Father, as I seek You with my whole heart, please reveal yourself to me as You promised in Your Word. Help me not to waver but to trust and serve You wholeheartedly with a willing mind. In Jesus' name, Amen.

Additional Scripture reading: Jeremiah 29:13; Hebrews 11:6; 1 Chronicles 28

Not Without You

How long are you going to wait?

Then Joshua asked them, "How long are you going to wait before taking possession of the remaining land the Lord, the God of your ancestors has given to you?" (Joshua 18:3 NLT)

How long are you going to wait before you take possession of the life you were called to live? God gives each one of us assignments throughout our lives. Your assignment this year may not be the same as your assignment last year or the next year. In every season of our lives, we are called to demonstrate God's love in different ways but it is up to us to seek God to see what that looks like. Learn to discern, understand and obey His voice.

Once you are aware of what you should be doing in this season of your life, accept and pursue it wholeheartedly. Do not become discouraged or disheartened by how big or small you think the assignment is; your desire should be to please God and *love* people not please them. Oftentimes, as Christians, we get caught up in seeking praise and validation from people; this type of behavior is distracting and unproductive. Stay in alignment with the assignment that God has given you in this season of your life. Whatever that is, do it with all your heart unto the Lord.

Prayer for Today: Heavenly Father, thank You for the calling that You have on my life. Thank You for the reassurance that it is all about You and no one else. All glory belongs to You. I seek to please You with my life and live according to the way You have called me to live. Keep me from getting caught up in things that do not matter and do not bring You glory. In Jesus' name, Amen.

Additional Scripture reading: Joshua 18: 1-3; Isaiah 49:1 and 4; John 10:27; Colossians 3:23 and Jeremiah 29:11

Not Without You

Achieving God-given dreams

"My thoughts are nothing like your thoughts," says the Lord. "And my ways are far beyond anything you could imagine." (Isaiah 55:8 NLT)

I have a friend who once considered giving up on her dream. She made several unsuccessful attempts to achieve her dream and decided to take a safe route that would get her in the neighborhood but not at her "address" (as my pastor would say). As the Holy Spirit reminded me of this Scripture, I shared it with my friend. I'd like to share this with you: Even though you're going down the path chasing your dream and you experience road blocks, don't give up. Don't allow difficulties to destroy your dreams.

Dreams are God-given and He gives us vision to make them happen. We must spend time in His presence studying and praying to receive guidance and direction. Find a place to spend quiet, quality time with the Lord. He will surely speak when we are ready to listen and obey. We learn to discern God's voice by spending time studying His word. God will not tell us anything that is contrary to His word.

Let's not get so far removed from God that we don't hear His voice and follow His way. Let us also not make the mistake of hearing His voice and not recognizing that it is God speaking to us. His thoughts and ways are not ours. Even when it seems like it is taking longer than expected to accomplish your goal, there is a lesson to be learned that will better prepare you for where you are going. Just because there is delay, doesn't mean that it won't happen. Don't give up! If it's from God, it shall be accomplished!

Prayer for Today: Father in heaven, thank You for Your power and Your wisdom. Cleanse my heart and mind that I may be able to hear You clearly and determine where You would have me to go. I only want what You want for my life. Teach me to delight in Your will and Your ways. In Jesus' name, Amen.

Additional Scripture reading: John 10

Not Without You

Turn around

At times I might shut up the heavens so that no rain falls, or command grasshoppers to devour your crops, or send plagues among you. Then if my people who are called by my name will humble themselves and pray and seek my face and turn from their wicked ways, I will hear from heaven and will forgive their sins and restore their land. (2 Chronicles 7:13-14 NLT)

In this passage of Scripture, we learn about some of the ways the Lord disciplined the Israelites because of their sin. They did not always experience prosperity and fruitfulness; their sin caused God to shut up the heavens. Likewise, our sins will oftentimes cause God to do things to get our attention so that we will humble ourselves and return to Him.

The Lord promised the Israelites that He will hear from heaven, forgive their sins and restore their land if they became humble, prayed, sought His face and turned from their wicked ways. God desires the same things of us today: humility, repentance, prayer and worship. He requires wholehearted devotion because without fully turning to Him and giving up the sin, we end up in the same place learning nothing from the previous consequences.

Take a moment to humbly seek God's face and forgiveness. Strive to sin less and worship more.

Prayer for Today: Heavenly Father, I praise Your holy name. Please forgive me of my sins and help me to fully turn away from them so that I may honor You in all that I do. I thank You for Your forgiveness and restoration, in Jesus' name, Amen.

Additional Scripture reading: Psalm 51 and Hebrews 12:1

Not Without You

I want to see You

Then they scoffed, "He's just a carpenter, the son of Mary and the brother of James, Joseph, Judas, and Simon. And his sisters live right here among us." They were deeply offended and refused to believe in him.(Mark 6:3 NLT)

It is amazing how people will discount you when they do not know or understand the calling that has been placed over your life. Re-read today's key verse. "He's *just* a carpenter," they said of Jesus but little did they know, He is actually the Messiah.

We often fail to see Jesus for who He is in our lives because He doesn't present Himself the way we think He should. Consider the moment when Jesus walked on water and called Peter to get out of the boat. Peter asked if it was really Jesus because He wasn't expecting Jesus to be on the water. He then stepped out of the boat by faith to meet Jesus on the water but started to sink when he took his eyes off Christ.

We will constantly miss the Lord if we continue to put Him in a box. If we can see Jesus in all of His glory, our own lives will fall into place and we will begin to live according to the way God intended for us to live.

Prayer for Today: Heavenly Father, help me to see You in all of Your glory. Let me be receptive to Your Holy Spirit. I want to live a faithful and abundant life that pleases You. In Jesus' name, Amen.

Additional Scripture reading: Mark 6:1-6 and 2 Chronicles 15:2

Temptations from within

When the devil had finished tempting Jesus, he left him until the next opportunity came. (Luke 4:13 NLT)

As we learn from today's key verse, Satan is always looking for opportunities to tempt us. Do not be fooled; he is always looking for ways to trap you. It is best to be prepared by keeping your heart and mind filled with the Word of the Lord. This is why it is so important to meditate daily on God's Word.

Commit to spending time in prayer and studying God's Word each day. Keep your spiritual tank full. God has given you everything you need to be equipped for all of Satan's schemes. Satan uses your innermost desires to cause you to sin. See James 1:14-15. You must not give him room to use these desires by replacing the desire for those sins with desires for the things of God.

Prayer for Today: Father in Heaven, I ask that You give me strength to overcome the evil desires in my heart that Satan uses to draw me away from You. Help me to become more like You by removing those things from me. In Jesus' name, Amen.

Additional Scripture reading: Luke 4:1-13 and James 1:12-15

~Day of Reflection~

The future

Read: Deuteronomy 5:29; Jeremiah 29:11

Meditate: Do I believe that God has plans for my future? Do I trust His plans?

Apply: Pray. Study God's word. Don't worry about the future. Determine what makes you anxious or worry about the future and replace those thoughts with God's promises.

Friends with Faith

Seeing their faith, Jesus said to the man, "Young man, your sins are forgiven." (Luke 5:20 NLT)

In this particular Bible story, some men took their sick friend, who was lying on a mat, to Jesus. Since Jesus was teaching a crowd, they could not get to Him. Therefore, the friends went up to the roof, took off some of the tiles and lowered their friend down through the roof, right to where Jesus was. What great faith! They stopped at nothing to get their friend to Jesus because they knew that Jesus had what the friend needed!

We all need friends like this in our lives. Do you have any friends in your life who will get you to Jesus when you need Him? Do you have any friends who will pray and intercede for you? Do you have any friends who will tell you God's truth and not their own truth even when you don't want to hear it? If not, then you need to get some friends like this. You need friends who will make sure you get in the Lord's presence when you cannot get there on your own.

You will learn from this story that it was not the sick friend's faith but the faith of his friends that moved Jesus to heal him! This teaches that it is important to have friends of faith that will help position you to receive a blessing!

Prayer for Today: Lord, thank you for your mercy and grace. Thank you for friends who have faith to seek you on my behalf. I pray that you teach each of us to be steadfast and faithful in your Word and in your ways. In Jesus' name, Amen.

Additional Scripture reading: Luke 5:17-26 and 1 Corinthians 10:24

Not Without You

Call out to God

So when the Aramean chariot commanders saw Jehoshaphat in his royal robes, they went after him. "There is the king of Israel!" they shouted. But Jehoshaphat called out, and the LORD saved him. God helped him by turning the attackers away from him. (2 Chronicles 18:31 NLT)

Before the king of Israel and the king of Judah decided to go into battle, they summoned prophets to consult the Lord requesting His guidance on whether or not they should enter into battle to recover Ramoth-gilead. The king of Israel's prophets (all 400 of them) were inspired by a lying spirit. Micaiah, a prophet of the Lord spoke the truth. He told them not to enter into battle because they would not win. However, the king of Israel did not like him and refused to listen and they went forth in battle despite Micaiah's warning.

The Lord had already determined that the king of Israel would die in battle but favor was shown to the king of Judah, even though he went against the Lord's prophet. He simply called out to the Lord and the Lord saved him.

You may have stepped outside of God's will to do something even when you knew it was not the right thing to do. God desires that you repent, return to Him and trust Him. Today, I encourage you to call out to the Lord to save you from any distressful situation that you may be experiencing. He is full of mercy and grace and ready for you to reach out to Him.

Prayer for Today: My Lord and my God. I come into your presence to say thank You for your immeasurable grace and mercy. Help me out of this place and teach me to trust You without hesitation. In Jesus' name, Amen.

Additional Scripture reading: 2 Chronicles 18 and Psalm 84:11

Not your battle

He said, "Listen, all you people of Judah and Jerusalem! Listen, King Jehoshaphat! This is what the LORD says: Do not be afraid! Don't be discouraged by this mighty army, for the battle is not yours, but God's. (2 Chronicles 20:15 NLT)

The battle that you and I fight each day is a spiritual battle not one of flesh and blood. It is important that you understand and believe this biblical truth.

In today's key verse, the Lord spoke through Jahaziel to the people of Judah and Jerusalem in response to their prayers and fasting. The word from the Lord is this: the battle is not yours to fight. In fact, all you have to do is stand still and watch the Lord's victory. He is with you, don't be afraid. Believe in God and His word and you will succeed. If you continue reading, you will find that is exactly what happened. They didn't have to fight. They Lord fought their battle for them.

Each day that you wake, you have a choice to make: believe in God's Word or not. This may not always be easy but this is exactly when your faith is tested: at that moment when you've been praying and fasting for something and all hell seems to be breaking loose. Even still, the battle isn't yours to fight. Equip yourself with the Word of God, stand firm, praise Him, believe in Him and His Word and watch what happens.

Prayer for Today: Heavenly Father, You are so awesome and mighty in power. Help me to remember daily that the battle is not mine but Yours and to trust that You already have the victory! Sometimes this can be a challenge for me but I give up my doubt and choose to replace it with faith in You and Your Word. In Jesus' name, Amen.

Additional Scripture reading: 2 Chronicles 20:1-29; Ephesians 6:10-18; 2 Corinthians 10:4

Guidance brings success

Uzziah sought God during the days of Zechariah, who taught him to fear God. And as long as the king sought guidance from the Lord, God gave him success. (2 Chronicles 26:5 NLT)

The Lord desires that you seek Him in all that you do. In today's meditational verse, the Bible tells us that the Lord gave success to King Uzziah as long as he sought guidance from Him.

It doesn't matter what you're dealing with or what task you're undertaking, seek the Lord first. When you diligently and faithfully seek God, He will show himself to you. He will give you the answers that you seek and most importantly, your relationship with Him will be strengthened. How so? You will learn to trust and rely on Him in all that you do. The Lord will reward your faithfulness.

Prayer for Today: Most holy God, I come into Your presence thanking You for all that You are and all that You have done in my life. I come seeking You as I start my day because I desire a closer relationship with You and Your will for my life. In Jesus' name, Amen.

Additional Scripture reading: 2 Chronicles 26:1-15; 1 Kings 2:3; Proverbs 15:22

Wise Counsel

Without wise leadership, a nation falls; there is safety in having many advisers. (Proverbs 11:14 NLT)

Do you have any spiritual mentors? Do you have anyone who you trust and from whom you can seek Godly wisdom? When we're seeking to become all God has created us to be, the Bible teaches that we need to seek wise counsel. Just as a nation will fall without having wise leadership, so will we. It is helpful to secure wise mentors for different areas of our life – from financial guidance to career and spiritual guidance.

Before we seek counsel, we must first determine our direction and what we hope to accomplish. Direction is determined by seeking the Lord and receiving wisdom. Counselors and advisors are not supposed to tell us what to do; their role is to help us get to where we're going in life by providing guidance. We should seek mentors who are trustworthy and who may have already accomplished what we're trying to achieve.

How do you know the people you seek out will give wise counsel? They will confirm what God has already told you and give Godly advice. Their advice will not and should not contradict God's word.

Prayer for Today: In the name of Jesus, Lord I come to You with praise. I praise You with everything that is within me! Thank You for being who You are! I ask that You give me wisdom. Give me direction. Help me find wise counselors who may help me achieve safety and success. I only want to follow You and do what brings honor to Your name. In Jesus' name, Amen.

Additional Scripture reading: 1 Kings 12:8-16 and Exodus 18:17-23

God's blessings should not make us prideful

But when he had become powerful, he also became proud, which led to his downfall. He sinned against the Lord his God by entering the sanctuary of the Lord's Temple and personally burning incense on the incense altar. (2 Chronicles 26:16 NLT)

When you live a righteous life and experience the many blessings and promises of God, it is important to remain humble and know your place. In today's meditational verse, King Uzziah was blessed with success in all that he did. However, he allowed his success and favor with God to go to his head and lost humility. His pride led to his destruction.

God desires that you keep a humble heart no matter how blessed you are. Remember that everything that you have and all that you have accomplished is a gift from God. Keep this in the forefront of your mind because just as God gave it to you, He can and may take it away.

Prayer for Today: Lord, I thank You for your many blessings. Please help me keep a humble heart. May You forever receive all the praise, honor and glory in all that I do. Let me always be reminded of who You are in my life and what You have allowed me to accomplish. In Jesus' name, Amen.

Additional Scripture reading: 2 Chronicles 26:16-23; Proverbs 8:13; 11:2; 16:18

~Day of Reflection~

Do your best

Read: Genesis 31:42; Ecclesiastes 9:10

Meditate: Am I giving my best at work, home or school? Am I working in the same way that I would work for God? Why or why not? When am I most productive?

Apply: Determine the changes that need to be made so that you can give your best in all areas of your life.

God's will shall be accomplished

Then the local residents tried to discourage and frighten the people of Judah to keep them from their work. They bribed agents to work against them and to frustrate their plans. This went on during the entire reign of King Cyrus of Persia and lasted until King Darius of Persia took the throne. (Ezra 4:4-5 NLT)

The people of Judah began to rebuild the temple of God after returning from exile. When they purposed in their hearts that they would complete this task, they faced continuous opposition. Their enemies sought to discourage, distract and defeat them. They went to their king to issue decrees to get them to stop rebuilding. If you continue reading, their enemies succeeded once. However, this did not stop God's plan for His temple to be rebuilt.

Just as the people of Judah faced difficulty when they determined to pursue God's plan, you will also encounter difficulty when you decide to follow God's will for your life. As you walk according to God's Word and decide to live according to His will, the enemy will whisper in your ear to distract you. He will attempt to frustrate you so that you will give up and return to your old ways. He will do all that he can to discourage and distract you from living out God's plan for your life.

When the enemy comes your way, there are several things that you must keep in mind:

1. He comes to kill, steal and destroy your spirit.

2. Greater is He that is in you than he that is in the world.

3. God's will shall be accomplished regardless of circumstances. The same people or situations that are meant to destroy you may very well assist you in accomplishing your goal.

Prayer for Today: Lord God, I thank You for Your plans for my life. I thank You that You have already given me strength and power to defeat the enemy. I thank You that I am victorious through your Holy Spirit. I can do all things through Christ who strengthens me. In Jesus' name, Amen.

Additional Scripture reading: Ezra 4; 1 John 4:4 and John 10:10

Keep going

At that time the prophets Haggai and Zechariah son of Iddo prophesied to the Jews in Judah and Jerusalem. They prophesied in the name of the God of Israel who was over them. Zerubbabel son of Shealtiel and Jeshua son of Jehozadak responded by starting again to rebuild the Temple of God in Jerusalem. And the prophets of God were with them and helped them. (Ezra 5:1-2 NLT)

During this particular time, the people of Judah and Jerusalem were called to rebuild the Temple of God in Jerusalem. They encountered difficulty and the work was temporarily put on hold. God's people were encouraged when the prophets prophesied, in the name of God, over them. This encouragement led them to begin working again.

What is your response when the Word of God is spoken over your life? When you read it? Study it? Hear a sermon? Receive prayer? Do you become encouraged and begin to work? Does hearing and receiving the Word of God cause you to want to continue on in what God has called you to do?

Allow the Word of God to penetrate your heart daily so that you may be encouraged to always walk in the will of God, living according to His purpose.

Prayer for Today: Father in Heaven, thank You for your Word. Thank You for the plans You have for my life. Let me always be encouraged and empowered by Your Word. Let Your Word accomplish the purpose for which it was sent. In Jesus' name, Amen.

Additional Scripture reading: Ezra 5; 7:28 and Isaiah 55:11

Not Without You

Interruptions are not always what they seem

"Moreover, I hereby decree that you are to help these elders of the Jews as they rebuild this Temple of God. You must pay the full construction costs, without delay, from my taxes collected in the province west of the Euphrates River so that the work will not be interrupted." (Ezra 6:8 NLT)

Once again, the enemies of God's people were attempting to stop the rebuilding of the Temple of God. They went to the king complaining and requesting that he search the archives to see if God's people were really given permission to rebuild the temple. When the king searched the archives and found this to be true, he ordered them to assist God's people in rebuilding the Temple.

God sometimes chooses to work through people and circumstances we least expect to help fulfill His purpose. Therefore, do not become discouraged about the temporary distractions that come up against you. God's plan is perfect and will be accomplished no matter who disagrees. God will receive His glory through it all.

I encourage you to keep an attitude of expectancy when you are doing what God has called you to do. When you come across interferences, know that they will help you fulfill your purpose. Expect these disturbances to help you grow and propel you to the next level in your relationship with God.

Prayer for Today: Father in Heaven, thank You for the power of the Holy Spirit that You have given me. Keep me focused on Your will in every situation that I encounter. Teach me to be strong and steadfast. In Jesus' name, Amen.

Additional Scripture reading: Ezra 6 and Romans 8:28

Character

Until the time came to fulfill his dreams, the Lord tested Joseph's character. (Psalm 105:19 NLT)

Many times when God places dreams in our hearts and we purpose in our heart to seek after it, we encounter many obstacles along the way. Our scripture today tells us that the Lord is the one who tested Joseph's character. Do you remember all of the things that Joseph encountered before Joseph's dreams had been fulfilled?

Let us first recount Joseph's dreams. His first dream (Genesis 37:6) is that he is in a field with his brothers, tying up bundles of grain. Suddenly his bundle stood up, and his brothers' bundles all gathered around and bowed low before his. His second dream (Genesis 37:9) was that the sun, moon, and even stars bowed low before him! Both dreams signified that Joseph would be ruler.

Let us revisit the obstacles he encountered before his dreams came to past. First, his brothers sold him into slavery. (Even as a slave to Potiphar, God was with him and still gave him success in everything he did). Second, Joseph was put in prison because Potiphar's wife lied on him. (Still the Lord was with Joseph in prison and made him a favorite with the prison warden.)

One day, Joseph was called upon to interpret Pharaoh's dream. After Joseph interpreted Pharaoh's dream, Pharaoh put Joseph in charge of the entire land of Egypt! Dream fulfilled! No matter what obstacles you are facing, remember that they are just stepping stones to get you where you need to be. This is just a testing of your character. The obstacles will only make you a better person and you will be better equipped when the time comes for the dream(s) to be fulfilled.

Prayer for Today: Father in heaven, I honor and praise Your holy name today! Sustain me during the times when my character is being tested. Give me strength and help me not lose sight of what you have in store for me! In Jesus' name, please be my strength, Amen.

Additional Scripture reading: Genesis 37; Jeremiah 29:11 and Psalm 109

Jesus first

"And please give me a letter addressed to Asaph, the manager of the king's forest, instructing him to give me timber. I will need it to make beams for the gates of the Temple fortress, for the city walls, and for a house for myself." And the king granted these requests, because the gracious hand of God was on me. (Nehemiah 2:8 NLT)

Nehemiah found favor with both God and man. Why? If you refer back to chapter 1, Nehemiah sought God desperately. He delighted in God. He repented of his sins. Because Nehemiah did these things, God showed him favor. He not only received favor from God but from the person placed in authority over him here on earth.

Wouldn't you like to experience that kind of honor from both God and man? The kind where you do not have to compromise your belief in God's principles to win the respect of man? You can surely experience this. Proverbs 3:1-4 encourages us to get wisdom, store it in our hearts, be loyal and kind and then we will find favor with both God and people. In Luke 2, the Bible also teaches us that even Jesus grew in favor with both God and man. If we follow Jesus' example, we can experience this as well. He was obedient and He grew in wisdom.

Essentially, in order to have favor with both God and people, you have to put God first. You must be uncompromising in your faith. God will honor those who honor Him. You cannot put the world and those in it before the Lord. God's first commandment was to "not have any other god but him."

Prayer for Today: Father in Heaven, I just want to thank You for being who You are. I ask that You give me wisdom that I may honor You first wholeheartedly. I want favor with both You and those around me but not at the expense of my relationship with You. Help me to be mindful of my actions and who I am putting first. In Jesus' name, Amen.

Additional Scripture reading: Nehemiah 1-2:10; Proverbs 3:1-4; Luke 2:41-52

Pray, Guard, Protect

"But we prayed to our God and guarded the city day and night to protect ourselves."(Nehemiah 4:9 NLT)

In Nehemiah 4, Nehemiah discusses how the enemies of God's people opposed them rebuilding the wall of Jerusalem. Their enemies were disgusted with them continuing on with what God called them to do. Nehemiah and the rest of God's people who were committed to rebuilding were scoffed at and talked about as they were doing their work. If you refer to verse 9, our meditation verse, you will see Nehemiah and his team's response. They prayed and guarded the city to protect themselves and the work that they were committed to.

When you're committed to doing the will of God, the enemy is going to be in your ear - whispering (sometimes shouting) about what you cannot do, will not accomplish, shouldn't do, or have no business doing. Since you know this: Be ready! Arm yourself with the Word of God to remind yourself of why you're doing it and who you're doing it for! Nehemiah took very important steps that we should all take:

- PRAY! Do not neglect your time alone with God praying and seeking guidance. This is a time of refreshing, spiritual renewal and empowerment.
- Be on Guard! Guard the dream/vision that God has placed in your heart and don't allow anyone to stop you from accomplishing it.
- Protect yourself! How? Become equipped with God's truth. Fight the enemy with the word of God - what you already know to be true.

Prayer for Today: Father God, keep me on track with the vision that You have planted in my heart. Give me the courage to remain steadfast in the midst of the attacks of the enemy. Thank You for choosing me for this great work. In Jesus' name, Amen.

Additional Scripture reading: Nehemiah 4

~Day of Reflection~

Complaining

Read: Psalm 142:1-2 and Jude 1:16

Meditate: Am I a complainer? Do I take my complaints to God? Do I complain to God because I want my own way?

Apply: Focus on being thankful. What must I change to become less of a complainer and more of a praiser? Identify five things that you can be thankful about and say a prayer of thanksgiving to God.

Work and Wait

For the revelation awaits an appointed time; it speaks of the end and will not prove false. Though it linger, wait for it; it will certainly come and will not delay. (Habakkuk 2:3 NLT)

Whatever the vision, goal or dream that God has planted in your heart, it will come to pass. God will not give you a dream or vision that He has not already equipped you for. He has not placed anything within you that you cannot attain.

As you wait for the appointed time for your dream to come to pass, I'd like to encourage you to work while you wait. Do not just sit around doing nothing. Write it down (v.2) and put it in a place where it will constantly be before you: refrigerator, bible, car dashboard. Position yourself by preparing yourself so that you may be ready when the opportunity presents itself to you. You must diligently work to accomplish or attain your goal.

Proverbs 10:4 NLT says "Lazy hands make a man poor, but diligent hands bring wealth." Whatever it is that you are trying to achieve will not happen on its own. God gave you the vision for a purpose; He wants you to work for it. If He said that it is going to happen, it will happen, but you also have to do what He has purposed in your heart to do.

Prayer for Today: Father God I come to You in the holy and powerful name of Jesus seeking Your will for my life. I pray that You speak to me like never before and just breathe Your purpose into my life. Give me understanding and wisdom so that I may know that it is You and that I may seek after that which You have called me. In Jesus' name, Amen.

Additional Scripture reading: Proverbs 13:4; Psalm 32:6-8 and Habakkuk 2:1-5

Not Without You

Spiritual fortitude

"Four times they sent the same message, and each time I gave the same reply."(Nehemiah 6:4 NLT)

Sanballat and his team continued to oppose Nehemiah's rebuilding of the wall. They were very persistent in trying to stop Nehemiah's work. In fact, the text shows in this particular instance, they sent the same message four times.

The enemy is pretty persistent and determined to keep you from doing God's will. You said "no" and prevailed against his attacks the first time. What about the next time he approaches you with the same message trying to get you off track? You have to have more determination than the enemy when you've made up your mind to follow God. The enemy never stops trying to discourage you and point out the many disadvantages that lie ahead. However, do not let this stop you from forging ahead and continuing the work with even greater fortitude and passion.

Remember that the enemy knows your potential and the magnitude of what you can accomplish through the power of the Holy Spirit if you remain in alignment with God; Satan's goal is to stop you from getting there.

Prayer for Today: Heavenly Father, thank You for Your Word. Thank You for the spirit of determination and courage that You have given me. Guide me so that I may stay focused on Your will and the assignments that You have placed before me. Thank You for choosing me. In Jesus' name, Amen.

Additional Scripture reading: Nehemiah 6 and Luke 4:13

God seeker

"But as soon as they were at peace, your people again committed evil in your sight, and once more you let their enemies conquer them. Yet whenever your people turned and cried to you again for help, you listened once more from heaven. In your wonderful mercy, you rescued them many times!" (Nehemiah 9:28 NLT)

In this passage of Scripture, the people of God were praying and confessing their sins to God. This particular line in the prayer stood out to me because it reminds me of how many of us act today: When things are going well in our lives, we generally don't seek God as much as we would if our lives were in shambles and we knew we needed God to move on our behalf.

Think about your life right now. Does this describe your relationship with God? When you are experiencing peace in your life, do you neglect your relationship with God? When you are experiencing havoc, do you seek God like never before? Going to church, praying more often, reading your Bible every day, etc.? If this does describe your relationship with God, I encourage you to seek Him wholeheartedly regardless of your present circumstances.

Do not allow your circumstances to drive your relationship with God; instead, seek Him every day. When you began to stray away, God will allow you to encounter situations that will bring you back to Him. God loves you and desires to have a strong, intimate relationship with you.

Prayer for Today: Heavenly Father, thank You for loving me wholeheartedly even when I am being unfaithful. Thank You for your grace and mercy. Give me wisdom that I may cherish and nurture my relationship with You regardless of what is going on in my life. In Jesus' name, Amen.

Additional Scripture reading: Nehemiah 9:5-37 and Psalm 37.

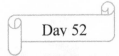

Not Without You

Separation for a better you

Then the rest of the people-the priests, Levites, gatekeepers, singers, Temple servants, and all who had separated themselves from the pagan people of the land in order to obey the Law of God, together with their wives, sons, daughters, and all who were old enough to understand joined their leaders and bound themselves with an oath. (Nehemiah 10:28-29a NLT)

Take a moment and think about the people in your life and the activities that you're involved in. Do these people and activities pull you closer to God or push you further away?

Sometimes you have to separate yourself from people and situations in order to fully obey God. There is nothing wrong with that. You must get to a place in your life where your relationship with God is more important than the opinions of others. You must also recognize that no one is exempt from being led away from God and into sin. Your title and status do not matter. Take King Solomon for example; even he was led into sin by his foreign wives. (see Nehemiah 13:26) This is proof that the people in your life can cause you to sin. You must be careful about whom you allow into your life because they influence your behavior.

Prayer for Today: Heavenly Father, thank You for Your mercy and grace. Give me wisdom to discern the character of those who are in my life. Let me not be influenced by those who do not find joy in Your presence. Show me activities and people in my life that I need to separate from in order that I may fully obey You. In Jesus' name, Amen.

Additional Scripture reading: Nehemiah 10 and Nehemiah 13

Not Without You

Don't miss your opportunity

"If you keep quiet at a time like this, deliverance and relief for the Jews will arise from some other place, but you and your relatives will die. Who knows if perhaps you were made queen for just such a time as this?" (Esther 4:14 NLT)

In the previous verses, the Bible tells us that the king allowed Haman, the most powerful official in the empire, to issue a decree that all the Jews be killed. Haman did this because of Mordecai's disobedience. Mordecai was a Jew and refused to bow to Haman therefore Haman thought that it wasn't enough to simply punish Mordecai but the entire Jewish race must be wiped out.

Mordecai sought the help of his cousin, Queen Esther when he learned of the decree. As Mordecai spoke with her messenger, Esther sent a message back to him as to why she wouldn't be able to do anything just yet. Today's key verse is his reply to her. This is an amazing reply and we can learn from it.

You are placed in certain positions and situations to complete a specific task. Many times you are not aware of what the task may be until the situation presents itself, as it did for Queen Esther. It is important to be mindful that God is always working through you and for you to accomplish His perfect will.

Don't allow fear to cause you to miss your moment of opportunity to do God's will.

Prayer for Today: Father in Heaven, thank You for Your design for my life. I am willing to be a vessel for You so help me not to miss my moment of opportunity to do what You have called me to do. In Jesus' name, Amen.

Additional Scripture reading: Esther 3 and 4

Faith like Job

Then the LORD said to Satan, "Have you considered my servant Job? There is no one on earth like him; he is blameless and upright, a man who fears God and shuns evil."(Job 1:8 NIV)

How about that? God knows Job's heart. In the text, we can see that God already knew what Job would do. He knew that whatever came upon Job, Job would still praise Him and give Him glory. When all of those trials came upon Job, he didn't stop believing in God. (Notice that whatever happens to you has to be run by God first. Satan has to get permission to bother you). In fact, at one point in the text, Job said "The Lord gives and he takes away, blessed be the name of the Lord."

Can God say that you are blameless? If He allows you to go through trials/tribulations, do know that it is not for naught. There is a *purpose*.

So, my question to you today is: Can the Lord say to Satan: "Have you considered my servant [insert your name here]?" Is your heart in the right place? When you're going through trials, are you focusing on God or the trial? Do not magnify your problems but magnify your God! God is *awesome*!

Prayer for Today: Father in heaven, I come to You right now thanking You for being who You are. I thank You that Your ways are greater than my ways and Your thoughts are higher than my thoughts. I thank You for having a plan already laid out for my life. Lord I seek to do Your will and not my own. Lord, I live to give You praise, honor, and glory. Thank You for loving me just as I am. I do not wish to stay as I am because I want to go higher in You. In Jesus' name, Amen.

Additional Scripture reading: Job 1

~Day of Reflection~

Clear conscience

Read: Proverbs 28:13; Romans 9:1; 1 Timothy 1:18-19; 1 Peter 3:16; Hebrews 9:14

Meditate: A clear conscience helps believers live in a way that honors God. Do I accept Jesus' forgiveness so that I may have a clear conscience? Is anything currently keeping me from having a clear conscience?

Apply: What is keeping you from having a clear conscience? Unforgiveness, pain, sin? Turn over it over to God. Free yourself of anything holding you back from living a victorious life.

Not Without You

Comfort in God's Word

At least I can take comfort in this: Despite the pain, I have not denied the words of the Holy One. (Job 6:10 NLT)

At this point in Scripture, Job was experiencing much pain physically, spiritually and emotionally. Job lost all of his wealth. His health was compromised because his body was covered in boils. His wife thought he was losing his mind and urged him to curse God because of his condition. Job's words in today's meditational Scripture are encouraging.

In all that Job was dealing with, he remained faithful. He did not deny the Lord or His word. He held on to who he knew God to be in spite of what was happening to him.

Although it is very difficult to trust in God and not doubt in times like these, it is important to hold on to God's Word. Remember everything that He has said. The Bible tells us that God will never leave nor forsake us.

No matter what you're facing today, God is forever faithful. Your situation is temporary and He will see you through it. It is for a purpose. Search for Him and the life lesson through it all.

Prayer for Today: Heavenly Father, through my pain, help me to see You and remember that Your mercy endures forever. Give me a faithful heart so that I may not deny You or your Word during my trials. I trust that You will see me through them. In Jesus' name, Amen.

Additional Scripture reading: Job 2:9; Job 6; Deuteronomy 31:6

Day 57

Anger does not rule you

Don't sin by letting anger control you. Think about it overnight and remain silent. (Psalm 4:4 NLT)

The Bible cautions us that our anger can lead us to sin. Jesus even speaks about this by saying "be angry but sin not." In this verse alone, the Bible shares three ways to deal with anger:

1. Don't allow anger to control you. You allow anger to control you when it drives your thoughts and actions.
2. Think about it overnight. Give yourself some time to cool down. Think about why you are angry. Is the situation or person that's causing you to be angry going to matter tomorrow? Next week? Next month? Next year?
3. Remain silent. When you're angry, it is quite possible to say things that will lead to even more trouble and possibly destroy relationships. Hold your peace and don't spew words when you're angry. You do not want a situation to get out of control because you were upset.

When you take time to walk away from the situation and cool down, you'll often find that it isn't worth the energy to stay angry. You may even forget what you were upset about in the first place.

Prayer for Today: Heavenly Father, teach me to control my anger and not allow my anger to control me. Give me wisdom in dealing with my anger so that I may not destroy relationships or find myself further away from You. In Jesus' name, Amen.

Additional Scripture reading: Psalm 4 and James 1

Time for a check-up

Even Death and Destruction hold no secrets from the Lord. How much more does he know the human heart! (Proverbs 15:11 NLT)

Self-examination: What is the condition of your heart? As often as possible, perform self-examinations to assess the condition of your heart. We learn in Proverbs 4:23 that out of the heart, flows the issues of life. The way we walk, talk and speak is a direct reflection of what's in our hearts.

God already knows your heart. Do not dwell in all of the things that you've done wrong and have a pity party. Instead, seek the Lord and abandon your old ways. You cannot allow the same things to damage your heart time and time again (which in turn damages your daily life). You must decide to change because change starts with a made up mind and then in your heart. An impure heart does not please God because actions are an outward manifestation of what's inside of your heart.

The word says that even your enemies will be at peace with you when your life pleases the Lord! Getting your heart right and pleasing God will prove beneficial to you not only spiritually but in day-to-day life as well.

Prayer for Today: Heavenly Father, forgive me of my sins. Take an inventory of my heart. Remove everything that's not like You. Purify me. Help me to turn away and never return to those things that do not please You. Help me to remain steadfast in Your Word and in Your Way. Let me purpose in my heart to remain diligent and seek to become more and more like You each day. I know it's not easy but it's worth it! I love and honor You today. In Jesus' name, Amen.

Additional Scripture reading: Proverbs 16 and Luke 6:45

Day 59

No interference

The wicked conceive evil; they are pregnant with trouble and give birth to lies. They dig a deep pit to trap others, then fall into it themselves. The trouble they make for others backfires on them. The violence they plan falls on their own heads. *(Psalm 7:14-16 NLT)*

When you plan to hurt others or set a trap for them, it is often set for you. When you make trouble for others, you are often the one in trouble. (Consider Haman and his hatred for Mordecai in the book of Esther.) This follows the premise that you reap what you sow. You cannot wholeheartedly follow God and harbor evil in your heart for other people.

You must operate in the love of God at all times, no matter what your enemies are doing. When you accepted Christ, you accepted the life of Christ which is to love others.

If you conceive or wish evil in your heart for another, ask the Lord to search you to determine why you have those feelings. Repent and combat those feelings with love. Focus on what you like about them instead of what bothers you about them. Pray for that person and do good to them but do not allow it to interfere with your relationship with Christ. You should remain pure in heart.

Prayer for Today: Create in me a clean heart oh Lord. Do not let me get to a place where I am holding grudges or harboring evil in my heart for my brother or sister. Teach me to love as You love and live according to the way You have predestined for me to live. In Jesus' name, Amen.

Additional Scripture reading: Psalm 7; Galatians 6:7 and Esther 7

Holy Shift

I will praise you, Lord, with all my heart; I will tell of all the marvelous things you have done. I will be filled with joy because of you. I will sing praises to your name, O Most High. (Psalm 9:1-2 NLT)

Here is a very powerful lesson to learn from David – Keep your eyes and heart on the Lord. With all that David encountered, (including running for his life twice), he kept his focus on the Lord.

Instead of fretting over future circumstances, give your attention to God. How? Sing praises to Him. Meditate on His goodness and sovereign power. Talk about how great God is instead of talking about your problems. Many situations arise simply to get your attention off God but you do not have to succumb to this trick of the enemy.

When you shift your focus from your problems to God, you will be filled with joy. Be encouraged to allow the Holy Spirit to fill your whole heart so that there won't be any room for anything else.

Prayer for Today: Most holy God, I give reverence and praise to Your name. Thank You for goodness and mercy. Teach me to magnify You and not my problems. Help me to fill my heart with thoughts of Your greatness. In Jesus' name, Amen.

Additional Scripture reading: Psalm 8 and 9

To know Him is to trust Him

Those who know your name trust in you, for you, O Lord, do not abandon those who search for you. **(Psalm 9:10 NLT)**

To trust God is to rely on Him. In order to truly know God's name, you must spend time with him. Spend time with God meditating on His word and seeking Him in prayer. When you do this, your confidence is built up in that you are truly able to rely on Him. It is very difficult to rely on someone you do not know.

When you trust in God, the Bible says that He will not abandon those who search for Him. I can attest that every time I have wholeheartedly and diligently sought God, I found Him. He has shown Himself to be true to His word. He will surely answer your prayers and give guidance when you seek Him. God answers prayers through His Word, prayer, through circumstances and through sermons.

If you haven't truly been seeking God, I challenge you today to begin seeking Him daily so that you may increase in faith and become more of the person He has created you to be.

Prayer for Today: Heavenly Father, I want to trust in You without question. Please remove anything from me that will prevent me from trusting You. Your word that says if I seek You, I will find You. I want more of You in my life. I desire Your will. In Jesus' name, Amen.

Additional Scripture reading: Psalm 34:10; 1 Chronicles 28:9; Hebrews 11:6

~Day of Reflection~

Courage

Read: Psalm 112:8; John 16:33; Acts 4:31; 1 Corinthians 16:33; Ephesians 6:19-20

Meditate: Am I a courageous believer? What gives me courage? What keeps me from living a courageous life?

Apply: Pray to God for courage. Choose not to live in fear. It is perfectly fine to be afraid of the unknown but do not let that stop you from living a courageous life. Do *it* afraid if you have to; but just make sure you do *it*.

Not Without You

Reasons to sing

I will sing to the Lord because he is good to me. (Psalm 13:6 NLT)

Do you need a reason to sing to the Lord? Here it is: He is good to you! He has shown you an abundance of love, grace and mercy! God has shown you an abundance of love by sending His Son Jesus to die for your sins.

God has shown you an abundance of grace because He has given you blessings that you do not deserve.

God has shown you an abundance of mercy because He has not punished you according to your sins. He has not dealt with you in the way that you deserve.

If you need reasons to sing and praise God, think of these things. God is always blessing you even when you do not realize it.

Prayer for Today: Heavenly Father, thank You for Your love, grace and mercy. Thank You for Your kindness and goodness towards me. I pray that You keep before me your awesome deeds that I may remain humble. Thank You for all that You've done in my life. In Jesus' name, Amen.

Additional Scripture reading: Psalm 13 and 103:10; John 3:16

Prayer is key

I am praying to you because I know you will answer, O God. Bend down and listen as I pray. (Psalm 17:6 NLT)

Prayer is one of the most critical parts of the Christian life. Prayer is how Christians communicate with God and spend time in His presence. If your prayer life is lacking, your Christian walk is not all that it should be.

Oftentimes, Christians become disappointed when they feel as if God isn't answering their prayers fast enough. Perhaps God wants to hear more from you? Perhaps He wants a more intimate relationship with you?

God desires that you spend time with Him in prayer each day. If you haven't committed to doing so, today is a great day to start. Set aside time each day just to be in God's presence. You will experience tremendous growth in your faith by doing so.

Prayer for Today: Lord, forgive me for not spending time in Your presence as I should. I commit to seeking You daily to get to know You more. I desire to live the abundant life that I am predestined to live in You. In Jesus name, Amen.

Additional Scripture reading: Psalm 17

God rewards faithfulness

"The Lord rewarded me for doing right; he restored me because of my innocence." (Psalm 18:20 NLT)

You may be in a position where you have done what the Lord has called you to do. You have honored those in authority, loved your neighbor, tithed, prayed, treated others justly and still feel like God has forgotten about you.

Perhaps you're waiting on a prayer to be answered?

Today's Scripture is your encouragement. Keep doing what is right. Keep doing what God has called you to do; He will reward you. God honors diligence and faithfulness but you have to remember that your reward may not be the desired answer to your prayer; the answer may be no. God sees the entire picture so do not become disheartened if you don't receive the reward you were praying for.

Remain steadfast in your faith; your reward could very well be something much greater than you even imagined.

Prayer for Today: Sovereign God, thank You for your faithfulness. Lord, I choose to remain steadfast and faithful, waiting on You to fulfill Your promises to me. In Jesus' name, Amen.

Additional Scripture reading: Psalm 18:20-30

Not Without You

What did you do?

And the Lord sent you on a mission and told you, 'Go and completely destroy the sinners, the Amalekites, until they are all dead.' (1 Samuel 15:18 NLT)

In this passage, Samuel was basically calling Saul out on his sin. Saul did not fully obey the Lord when the Lord instructed him to destroy the Amalekites. Saul saved King Agag (King of Amalekites) and the best of the cattle, sheep, goats, and other animals. He only destroyed what *he thought* was worthless. The Lord became angry with Saul and rejected him. The Lord then chose someone else (David) to be king. Saul's disobedience caused him to lose his blessing (position and favor) with God. I think this is a good example of how our disobedience can cause us to lose out on our blessings. How many blessings have we missed out on or lost because of our sin against the Lord?

When God gives us guidance, whether through prayer, studying his word or through our pastors, we must be careful to do exactly what He has told us to do. Earlier in chapter fifteen, God gave clear instructions to Saul regarding his assignment. Yet, Saul didn't do all that the Lord asked; partial obedience is still disobedience. We learn in verse 22 that obedience is better than sacrifice! Saul's excuse for his sin was that he was going to use what he didn't destroy as burnt offering and sacrifice to the Lord but we learn that the Lord prefers obedience.

So today, ask the Lord to examine your heart. Repent for your disobedience and resolve to be obedient to God's word today and hereafter. Decide to do all that God has called you to do.

Prayer for Today: Heavenly Father, thank You for Your guidance. Help me not to make excuses for my disobedience. I know that once I receive Your word I am responsible for carrying it out. I ask that You forgive me for partial obedience and help me to fully obey Your word. In Jesus' name, Amen.

Additional Scripture reading: 1 Samuel 15

Not Without You

I want to please You, Lord

Keep your servant from deliberate sins! Don't let them control me. Then I will be free of guilt and innocent of great sin. May the words of my mouth and the meditation of my heart be pleasing to you, O LORD, my rock and my redeemer. (Psalm 19:13-14 NLT)

Some sins are easier not to commit than others. For those sins you have trouble with, pray and ask God to strengthen you in that area. King David asked God to keep him from deliberate sins and to not let them control him. Sometimes you can get so caught up in a sin that it becomes a part of you. You become desensitized to it and it doesn't even bother you when you do it.

An important message in today's meditational Scriptures is that your words and your heart need to be pleasing to God. Sin starts in your heart. It's great to keep your mouth from sinning but the sin must be dealt with where it starts– in the heart. Make a decision today to live a life pleasing with God, beginning with a pure heart.

Prayer for Today: Heavenly Father, thank You for Your patience. Cleanse me of my sins and unrighteousness. Create in me a clean heart and renew a steadfast spirit within me. I want my words and my heart to be pleasing to You. Guide my steps. In Jesus' name, Amen.

Additional Scripture reading: Psalm 19:7-14 and Psalm 51

Not Without You

Point me in the right direction

"Show me the right path, O Lord; point out the road for me to follow. Lead me by your truth and teach me, for you are the God who saves me. All day long I put my hope in you." (Psalm 25:4-5 NLT)

David had a very intimate relationship with God. He honored the Lord in all that he did and he communed with him daily. David cared what God thought about his actions and decisions. From reading today's meditational Scripture, we learn that David desired to go along the path that the Lord predestined for him.

What choices are you facing today? Have you consulted the wisdom of God? Are you relying on your own wisdom? Before you make any decisions, ask the Lord to show you the right path. Ask Him to lead you. Put your hope in Him. You can begin by searching the Scripture to see what God says about your particular issue. Consult wise counsel. Make sure that the heart of God is at the center of your decision.

Prayer for Today: Spirit of the living God, I come to You with a heart filled with praise and thanksgiving. I want to be led by You so I ask that You teach me Your ways, show me the right path and point out the road for me to follow. Let me be sensitive to Your voice and give me spiritual discernment. In Jesus' name, Amen.

Additional Scripture reading: Psalm 25:1-8 and Proverbs 2

~Day of Reflection~

Decisions, decisions, decisions

Read: Nehemiah 1:4; Psalm 119:105; Proverbs 18:15; James 1:2-8

Meditate: What is my decision-making process? Who do I consult before making a decision? Is prayer part of the process?

Apply: Consider any decision that you have before you today. There are three essential steps that should be part of your decision-making process: pray first, study God's word and seek counsel. Be sure to include each of these steps in your next decision: large or small.

Not Without You

God leads those who allow Him to lead

"He leads the humble in doing right, teaching them his way." (Psalm 25:9 NLT)

God desires to lead you and give you direction in every area of your life. However, your heart can be a hindrance to the Holy Spirit's gentle nudging. How? If your heart isn't pure, how can you receive what God is speaking to you through His messengers and His Word?

When you're not humble, you are prideful. The Bible teaches that pride cuts us off from God and others. Pride also leads to destruction. Humility positions your heart to be receptive to correction; therefore, you learn to do what is right.

Do not allow pride to get in the way of you becoming all that God has created you to be. It is difficult to remain humble and receive chastisement from the Lord but remember the Lord chastises those He loves. He wants you to be the best you that you can be.

Prayer for Today: In the name of Jesus, Lord God search my heart and remove any pride that is within me. Give me a humble and willing spirit so that I may learn Your ways. In Jesus' name, Amen.

Additional Scripture reading: Psalm 25:9-22; Proverbs 16; Luke 18:9-14

Filter

Your own ears will hear him. Right behind you a voice will say, "This is the way you should go," whether to the right or to the left. (Isaiah 30:21 NLT)

Earlier in this chapter, Judah sought help from Egypt. Judah seeking help from Egypt was contrary to God's plan for them. This chapter teaches us that seeking help outside of the Lord's will – will lead to destruction (v.12 -15). We will only experience lasting success and peace when we seek the Lord and follow the instructions of His voice.

Have you ever been faced with such a big decision that you've talked it over with everyone but God? Well, I'm guilty of that. I remember being faced with the decision to change jobs and talked it over with several of my friends. Many times, we choose to talk about our issues and decisions with everyone except our Father in Heaven. By the time we take the problem to Him, we are hearing so many voices and are so distracted that we cannot hear God's voice or the direction He is leading us. Today's verse says that our *own* ears will *hear* His voice and He will tell us which way to go.

I have since learned to go to God first to seek guidance. There have been times where I've been tempted to step outside of God's will in a rush to get a quick answer but the Holy Spirit gently reminds me of who I need to consult first to get direction. We should keep our minds and hearts clear of all the other voices by seeking God through prayer and His word. Should there be someone you need to discuss your situation with, He will reveal that too. (Remember godly counsel)

Prayer for Today: Father, in the name of Jesus, please give me wisdom, patience and strength to seek You first in all things. I pray that You let Your voice be so clear to me that I am certain that it is You speaking to me. I only want to do Your will. In Jesus' name, Amen.

Additional Scripture reading: Isaiah 30

Not Without You

Protect your purpose

After the wise men were gone, an angel of the Lord appeared to Joseph in a dream. "Get up! Flee to Egypt with the child and his mother," the angel said. "Stay there until I tell you to return, because Herod is going to search for the child to kill him." (Matthew 2:13 NLT)

In Matthew 2, King Herod heard about the birth of Jesus and became disturbed that people were going to worship Him. He even sent the wise men to search for baby Jesus so that he could learn of His whereabouts to kill Him.

The enemy knew that Jesus is the Messiah and that God sent Him for a great purpose. The enemy also knows that God created you for a purpose and the enemy's goal is to keep you from realizing your full potential. He is going to try to kill your dreams and destroy your spirit to keep you from being all that you were destined to be.

Just as the angel of the Lord appeared to Joseph to warn him, the Lord also gives warning signs to you as well. This is why it is very important to walk in the Spirit and use divine discernment. The enemy is not going to give up trying to stop you; so you must not relax and give the enemy any room in your life to penetrate your mind and heart.

Prayer for Today: Father God, there is no one like You in all the earth. How excellent is Your name! Thank You for the plans You have for my life. Thank You for going before me and making my paths straight for Your name's sake. Give me wisdom and discernment in every area of my life so that I may live to please You. In Jesus' name, Amen

Additional Scripture reading: Matthew 2

Not Without You

Fulfilled dreams

"Herod's brutal action fulfilled what God had spoken through the prophet Jeremiah:" (Matthew 2:17 NLT. See also verses 15 and 22)

What has God promised you? What dream has He spoken into your heart? What word is He constantly speaking to you through His messenger (your pastor)? In the scripture references above, things that the prophets spoke about Jesus were beginning to happen just as they said they would. This is important because the prophets' words came from God and they were fulfilled. Everything that God has spoken about us will be fulfilled as well.

Take some time to think about the sermons you've heard over the past few months? More likely than not, there have been consistent messages that God has been speaking and trying to get through to you. Generally, I find that when there is a question on my heart, God answers it many times through His Word, my pastor, other people or circumstances. Each time, the answer is the same. I mention this because I want to point out that God is constantly speaking to us. He is consistent. He confirms His word in our lives over and over again. He is forever showing us that our path has already been prepared for us; we just have to be obedient and walk in it.

Before I began writing books, I prayed and asked God for direction. He answered my prayers through His Word, dreams, sermons from my pastor and through an evangelist on TV that I wasn't even watching. Be encouraged that when God puts something in your heart, He will not allow you to let it go. You will not rest until it is done. It will continue to resurface time and time again. God's word will not return unto Him void (Isaiah 55:11). It will certainly accomplish the purpose for which it was sent. Whatever God has promised and predestined for you, it will be fulfilled!

Prayer for Today: Father God, You are most Holy and kind to me. I ask that You continue to speak to my heart. Empower and encourage me through Your word so that I may continue to walk in destiny and fulfill what You have predestined for me in this life. In Jesus' name, Amen.

Additional Scripture reading: Matthew 2 and Isaiah 55

Evidence

Prove by the way you live that you have repented of your sins and turned to God. (Matthew 3:8 NLT)

The book of Romans tells us that all of us have sinned and fallen short of the glory of God. Because of this, we must accept Christ as our Lord and Savior and live a life that is pleasing to Him.

The results of this change of heart should be manifested in the way that you live. In order to live a life pleasing to God, you must know what is pleasing to God. To know this, you must spend some time reading the Word of God and listening to a pastor who can rightly divide the Word of God and teach you the ways of the Lord.

Do not neglect time in God's presence. You must study to show yourself approved unto the Lord. You cannot live a life pleasing to God if you do not know what pleases Him. Commit to spending time each day studying God's word so that you may be able to prove by the way you live that you have repented of your sins and turned to God.

Prayer for Today: Mighty and awesome God, thank You for salvation. Thank You for Jesus' obedience up to and through the cross. I pray that You help me live a life that is pleasing to You. Let the words of my mouth and the meditation of my heart be acceptable in Your sight. Let my actions reflect that I know and love You. Let Your light shine through me so that You may be glorified. In Jesus' name, Amen.

Additional Scripture reading: Matthew 3 and 2 Timothy 2:15

Holy commitment

Trust in the LORD and do good. Then you will live safely in the land and prosper. Take delight in the LORD, and he will give you your heart's desires. Commit everything you do to the LORD. Trust him, and he will help you. (Psalm 37:3-5 NLT)

In today's passage of Scripture, David encourages the believer to do three things: Trust in the Lord (place total faith in Him); Delight in the Lord (take pleasure in His presence); and Commit everything you do unto the Lord (do everything as if you're doing it for God). David continues to explain the promises of God to us if we do these things: You will prosper; God will give you the desires of your heart and God will be your helper.

These are great promises of God. Just like many of the promises that are written in the Bible, you are required to do your part and live righteously to receive them. The Lord knows that you will stumble but He still requires and deserves the very best of you.

God is full of grace and oftentimes gives what you do not deserve. God desires that you live and experience an abundant life; you will experience this life when you walk according to God's Word. A great way to start is to take David's advice in today's passage of Scripture.

Prayer for Today: Heavenly Father, thank You for your unearned favor and grace. I ask that You help me trust, delight and commit my all to You even more. I want to experience the life that You have predestined for me to live. In Jesus' name, Amen.

Additional Scripture reading: Psalm 37 and Romans 5:1

~Day of Reflection~

Walk, stand, sit

Read: Psalm 1

Meditate: Whose advice do you follow? Consider who you spend time with. What are you doing when you're with your companions?

Apply: What can you do to ensure that you are following wise counsel and delighting in the ways of the Lord?

Know the Word

Then the devil took him to the holy city, Jerusalem, to the highest point of the Temple, and said, "If you are the Son of God, jump off! For the Scriptures say, 'He will order his angels to protect you. And they will hold you up with their hands so you won't even hurt your foot on a stone.' Jesus responded, "The Scriptures also say, 'You must not test the LORD your God.'"(Matthew 4:5-7 NLT)

The enemy will constantly test your faith and knowledge of God's holy word because he hates God. He comes to kill, steal and destroy your spirit and your faith in God. He wants to confuse you and leave you in a puddle of doubt.

In today's Scripture passage, Satan was telling Jesus what the word of God says. It is important to see that Satan knows what the Scriptures say. Since the one who is totally against God knows what the Scriptures say, how much more should believers know the word of God?

I encourage you to spend time studying and living the Scriptures so that you will not be fooled or tricked by the enemy. He searches your weakest areas and looks for every opportunity to exploit those areas to cause you to stumble and fall. Be smarter than the enemy and know your God intimately for your own sake.

Prayer for Today: Most holy God, thank You for Your Word. I pray that as I study and learn Your Word that You let it penetrate and fill my heart so that I can remember and live it daily. Thank You for Your wisdom and discernment. In Jesus' name, Amen.

Additional Scripture reading: Matthew 4:1-11; Psalm 91:11-12; and Deuteronomy 6

Consistency

This fulfilled what God said through the prophet Isaiah: "In the land of Zebulun and of Naphtali, beside the sea, beyond the Jordan River, in Galilee where so many Gentiles live, the people who sat in darkness have seen a great light. And for those who lived in the land where death casts its shadow, a light has shined." (Matthew 4:14-16 NLT)

Throughout the book of Matthew, the Bible constantly reminds readers of the fulfillment of God's word through prophets regarding Jesus. Hundreds of years span the time from when the prophets spoke about Jesus until He was actually born and the prophecies began to be fulfilled. We learn from this that God and His Word are consistent.

This consistency should encourage you to trust in God even more because His Word is reliable. He can be trusted. This is evidence that what He has said will happen. Though things may not occur when you think they should or you want them to, God's Word will prove true.

Take comfort in knowing that God's promises will not go unfulfilled in your life. Remain in faith and remember that His Word has never failed.

Prayer for Today: Heavenly Father, thank You for being trustworthy and consistent. I thank You that Your Word never fails but stands forever. Let this serve as a reminder to me while I wait for Your promises to be fulfilled in my life. In Jesus' name, Amen.

Additional Scripture reading: Matthew 4:12-25; Isaiah 40:8; 1 Peter 1:23-25

Not Without You

Let your light shine

In the same way, let your good deeds shine out for all to see, so that everyone will praise your heavenly Father. (Matthew 5:16 NLT)

The way you live each day is a reflection of God. You are God's ambassador, His representative here on earth. Is that enough pressure?

You are able to win others over to Christ when you properly represent Him by living righteously. Let your light shine at home, work, with friends, in the grocery store, in the parking lot, in traffic, etc. It doesn't take much to be courteous and kind. Essentially, as a Christian, you should have the heart and mind of Christ.

In order to have the heart and mind of Christ, you must spend time getting to know Him by studying and applying the Word of God to your life. God is pleased when you represent Him in a positive light. When you exemplify Christ-like behavior, you may draw others to Him and cause them to desire a relationship with Christ as well.

Prayer for Today: Heavenly Father, let me allow Your light to shine through me so that You will be glorified in all that I do. Let me be mindful that I am a reflection of You because I only want to bring glory to Your name. Lead me in the paths of righteousness for Your name's sake. In Jesus' name, Amen.

Additional Scripture reading: Matthew 5:13-16; 43-48 and 2 Corinthians 5:20

Not Without You

No end to God's greatness

O Lord my God, you have performed many wonders for us. Your plans for us are too numerous to list. You have no equal. If I tried to recite all your wonderful deeds, I would never come to the end of them. (Psalm 40:5 NLT)

One can always find something to complain about. However, I encourage you to choose to meditate and think about the many blessings that the Lord has bestowed upon you. You may not think about it much, but it is a blessing to have electricity, clean running water, and many other things that we so often take for granted. You have eyes to read the words on this page or ears to listen to someone read it to you!

Think of the personal blessings that God has granted to you, blessings that you did not even deserve. In addition to this, God has many other great things in store for you. They may not be what you have in mind but I can assure you that these blessings are exactly what you need and far exceed what you can imagine.

Just like David, even if you tried to list all of the great things that God has done for you, you would never stop talking. There would be no end. No matter what you are going through today, regardless of what isn't right in your life, take a moment to thank God for His countless blessings! Find something to be thankful for because at any moment, it can all be taken away.

Prayer for Today: Heavenly Father, oh how I thank You for Your many blessings! There is no one like You in Heaven or on earth! Thank You for Your sovereignty and abundant grace, love and mercy. There is no end to Your goodness and I praise You for that. Teach me to be thankful in every situation, knowing that I have been blessed by You. In Jesus' name, Amen.

Additional Scripture reading: Psalm 40

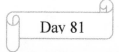

Day 81

Stand for God

"God blesses you when people mock you and persecute you and lie about you and say all sorts of evil things against you because you are my followers." (Matthew 5:11 NLT)

Have you ever been talked about or chastised because you chose to do the right thing or live your life in such a way that it pleases God? Or have you ever mocked someone else for this very thing?

God has called you to live a life of purpose and passion for Him. It is perfectly fine to say no to people and situations that will tarnish your testimony because your goal is to please God and not those around you. People are often intimidated by those who do what is right and will attempt to make the righteous person feel ashamed for standing for Christ.

Do not allow the enemy to shame you into covering up your light. Remember that you may win others to Christ just by being obedient and doing what God would have you do. Remain steadfast in your walk of faith and you will be greatly rewarded.

Prayer for Today: Heavenly Father, thank You for being the light that shines through me. I pray that my actions bring Your name glory and draw others to You. Help me to remain courageous and stand in faith. In Jesus' name, Amen.

Additional Scripture reading: Matthew 5: 1-16

Get rid of it

"And if your hand - even your stronger hand - causes you to sin, cut it off and throw it away. It is better for you to lose one part of your body than for your whole body to be thrown into hell." (Matthew 5:30 NLT)

Sin will cause you to go to hell if you aren't saved. However, once you are saved, you are not exempt from falling into temptation and sinning. The Bible reminds us in Romans 3:23 that all have sinned and fallen short of the glory of God, but we must also remember that we are *"more than conquerors through Jesus Christ."*

Through the power of the Holy Spirit, we can overcome those things that attempt to separate us from God. It is better to stay away from the very appearance of sin and from the people who you know will try to entice you to sin. Be mindful that the desire to sin begins in your heart and then moves into your thoughts, therefore causing you to act.

In today's meditational verse, Jesus says to rid yourself of whatever causes you to sin. Separate yourself from the things and people in your life that lead you into sin and assist you in living a life that is not pleasing to God. If it is something you're watching, watch something else. If it is something you're listening to, listen to something else. If it is a person, do not spend time with them. It is better to get rid of those things than to spend an eternity separated from the Lord.

Prayer for Today: Heavenly Father, I desire to spend eternity with You. I want to please You so I ask that You remove anything in my life that is not pleasing to You. In Jesus' name, Amen.

Additional Scripture reading: Matthew 5:27-30 and Romans 3:23-26

~Day of Reflection~

Envy

Read: Psalm 37:1; Psalm 73:2-3; Proverbs 14:30; Proverbs 27:4; Ecclesiastes 4:4; Titus 3:3

Meditate: Envy steals your peace and can cause you to act irrationally. Have you allowed envy to rob you of peace and contentment?

Apply: Consider why you have been envious. What is the root of your envy? Are you comparing yourself to someone else? What will you do to rid yourself of envy and start to love and embrace the person God created you to be?

Love the unlovable

"You have heard the law that says, 'Love your neighbor' and hate your enemy. But I say, love your enemies! Pray for those who persecute you! In that way, you will be acting as true children of your Father in heaven. For he gives his sunlight to both the evil and the good, and he sends rain on the just and the unjust alike." (Matthew 5:43-45 NLT)

This is tough! Isn't it? However, this is a true test of your maturity in the Christian faith. It is quite easy to love and help those in your life who you believe deserve it, but it is another thing to do the same for those who you believe do not deserve it.

You must make a conscious decision to love and treat everyone justly regardless of how they behave. To truly "love your neighbor," you cannot operate on feelings. In fact, you will have to completely remove your feelings from this altogether. You have to learn to love as God loves and be merciful even to those who do not deserve it. This is how God acts towards you and me. He gives us mercy and grace even when we don't deserve it. It isn't based on how we act but on His character.

I'm sure there are some people in your life who are "character builders." Choose to love them in spite of differences and pray for them. That is probably what they need anyway. Oftentimes, the difficult neighbor is the one who is hurting and needs to be shown extra kindness and mercy. Allow God to use you to intercede on their behalf.

Prayer for Today: Lord, it can sometimes be very difficult to love all of my neighbors. Teach me to love as You love even when I don't want to. Show me those who need intercession so that I may intercede. In Jesus' name, Amen.

Additional Scripture reading: Luke 6:36; Matthew 5:7 and 43-48; 1 Peter 4:8

Not Without You

A giving vessel

Watch out! Don't do your good deeds publicly, to be admired by others, for you will lose the reward from your Father in heaven. (Matthew 6:1 NLT)

You are God's hands here on earth. God uses each of us at some point as channels through which His blessings flow. As you trust God to guide you to give to others, ask the Lord to search your heart and reveal the condition of it to you. You should give with pure intentions: to help others and glorify God.

It doesn't matter if anyone else knows of your good deeds; God knows it and will reward you for it. He will reward you openly if you do it in private (that is, not doing it to receive recognition). Don't give so that you may receive praises from people for your good works. Give to others so that your Father in Heaven will be pleased.

God may be trying to use you today. Be open to being a blessing to someone in need whether it's open arms, listening ears or tangible gifts. God desires to use you for His glory, so keep a sensitive, discerning ear to His voice.

Prayer for Today: Heavenly Father, thank You for using me as a vessel to bless others. Give me the desire to be used by You. Give me a discerning heart so that I may give as You desire me to give. In Jesus' name, Amen.

Additional Scripture reading: Matthew 6:1-4

Power over temptation

And don't let us yield to temptation, but rescue us from the evil one. (Matthew 6:13 NLT)

Temptation arises every day. The enemy seeks to destroy your spirit and to have you living a defeated and broken life. It is important that you begin your day asking God to keep you from giving in to temptation.

Here are few things about temptations:

1. Satan tempts you with what you desire.

2. The Lord always gives you a way out.

3. You have to make a choice to flee from evil.

In knowing this, you must continually pray and discern the tricks of the enemy. Remember his cause: kill, steal, and destroy. Remember our cause: to live like Christ.

Know what God desires of you and learn His ways. There is a very distinct line between God's way and the way of Satan.

Prayer for Today: Father in Heaven, I give You praise for being a forgiving God. Give me the strength not to yield to temptation and give me wisdom to discern and take the way out. In Jesus' name, Amen.

Additional Scripture reading: Matthew 18:7-9

No worries

Can all your worries add a single moment to your life? (Matthew 6:27 NLT)

Are you a worry wart? Do you worry about the inconveniences in your life? Do you worry about the things beyond your control? Whether it's something you can or cannot control, worrying will not change the situation. Worrying *will* cause you to have headaches and sleepless nights.

Sometimes, it is difficult not to worry. We all want things to turn out well for us, our families and those we love. So how do we stop worrying? Worry has to be replaced with something else: Faith. You have to start trusting God to take care of those situations that cause you to worry. Each time you begin to worry, combat it with a "faith thought." Faith thoughts are what God has promised in Scripture. Study God's word when you begin to worry. If you aren't in a place where you can study, take a moment to pray. Meditate on previous victories. God already knows your thoughts and what's causing you distress. God already knows what you need before you ask. Just earnestly seek and trust in Him.

Prayer for Today: Lord, I thank You for being more than willing and able to take care of my worries. I am thankful that I can cast all of my cares on You. Thank You for loving me enough to give me peace in my troubles. In Jesus' name, Amen.

Additional Scripture reading: Matthew 6:25-34 and 1 Peter 5:7

Block prayer distractions

So Ahab went to eat and drink. But Elijah climbed to the top of Mount Carmel and bowed low to the ground and prayed with his face between his knees. (1 Kings 18:42 NLT)

When Elijah prayed for rain, he prayed with head in between his knees. This is significant because this demonstrates that he could not see or hear others. He recognized that in order to truly get in the Lord's presence, he had to block everything else out. This is the same with you and me.

When you set aside time to pray:

1. Go off by yourself so that you won't be distracted.
2. Clear your mind so that your mind won't be wandering off.
3. Protect your ears so that outside noises are eliminated.

Your personal prayer time should be all about you and the Lord. The purpose of prayer is to strengthen your relationship with God, praise God, worship God, strengthen you, receive guidance and commune with Him. Remove yourself from anything going on around you that will hinder that.

Prayer for Today: Heavenly Father, I desire a stronger prayer life with You. I want to get to know You more so that I can live a life more pleasing to You. Help me to make my time with You a priority. In Jesus' name, Amen.

Additional Scripture reading: 1 Kings 18:41-46

Love others not judge them

"Do not judge others, and you will not be judged. For you will be treated as you treat others. The standard you use in judging is the standard by which you will be judged." (Matthew 7:1-2 NLT)

Have you ever thought of your sins as less significant or not as bad as your neighbor's sin? For example, have you ever said or thought, "Well at least I'm not fornicating or getting drunk or committing adultery like ____?"

We often use a different measuring stick for our sins than we use for others when in fact, we shouldn't be using a measuring stick at all. Sin is sin in God's eyes. We sometimes even judge ourselves by saying things like, "I could be doing something worse like ____."

We judge others and ourselves in an attempt to make ourselves feel less guilty. The truth is that God hates all of it. Matthew 7:1-2, admonishes believers not to judge others and if we do, we will be judged by the same standards.

There is no condemnation for those who are in Christ, so we should not be condemning others for God. Everyone has sinned but God gives grace and salvation.

Jesus is the measuring stick. Live by His standards and His alone. He is the one true judge so make sure you aren't taking His job. Treat your brothers and sisters in Christ with love and not judgment.

Prayer for Today: Heavenly Father, teach me to love as You love and not pass judgment on fellow believers. You are the only judge so help me not to judge on Your behalf but to uplift my brothers and sisters. In Jesus' name, Amen.

Additional Scripture reading: Matthew 7:1-6

~Day of Reflection~

Doubt

Read: James 1:5-7; John 20:24-29

Meditate: Do you doubt God in any way? Consider why. Is it because of some past hurts or unanswered prayers?

Apply: Pray and ask God to help you overcome your doubt. Focus on God's character and what He has done.

Praying with expectancy

"Keep on asking, and you will receive what you ask for. Keep on seeking, and you will find. Keep on knocking, and the door will be opened to you. For everyone who asks, receives. Everyone who seeks, finds. And to everyone who knocks, the door will be opened." (Matthew 7:7-8 NLT)

How persistent are you? How many times do you ask God for something? Do you ask once and then leave it alone? Do you ask continuously? You should keep asking until your prayers are answered. I think that children are the most determined. Children will continue to ask their parents for something until they receive it. Sometimes the parent's answer is "later" "maybe" or "not yet." It may even be "no." However, many children still maintain a tenacious and expectant spirit.

With the same spirit, Christians should continue to seek God. He instructs us to keep on seeking, keep on asking, and keep on knocking. This lets us know that what we're asking for will not always be given immediately. Sometimes His answer is "no" "later" or "not yet." However, God is more concerned with hearing from us so He desires that we continue to seek Him.

Prayer for Today: Heavenly Father, thank You for Your faithfulness. Keep me from becoming weary when seeking You. Give me perseverance and strength as I wait on You. In Jesus' name, Amen.

Additional Scripture reading: Matthew 7:7-10

Not Without You

Say good-bye to yesterday

Forget the former things; do not dwell on the past. (Isaiah 43:18 NLT)

Thinking about your past can cast a slight shadow of doubt regarding current endeavors and cause you to question if you can really get to your God-chosen destiny. I heard a sermon a few years ago entitled, "*A Conversation About the Future.*" One of the most memorable comments in the sermon was this: "Don't let what you have not done, stop you from what you can do." Just because your current assignment does not look like your past assignments, do not stop moving forward. God knows what your resume looks like. He did not choose you in error. He chose you because there is something within you that He wants to use to help someone else.

If we spend too much time thinking about our past, we can become consumed with it. When we become consumed, all we're thinking or even talking about is what we did or did not do last month, last year or even 5 years ago. (Remember that thoughts manifest into actions, and in this case, our speech). When we're focused on our past, we can't possibly be focused on our future.

Today, I'd like to encourage you to stop dwelling on the past. Instead focus your mind on what you can actually do something about – your future –you cannot do anything about your past. Note that the enemy wants you to focus on your past because in this way, you are not doing anything about your future. You are not moving forward. The enemy wants you to be preoccupied with anything that will keep you from becoming all you should be.

In verse 19, the Lord says that He is going to do a "new thing." Isn't that exciting? I believe that God wants to do something new in your life. Seek God for the "new" and forget the old.

Prayer for Today: Heavenly Father, thank You for the *new* thing that You are going to do in my life. Keep me from dwelling on past accomplishments and disappointments. Thank You for all that You're going to do in my life. In Jesus' name, Amen.

Additional Scripture reading: Isaiah 43 and Philippians 3:12-14

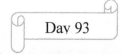

Day 93

Identified by actions

Yes, just as you can identify a tree by its fruit, so you can identify people by their actions. (Matthew 7:20 NLT)

The fruit that Christians should produce are love, joy, peace, grace, mercy. The Scripture today reminds us that we are identified by this fruit; this is how the world knows that we belong to Christ. Living a life that mirrors Christ and pleasing God is how Christians are set apart from the world.

After accepting Christ (believing in your heart and confessing with your mouth that Jesus Christ was crucified for your sins and God raised Him from the dead), our actions should reflect our faith.

Although we have all sinned, we do not have to continue living in sin. Instead, choose to live righteously. When you fall, get back up, repent and start again. Do not allow Satan to condemn you and do not use God's grace as a crutch. Serve God with your whole heart and seek to do God's will in all things.

Prayer for Today: Heavenly Father, I want others to look at me and see Your Spirit at work within me. Touch my mind and heart today so that I may produce the fruit of Your Holy Spirit. In Jesus' name, Amen.

Additional Scripture reading: Galatians 5:22-23

Not Without You

Leaders

Work hard and become a leader; be lazy and become a slave. (Proverbs 12:24 NLT)

I read this book titled, "You Don't Need a Title to Be a Leader," by Mark Sanborn. The book gives several examples of people who worked very hard but did not have leadership titles; these people were not managers or CEOs of their companies. These people weren't even working hard because they wanted a title; it was just their character. They loved their jobs and each had a passion for what they were doing each day.

Many of these people came up with ways to improve efficiency and boost productivity. They also motivated those around them. Eventually, many of the people mentioned in Mr. Sanborn's book did receive the "title." However, that was not their purpose for being great at their jobs; they simply wanted to make things better. They weren't looking for special recognition. Many times we do something "special" at work or church to try to gain recognition or to get "an edge" over the next person. When the outcome is not as expected, we're upset. We should make sure that whatever we're doing, we're pursuing it for the right reason – to please God.

Today I encourage you to work hard regardless of your title. *Proverbs 13:4 NLT says "Lazy people want much but get little, but those who work hard will prosper."* So even when it seems like no one notices your hard work, God sees it! He will promote you in His timing. Your hard work will pay off in due season. You will accomplish your goals. The Bible promises us that we will prosper if we work hard.

Prayer for Today: Father, in the mighty and powerful name of Jesus, I honor and praise Your Holy name! I ask that You give me the strength to continue to work hard even when I haven't received my promotion. Change my heart so that my purpose for working hard won't be because I want a promotion, but that I'll work hard because that's who I am and it's pleasing to You. In Jesus' name, Amen.

Additional Scripture reading: 2 Chronicles 19:5-7 and Matthew 20:26-28

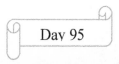

Day 95

The art of wisdom

Anyone who listens to my teaching and follows it is wise, like a person who builds a house on solid rock. (Matthew 7:24 NLT)

God gave us pastors and ministers to teach us His ways. The word of God tells us that we are wise when we listen to and live out His word. When trouble, trials and tribulations come, we won't fret because we have been doing the will of God and we know what God's word says. When we do not follow God's word that we have been taught, the Bible says that is foolish. When trouble arises, we are proven weak, and as a result, we stumble because we haven't been applying God's truths to our lives.

To learn and build upon what we've been taught, here are a few things that we should do:

1. Take notes during sermons
2. Study the notes during the week.
3. Learn the Scriptures associated with the lesson so that they will be implanted in our hearts and become a part of our lives.

Trust God to lead you as you learn to live out His principles.

Prayer for Today: Heavenly Father, thank You for the pastors and ministers that You have placed in my life. Help me not to harden my ears and heart towards Your word. I desire to live out Your teachings in my daily life. In Jesus' name, Amen.

Additional Scripture reading: Matthew 7:24-27

Because you believe

Then Jesus said to the Roman officer, "Go back home. Because you believed, it has happened." And the young servant was healed that same hour. (Matthew 8:13 NLT)

Your faith is what will cause God to move on your behalf!! How much faith do you have in God to answer your prayers? How much faith do you have in God to do what the Bible says He will do in your life? You should have complete and unwavering faith! You must believe wholeheartedly and not doubt. Hebrews 11:6 reminds us that it is impossible to please God without faith.

Take a moment and reflect on your recent prayers. Have you had unwavering faith in God as you wait for His guidance? In today's Scripture, Jesus healed the servant because of the Roman officer's faith. In fact, He told Jesus not to come to his house but to simply speak it! All it takes is a word from the Lord.

I encourage you to trust God today like never before to guide you and answer your prayers. Cast away all doubt and fear.

Prayer for Today: Heavenly Father, today I choose to trust in You. I choose to have faith and not doubt as I wait on You to guide me. Thank You for Your faithfulness. In Jesus' name, Amen.

Additional Scripture reading: Matthew 8:5-13

~Day of Reflection~

Fear

Read: Psalm 27:1; Psalm 25:12; Psalm 91

Meditate: God has not given us the spirit of fear. Are you allowing fear to hold you back from doing what you have been called to do? Is fear keeping you from pursuing some goal or dream?

Apply: Consider the cause of your fear. Combat your fear with action by doing that which is causing you anxiety. Do not spend time worrying about something that may not happen.

Not Without You

Stand firm

Unless your faith is firm, I cannot make you stand firm. (Isaiah 7:9b NLT)

Have you ever set your heart and mind out to accomplish something and issues seem to keep popping up? A family member gets sick, unplanned expense puts your finances in a bind. Someone attacks your vision. You're wondering if you are really doing the right thing and now you have shifted from a spirit of excitement to worry. Worrying is an attack of the enemy. If you spend your time worrying about what might happen, you're distracted from what you're supposed to be doing; you're not focused on your assignment.

As I read our scripture text, the Holy Spirit reminded me to stand firm in the faith and to remain unmovable and unfazed by the things that are going on around me. The Holy Spirit also reminded me not to worry about things that might or could happen. My job is to complete the assignment given to me. It is often easy to start something and harder to finish it. Earlier in the chapter, King Ahaz received word that Jerusalem was about to be attacked. This caused him to tremble with fear. Later on in the chapter, the Lord sent Isaiah to King Ahaz to tell him to stop worrying and confirmed to him what *will* happen. Even though plans were made to attack Jerusalem, they were not carried out. Remember that the Lord has the ultimate power and nothing can happen unless He allows it. So instead of focusing on your attacks you should keep the focus on God and your assignment.

Today I want to encourage you to ignore the negative voices. Keep your feet firmly planted on the track to complete your assignment. Continue to let the Holy Spirit guide you. Be firm. Be steadfast. Be faithful. God will surely make you stand firm (give you success) if your faith is firm!

Prayer for Today: Heavenly Father, thank You for Your timely word. As I lift up Your name right now, I take comfort in knowing that You care for me and that You know exactly what I need. Thank You for reminding me of who You are and what You have called me to do. Help me to be steadfast in my faith. In Jesus' name, Amen.   *Additional Scripture reading*: Isaiah 7

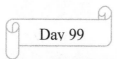

Day 99

Meditate on God's love

O God, we meditate on your unfailing love as we worship in your Temple. (Psalm 48:9 NLT)

What do you spend your time meditating on? Are you thinking about the chaos that's going on around you in this world? In your neighborhood? In your church? In your home? Replace those thoughts with meditation on God's unfailing love for you. Meditate on the truth that even in the midst of every uncomfortable situation, the Lord has kept you.

When you go to worship services, clear your mind so that you may only be focused on God and His love for you. Focusing on God will allow your spirit to worship fully because you are meditating on the One the worship service is all about.

Each day (and even before worship) take a moment to purge your thoughts. Write down the things plaguing your thoughts or talk them over with someone. Do whatever you need to do to clear your mind. Then shift your thoughts to God's love for you.

Prayer for Today: Heavenly Father, I submit my mind to You today. Let my meditations be pure and pleasing in Your sight. Remove everything that doesn't please You and help me to focus on the things that bring You joy. In Jesus' name, Amen.

Additional Scripture reading: Psalm 48 and Psalm 19:14

Not Without You

Don't remain in sin

For I was born a sinner—yes, from the moment my mother conceived me. But you desire honesty from the womb, teaching me wisdom even there. (Psalm 51:5-6 NLT)

The Bible tells us here that we were sinners from the time we were conceived. However, the Bible also says that the Lord still desires honesty. Essentially, being born into sin is not an excuse to live a life filled with sin.

Commit to living a life pleasing to God. Whatever you do, do it as unto God. In today's Scripture, we learn that God begins giving wisdom in the womb. Seek the Lord for His wisdom in how to live in the various situations you encounter. Begin seeking Him by reading and studying His word. When you know Him, you will be able to discern how He would want you to behave in any given situation. Listen to the voice of the Holy Spirit who dwells within you.

Remember the phrase "What would Jesus do?" As you get to know Him more, you will be able to discern what He would do. Jesus' way may not be easy or the popular way to do things, but it is the right way. Do not be deceived; the gate to heaven is narrow but the gate to hell is broad.

Prayer for Today: Heavenly Father, I submit my will to You. Let me always listen to the voice of Your Holy Spirit and let me forever desire to do Your will. In Jesus' name, Amen.

Additional Scripture reading: Psalm 51 and Matthew 7:13

Jesus, the sin doctor

When Jesus heard this, he said, "Healthy people don't need a doctor— sick people do." (Matthew 9:12 NLT)

Why do we need Jesus? Jesus is the doctor for our souls. Our souls needed healing and saving - restoration unto our heavenly Father – and this is what Jesus came to do.

Jesus explains in the text that only sick people need doctors. Each person must come to the realization that s/he is a sinner and needs to be saved (from the sickness of sin). Our role as Christians is to point people toward Jesus by the way that we live our lives. When a person accepts Christ, they are made spiritually new. This inner change should bring about an outward manifestation of change through actions and speech.

Can others see that you've been to the doctor?

Prayer for Today: Heavenly Father, I am in need of Your healing power in my life each day. Thank You for saving me and restoring me unto You. I pray that my ways please and draw others to You. In Jesus' name, Amen.

Additional Scripture reading: Matthew 9:9-13

Not Without You

Labor for the Lord

He said to his disciples, "The harvest is great, but the workers are few."
(Matthew 9:37 NLT)

God desires that we labor for Him. He desires that His people help and uplift one another, encouraging each other in His word. In this Scripture text, Jesus told His disciples that there is much work to be done but very few people to do it. Jesus had compassion for the people because He saw that they were lost and needed more of God's word. His compassion led Him to act; and we must also allow ourselves to be led to action.

We live in a society where people need hope and encouragement. Someone needs to hear about and see your faith in God. Your neighbors need to know how God has moved in your life and that He can do the same for them if they have faith.

Commit to labor for the Lord by letting your light shine. Allow the Lord to direct you to work for Him by being an earthly vessel. Whether the task is giving, praying, working in a specific ministry or charitable organization, commit to being the Lord's hands on earth.

Prayer for Today: Heavenly Father, teach me to be Your hands here on earth. Give me a heart to serve others on Your behalf. In Jesus' name, Amen.

Additional Scripture reading: Matthew 9:35-38

Not Without You

Opportunities to show your faith

You will stand trial before governors and kings because you are my followers. But this will be your opportunity to tell the rulers and other unbelievers about me. (Matthew 10:18 NLT)

Oftentimes, we do not see uncomfortable situations as opportunities but that is exactly how we should view them. When you are under pressure or in a position where things don't go as you planned, use that as an opportunity to show your faith. It is even more beneficial for others to see your faith in troubling times.

Choose to let unpleasant circumstances be your avenue to allow the Holy Spirit to use you. Speak about and show your faith in God. Let those around you witness you giving God glory and praise throughout the situation. Your actions will encourage them and God will be glorified in the process. This will serve as your testimony.

As the Scripture says, don't worry about what you will say because the Holy Spirit will give you the right words at the right time. Make the choice to be a willing vessel.

As you go throughout your day today, choose to glorify and uplift God no matter what happens. Your countenance just may be someone else's comfort and hope.

Prayer for Today: Heavenly Father, I come into Your presence seeking Your face. I desire Your will and Your way. Help me to live in such a way that You will be glorified and others will be drawn to You. In Jesus' name, Amen.

Additional Scripture reading: Matthew 10:16-20

Not Without You

Giving

Read: Ezra 2:68-69; Mark 9:41; 1 John 3:17-22

Meditate: Are you selfish? Do you have trouble giving to others?

Apply: Give within your ability to someone in need or a local charity. Consider volunteering your time in an area you're passionate about to help others in need.

Produce good fruit

A good person produces good things from the treasury of a good heart, and an evil person produces evil things from the treasury of an evil heart. (Matthew 12:35 NLT)

If you never breathed a word to anyone else regarding your faith, would they know that you are a follower of Jesus Christ? How would they know? They should be able to identify you by the fruit that you produce.

As a Christian, you should be producing the fruit of the Spirit: love, joy, peace, kindness, goodness, mercy. To produce this type of fruit, you must have a pure heart that is willing to be led by the Holy Spirit. Be mindful that your thoughts and actions are a direct reflection of the condition of your heart.

In addition to having a pure heart, you must also choose to reflect the nature of Christ in your daily life. You choose what you say and how you live your life each day. Just because you have the freedom to say and do what pleases you, doesn't mean that you should. Develop a habit of asking yourself if what you're about to say or do reflects Christ in you. Consider: "Will this bring shame to the body of Christ? Is this beneficial? Will this draw others closer to God or push them away?"

Prayer for Today: Father in Heaven, as I go throughout my day, give me a spirit of conviction before I do or say something that doesn't please You. Help me to be mindful of my thoughts, speech and actions so that my ways will reflect Your Spirit within me. In Jesus' name, Amen.

Additional Scripture reading: Matthew 12:33-37 and 1 Corinthians 10:23

Not Without You

Praises for promises

I praise God for what he has promised. I trust in God, so why should I be afraid? What can mere mortals do to me? (Psalm 56:4 NLT)

What has God promised you? There are thousands of promises from God to you throughout His word. In order to know them and hide them in your heart, you must study His word.

When you are obedient and walk in faith, God promises to bless you. God promises not to withhold any good thing from you if you live righteously. He promised to be with you forever and not forsake you. The most important promise is eternal life for believing that the Lord sent Jesus Christ to die for your sins and that God raised Him from the dead.

God is faithful and He doesn't change. Study God's word to learn about all He has promised. Your faith will increase and you will live a more abundant life.

Prayer for Today: Heavenly Father, thank You for Your promises. Thank You for all that You are going to do in my life when I choose to do Your will. Give me the wisdom to follow along Your path. In Jesus' name, Amen.

Additional Scripture reading: Deuteronomy 28 and Psalm 84:11

Can you handle God's favor?

But Noah found favor with the LORD. (Genesis 6:8 NLT)

Being favored by God is not always easy. Sometimes it will mean that you won't be supported or that no one will believe in the vision that God has given you. However, do not allow what others can't handle to cause you to become discouraged.

Noah walked in close fellowship with God and found favor in God's sight above everyone else on earth at that time. Because of God's favor, Noah was chosen to do something that had never been done to prepare for something that had never happened (build a large boat to prepare for rain). No one believed Noah or supported him. Guess what? They perished for their lack of faith.

I once heard a pastor say that you need to be strong if you're going to be blessed, because that's when you will experience the most discomfort. People will dislike and plot against you for unknown reasons. Not everyone will be able to handle the favor of God on your life. Do not allow that to discourage you from carrying out the assignment(s) before you: large or small.

Prayer for Today: Heavenly Father, thank You for the favor that You have given me. Thank You for choosing me to do such great things in Your name. Strengthen me daily so that I may stand firm and continue to do the work that You have called me to do. In Jesus' name, Amen.

Additional Scripture reading: Genesis 6

Not Without You

Worship in uncertainty

After that, Abram traveled south and set up camp in the hill country, with Bethel to the west and Ai to the east. There he built another altar and dedicated it to the LORD, and he worshiped the LORD. (Genesis 12:8 NLT)

The Lord called Abraham (Abram at the time) to leave his home to go to a land that the Lord would show him. He was obedient; he packed up his wife, nephew Lot, and all of his wealth and began traveling as the Lord instructed.

At the time of his departure, Abraham did not know where the Lord was leading him. Instead he relied on God's faithfulness and trusted Him to lead him into the Promised Land. Although he didn't know where he was going, he did not allow that to keep him from worshiping the Lord.

Today, I encourage you to continue following God even if you don't know the end result. Don't focus on that but on the Lord. Keep worshiping and praising because your worship will draw you closer to God and set your focus where it needs to be - on Him.

Prayer for Today: Heavenly Father, today I choose to wholeheartedly follow You. I will worship and praise You as I follow You along the path that You have predestined for me. In Jesus' name, Amen.

Additional Scripture reading: Genesis 12

Not Without You

Who's in your circle?

But the LORD sent terrible plagues upon Pharaoh and his household because of Sarai, Abram's wife. (Genesis 12:17 NLT)

As Abraham and his wife Sarah were traveling to the land God was leading them to, they passed through Egypt. While there, Abraham instructed his wife to tell everyone she was his sister. When he did so, Pharaoh took her as his wife. The Lord then sent plagues upon Pharaoh and his household because of her. It is important to know that having the wrong person in your camp can be destructive!

On the surface, it may seem like a good idea to quickly allow someone into your inner circle. Many times people present to you the person they want you to see. Take your time getting to know people and who they are connected to before you allow yourself to become close to them.

Resist the temptation to do this in your social, professional and spiritual life. Consider what happened to the ship that Jonah jumped into when God instructed him to go to Ninevah. The people on the ship experienced turmoil because of Jonah. Check your connections in your life to make sure there are no Jonahs.

Prayer for Today: Heavenly Father, thank You for Your Holy Spirit who gives discernment. I pray that You give me wisdom to use discernment in my daily life. In Jesus' name, Amen.

Additional Scripture reading: Genesis 20 and Jonah 1

Look straight ahead

Look straight ahead, and fix your eyes on what lies before you. Mark out a straight path for your feet; stay on the safe path. Don't get sidetracked; keep your feet from following evil. (Proverbs 4:25-27 NLT)

When God gives you an assignment, you have to stay focused. Once you purpose in your heart to follow God's instructions, there will be many distractions to come up against you in an attempt to get you off course. The scripture says to fix your eyes on what lies before you. Your actions usually follow the direction of what you have your sight set on. Think about the driver who turns his head to the left or right to stare at a sign. His car will drift toward the direction in which he is looking. The same thing happens in your life each day. Your life will head in the direction that your heart is fixed on.

The scripture also says to "mark out a straight path for your feet." Make a plan to get to what lies before you! When you have a written plan, you are more likely to accomplish your goals. You will have something to work toward and keep your eyes focused upon. Write down your plans and keep them before you to constantly remind yourself of where you are going.

Today, I encourage you to think about what it is that you have your eyes fixed upon. Make sure you have a written plan on how to get there because there will *always* be things, situations and people that will try to get you off track and fix your eyes on anything and everything that is not leading you to your goal. When you're certain about your direction and you encounter a distraction, you'll be able to identify it as such, dismiss it and keep moving forward.

Prayer for Today: Heavenly Father, I am trusting You and keeping my mind fixed on what lies before me. Strengthen me to stand against distractions and remain focused on Your will for my life. In Jesus' name, Amen.   *Additional Scripture reading*: Psalm 23 and Psalm 25:9

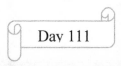

Day 111

~Day of Reflection~

Guidance

Read: Psalm 25:4-5; Psalm 32:8; Psalm 119:133; Proverbs 3:5-6

Meditate: Are you allowing God to guide your steps in your decision-making, relationships and everyday walk? Do you seek God for guidance? Do you trust His guidance?

Apply: Is there anything that hinders you from receiving God's guidance? What can you do differently to discern God's guidance for your daily life?

Not Without You

An appointed time

After four generations your descendants will return here to this land, for the sins of the Amorites do not yet warrant their destruction. (Genesis 15:16 NLT)

As people of God, we often want God's blessings without going through the process to receive them. Today's Scripture reminded me of the Israelites and their oppression in Egypt. They spent 400 years poor, beaten and oppressed. The good news about this is that God already had an appointed time for their deliverance as stated in today's Scripture reference.

While going through their troubles, the Israelites did not know how long they would last. Just like the Israelites, you don't know the duration of your trials. However, you can rest assured that they will expire, because there is an appointed time for you to receive every blessing that God has established for you. In the meantime, continue to praise and grow in God. You are going to come out of it much better spiritually. Remain faithful.

Prayer for Today: Heavenly Father, thank You for the plans of restoration You have for my life. I give You praise that even before I enter into trials You have already established my deliverance. I bless Your holy name! In Jesus' name, Amen.

Additional Scripture reading: Genesis 15 and Jeremiah 29:11

Fixers

So Sarai said to Abram, "The LORD has prevented me from having children. Go and sleep with my servant. Perhaps I can have children through her." And Abram agreed with Sarai's proposal. (Genesis 16:2 NLT)

Are you a fixer? How do you know if you are a fixer? Here are a couple of clues to help you out:

1) You begin thinking or taking action to fix a problem as soon as it arises.
2) Perhaps a friend comes to you with a problem and instead of listening, you want to fix it.
3) Maybe you feel like it takes God too long to answer your prayers so you begin coming up with your own solutions without guidance from Him.

Do any of these sound familiar?

My fellow fixer, you and I acted just like Sarai when it was taking quite a while for her to conceive a child. She went and found what she thought was the solution to God's plan. As a fixer, you or I might have done the same thing.

One thing about fixers is that they are impatient. I pray that you will join me and learn to be patient and wait on God. In the process of waiting, let's try really hard not to attempt fixing things ourselves.

Prayer for Today: Heavenly Father, forgive me for my impatience. I admit that I often want immediate results and get in the way of Your timing and plans for my life. Help me resist the urge to do things on my own but to trust and wait patiently on You. In Jesus' name, Amen.

Additional Scripture reading: Genesis 16

Generational blessings

And through your descendants all the nations of the earth will be blessed—all because you have obeyed me. (Genesis 22:18 NLT)

Obedience to the Lord can sometimes be really challenging, especially when your heart and flesh desires the opposite of what God commands.

The Lord instructed Abraham to sacrifice his only son. Abraham proceeded to do as the Lord asked because he trusted the Lord. He had already experienced the fruit of God's promises, so he knew God to be faithful and decided to obey. His trust in God led him to believe that God would provide a way, though he didn't know how or when. Earlier in the chapter he told his servants that they (not just him but Isaac as well) would return and that God would provide a sacrifice for the burnt offering. The Lord did provide! As Abraham was about to sacrifice his son, the Lord sent the ram in the bush.

Abraham's obedience moved God to bless him and his descendants. Remember, no matter how significant or not you think your obedience is, it can be the difference between blessings or curses for you and your children's children. Obedience = blessings.

Prayer for Today: Father in Heaven, thank You for blessings You've given me that I don't deserve. I desire generational blessings so I ask that You give me a spirit of conviction when I am about to do something against Your will. Give me the desire to be obedient to Your word. In Jesus' name, Amen.

Additional Scripture reading: Genesis 22 and Deuteronomy 28 and 29

Not Without You

God carries you

Praise the Lord; praise God our savior! For each day he carries us in his arms. (Psalm 68:19 NLT)

Get this Scripture deep down in your spirit today. Take comfort in knowing that not only is God with you but He is carrying you throughout the day. He is willing and able to take on your burdens and cares for this day.

Whether you are heading to a stressful job, looking for a job, staying at home with children, taking care of your family or teaching in a classroom, do not worry about what lies ahead. Instead, prepare mentally and spiritually by taking comfort in the fact that God sees you, hears you, cares for you and carries you.

Trust and rest in Him today.

Prayer for Today: Heavenly Father, thank You for carrying me. Thank You for loving me so much that you care about the condition of my heart and spirit. Give me peace throughout today as I trust and rest in You. In Jesus' name, Amen.

Additional Scripture reading: Psalm 68

Not Without You

With me, is God

All right then, the Lord himself will give you the sign. Look! The virgin will conceive a child! She will give birth to a son and will call him Immanuel (which means 'God is with us'). (Isaiah 7:14 NLT)

Several years ago, Pastor Benford, The Living Word Fellowship Church, preached a sermon titled *"With Me, Is God."* Throughout the message he used our scripture text as a reference. He reminded us that Immanuel meant "God with us." But he urged us to look at it this way: "With Me Is God." Now I must be honest. I don't remember many sermons (especially without studying them repeatedly) but this one has stayed with me since the morning I heard it. I can still hear his final words: "If y'all don't remember anything else, remember this: With Me Is God."

Immanuel is one of the many names of God. I know that we each experience moments in our lives when we pause to wonder if God is there and if He's listening to our prayers. Take comfort in knowing that He is there and He does hear them. His name describes who He is; He is with us! He will never leave us nor forsake us. He is omnipresent!

So today I want to pass this on to you: if you must remind yourself daily, then please do so. It is surely comforting and empowering to know that *With Me Is God.* In order to fully appreciate this fact, we must know the *power* of God's presence. I pray that you come to know, understand and appreciate what it means to be in God's presence and experience the power of God's presence in your life.

Prayer for Today: Heavenly Father, thank You for Your Holy presence in my life. Knowing that You are with me brings me joy and gives me peace. I choose to trust in Your power and rely on Your guidance. In Jesus' name, Amen.

Additional Scripture reading: Joshua 1 and Psalm 25:9

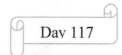

Day 117

Life interrupted

Jesus saw the huge crowd as he stepped from the boat, and he had compassion on them and healed their sick. (Matthew 14:14 NLT)

In today's scripture text, Jesus had just received news of John the Baptist's death. When He heard about it, He was on His way to be alone. Instead, the crowds followed Him and interrupted His alone time. He saw that they needed Him and was moved to action. What did He do? Healed the sick.

Meditating on this passage reminded me of life's interruptions. You may want or even need to take a moment alone, but sometimes those around you may need you even more. Someone needs your love and compassion. Someone needs to receive an outpouring of the love of God that dwells within you. They need to see Jesus.

Take a moment today to show love to someone who needs it. The Lord will certainly bless you for the compassion that you show to others.

Prayer for Today: Heavenly Father, give me wisdom not to ignore others when they need me. Let me allow Your love to flow through me to shower upon someone else today. In Jesus' name, Amen.

Additional Scripture reading: Matthew 14:1-14

Not Without You

~Day of Reflection~

God is always there

Read: Psalm 121

Meditate: Do you sometimes feel as if God isn't there or that He doesn't care what happens to you? Consider why you feel as if He isn't there. It is not God who is far away from us; it is often we who have strayed away from Him.

Apply: Focus on the words of this Psalm. God is always there and He cares what happens to you. Continue looking to Him for strength and guidance. Think back over your life and meditate on how He has protected and watched over you. Take comfort in Him.

Don't underestimate your gifts

"But we have only five loaves of bread and two fish!" they answered. (Matthew 14:17 NLT)

Oftentimes, we underestimate the value of that which we have in our possession to give. When you hold on to the notion that your gifts to the church, family, friends or strangers need to be of a certain amount to be of value and you allow this to keep you from giving, you miss the opportunity to be a blessing to someone else.

In your eyes and in your hands, five dollars may not be much but if it is all you have to give, in God's hands it can be plenty. When you give to others with the right spirit, God will bless you and your gifts.

In the text, the disciples told Jesus that they didn't have enough to feed all those people. But when they gave what they had to Jesus, it became more than enough.

God can use even the smallest gift to bless your neighbor, so don't allow the smallness of your gift to deter you from giving; it just may be what someone else needs.

Prayer for Today: Heavenly Father, give me a heart and mind to please You by blessing others with the gifts that I have. Help me to remember that when I put my gifts in Your hands, they can be life changing. Thank You for the gifts You've given me. In Jesus' name, Amen.

Additional Scripture reading: Matthew 14:13-21 and Proverbs 3:28

Not Without You

From problems to promises

But when he saw the strong wind and the waves, he was terrified and began to sink. "Save me, Lord!" he shouted. (Matthew 14:30 NLT)

The moment Peter stopped focusing on Jesus and began to focus on the troubles around him, he was overcome with fear and began to sink. He allowed his fear to overpower his faith.

Just like Peter, you will sink in life when you allow your troubles to overpower you. Things can get really bad, but that is when you must stand firm in your faith. Remember how God delivered you last time. Meditate on how God worked out the many troubles in your life before now. Stay in faith and praise. Praise redirects your focus from your problems to God's promises. God does not change. He is still the same merciful, forgiving, loving and faithful God that He was yesterday.

Prayer for Today: Heavenly Father, thank You for being unchanging. It brings my heart joy to know that You are faithful even when I am unfaithful. Today, I will praise You and not my problems. I choose to focus on Your goodness and mercy. In Jesus' name, Amen.

Additional Scripture reading: Matthew 14:22-36

Out of your heart, out of your mouth

It's not what goes into your mouth that defiles you; you are defiled by the words that come out of your mouth. (Matthew 15:11 NLT)

In Psalm 51, David asked the Lord to create within him a clean heart and to renew a right spirit in him. This Psalm was penned after David sinned with Bathsheba. David understood that he needed forgiveness and that his sinful actions stemmed from an impure heart.

All thoughts and actions start out as seeds planted in your heart. In order to change your life and live according to how God wants you to live, you need a clean heart.

Pray and ask God daily for a pure heart and a renewed spirit. Be mindful of what you allow into your heart. Seeds are planted in your heart by what you see and listen to.

Put pure in, get pure out. Put impure in and impurity flows out. Make your eyes study God's word and let your ears listen to what pleases Him. Remember that your life is a direct reflection of what's in your heart.

Prayer for Today: Father in Heaven, I praise Your holy name. Create in me a clean heart and renew within me a faithful and steadfast spirit. Let me be mindful of what I allow access into my spirit. Give me the desire to please You and only do Your will. In Jesus' name, Amen.

Additional Scripture reading: Matthew 15:1-20; Psalm 51 and 2 Samuel 11

Not Without You

Take the way out

What sorrow awaits the world, because it tempts people to sin. Temptations are inevitable, but what sorrow awaits the person who does the tempting. (Matthew 18:7 NLT)

There is no way around experiencing temptation. Today's verse tells us that temptations are inevitable, which means that you will certainly be tempted. You don't have to give in to temptation because when you are tempted, you are always given a way out.

Not only should you keep away from sin but you must not cause anyone else to sin. Do not bring your friends into your mess. Distance yourself from the things and people that bring out the worst in you and tempt you to sin. The Bible teaches that it is much better to be without such parts that cause you to sin than to be separated from God because of them.

Commit to taking the "out" that you're given when you are tempted, and determine not to lead anyone else down the path of unrighteousness. Commit to being the light that leads to Christ instead of the darkness that leads to sin.

Prayer for Today: Heavenly Father, lead me not into temptation but deliver me from all evil. Give me the wisdom and the strength to resist temptation and to take the exit that You provide. Help me to flee from sin. In Jesus' name, Amen.

Additional Scripture reading: Matthew 18:1-10 and Corinthians 10:13

Prayer partner

I also tell you this: If two of you agree here on earth concerning anything you ask, my Father in heaven will do it for you. (Matthew 18:19 NLT)

Do you have a prayer partner? Someone who will pray in agreement, believing with you for what you need from God? It is great to pray by yourself because you need a healthy prayer life. Prayer builds intimacy with the Holy God.

It is also a good idea to have someone to pray with you from time to time. Here are a few reasons why:

1) Jesus promises that God will do what you ask.
2) Jesus promises that He will be in the midst of those who pray.
3) It boosts your faith when you have someone who will truly believe with you.

Pray continually. Do not allow anything to interrupt your prayer life because this is one of the ways your faith in God and your relationship with God are strengthened. Consider praying in agreement because of what Jesus promises to you in the Scripture. God gave authority and power to Jesus: When you pray in His name, it is done.

Prayer for Today: Heavenly Father, thank You for Your word. Send me an accountability partner so that I may have someone to pray with and hold me accountable. I desire to be in alignment with Your will and experience the fullness that You promised. In Jesus' name, Amen.

Additional Scripture reading: Matthew 18:15-20

Not Without You

Forgive at all times

Then Peter came to him and asked, "Lord, how often should I forgive someone who sins against me? Seven times?" "No, not seven times," Jesus replied, "but seventy times seven." (Matthew 18:21-22 NLT)

God desires that you forgive others as often as He forgives you. You ask God for forgiveness daily. In the same way, you should forgive others daily.

Forgiveness benefits you more than it helps the person who offended you. Sometimes, the offender doesn't know that they did something wrong. When you harbor unforgiveness in your heart and become bitter at that person, you are destroying your own spirit.

Go to the person who has wronged you and let them know they offended you. S/he may ask for forgiveness and apologize. Forgive them. Do not hold a grudge. Even if they do not ask for forgiveness, forgive them so that you may have peace.

What if it's a *big* offense? God doesn't hold your sins against you based on the magnitude of them. In an effort to live as Christ desires you to live, forgive regardless of the magnitude. This does not mean that you give room for the offense to happen again. Use wisdom. Simply extend to others the same forgiveness that God daily extends to you.

Prayer for Today: Heavenly Father, give me the strength to forgive those who have wronged me. Help me to move past the hurt and forgive others as You have forgiven me. In Jesus' name, Amen.

Additional Scripture reading: Matthew 18:21-35 and Ephesians 4:32

Not Without You

~Day of Reflection~

Commitment to God

Read: Isaiah 40:29-31

Meditate: Have you been wavering on your commitment to God?

Apply: Consider why you have been wavering. Is it because of some unanswered prayer? Enticement of the enemy? What will you do to recommit yourself to God? God welcomes all of His children back to Him.

Not Without You

The shepherd and His sheep

The Lord is my shepherd; I have all that I need. (Psalm 23:1 NLT)

A shepherd's role is to protect and watch over the sheep. Here are a few things that a shepherd does:

- Leads the sheep
- Feeds the sheep
- Gives the sheep water
- Watches over the sheep
- Seeks out and finds the sheep to bring them back to the flock after they have gone astray
- Guards the sheep
- Protects the sheep

The Lord is your shepherd and you are His sheep. Just as a shepherd does these things for sheep, the Lord also does these things for you. The Lord provides all that you need. He is there to guide you, protect you and bring you back to Him after you have gone astray.

The Lord desires that you remain close to Him. When you stray away, He allows things to happen to bring you back to Him. There is safety in the arms of the Lord. Stay in His presence. It is not until you leave His presence that you forsake His presents.

Prayer for Today: Heavenly Father, thank You for being my shepherd and caring for me. Thank You for being faithful. Thank You for not giving up on me. Draw me closer to You. In Jesus' name, Amen.

Additional Scripture reading: Psalm 23 and John 10

Blessed by association

"Please listen to me," Laban replied. "I have become wealthy, for the L*ORD has blessed me because of you." (Genesis 30:27 NLT)*

Because of who Jacob was, his uncle Laban was blessed. Laban's wealth increased greatly because of Jacob's management of his flock and because God's blessing was on Jacob. (Remember that Isaac gave Jacob the blessing instead of his brother Esau.) Laban recognized that his association with Jacob resulted in him being blessed.

It is important to learn that those you are connected or associated with will have an impact on your blessings. What if Jacob was evil and God was not with him? I don't think Laban would have been as blessed.

Consider your circles: friends, spiritual partners, business associations. Are you a blessing or a curse to those around you? Are you adding value to them? Are those in your circle a blessing or a curse in your life? Are they adding value to you? Or is there subtraction? If there is subtraction, perhaps you should subtract them from your circle.

Prayer for Today: Heavenly Father, thank You for those in my life who are a blessing because of Your favor on their lives. Help me to be obedient to Your word so that I will be a blessing and not a curse to those in my life. In Jesus' name, Amen.

Additional Scripture reading: Genesis 30:25-43

Not Without You

The Lord is on your side

"In fact, if the God of my father had not been on my side—the God of Abraham and the fearsome God of Isaac—you would have sent me away empty-handed. But God has seen your abuse and my hard work. That is why he appeared to you last night and rebuked you!" (Genesis 31:42 NLT)

Jacob recounted to Laban the saving power of the presence of God in his life. Jacob recognized that if God were not on his side, Laban may have treated him badly and taken everything away from him.

Can you think of any situation in which you know that God was clearly on your side? He preserved you. He kept you from harm. He saved you from being destroyed. The Lord has kept you from seen and unseen danger.

Give God praise for all that He has done for you. Never forget to whisper a prayer of thanks to Him for His faithfulness. Even when things are bad, they can be much worse. He knows how much you can handle and He won't let anything greater than that happen. God loves you and is always looking out for you – even when it doesn't seem like it. God sees the whole picture when you only see a fraction of it. Be thankful and remain faithful.

Prayer for Today: Heavenly Father, thank You for being on my side. Thank You for preserving me. I know that You have saved me from things that I don't even know about. Thank You for being faithful and showing me favor. In Jesus' name, Amen.

Additional Scripture reading: Genesis 31:22-42

Transformation begins within

You blind Pharisee! First wash the inside of the cup and the dish, and then the outside will become clean, too. (Matthew 23:26 NLT)

God is concerned with what's in your heart and how you allow that to control your behavior. Although what you do should be pleasing to Him, your heart should please him as well. If your heart is not clean, then your actions aren't pure and true.

You should not pick and choose which Scriptures to obey. Some Scriptures are easier to obey because they can be done outwardly without the condition of your heart being apparent. These particular actions can become mechanical (e.g. tithing even the smallest part of your income because of habit not heart condition). What about truly loving and giving to those in need? What about allowing the Lord to use you as a vessel to bless your neighbor? Are you truly clean on the inside if you're not willing to be used by God? Love your neighbor? Forgive? Show mercy?

Ensure that your heart is in the right place. Once you're clean inwardly, your actions will reflect this cleanliness. Pray. Seek,. Love. Forgive. Study. Praise. Worship. Be transformed.

Prayer for Today: Heavenly Father, I want my deeds to be pure and reflective of Your Holy Spirit. Show me my heart's condition. Cleanse my heart and renew the right spirit within me. In Jesus' name, Amen.

Additional Scripture reading: Matthew 23:23-28

Difficulty propels you into destiny

"Come on, let's kill him and throw him into one of these cisterns. We can tell our father, 'A wild animal has eaten him.' Then we'll see what becomes of his dreams!" (Genesis 37:20 NLT)

Be very careful of who you decide to share your dreams with. God-given dreams will often cause others to be jealous or feel threatened. When God gives a dream: 1) It exceeds your current capacity; 2) You will need to rely on Him to provide the resources to make it happen and 3) No one can stop it from coming to fruition no matter what they try.

Consider how Joseph's brothers schemed to get rid of him to kill his dreams. Throughout everything that Joseph went through, he was propelled closer to the dream that God gave him, not away from it as his brothers would have liked.

Whatever issues you may be facing today, know that they are meant to teach you something and launch you further into your destiny. The issues are not meant to discourage you as the enemy would have you believe. Use your obstacles as learning tools and stepping stones as you stay in faith and strive to move forward.

Prayer for Today: Heavenly Father, give me eyes to see things as You see them. Help me use my issues as opportunities to trust You and grow in faith. Thank You for the spiritual lessons. In Jesus' name, Amen.

Additional Scripture reading: Genesis 37

Not Without You

Even in mess, God can bless

So Potiphar gave Joseph complete administrative responsibility over everything he owned. With Joseph there, he didn't worry about a thing—except what kind of food to eat! (Genesis 39:6a NLT)

I'm glad that God's love is unconditional. As I meditated on the story of Joseph in Potiphar's house, I realized that God is bigger than all of our problems.

Another thing to note is that God can and will bless you and cause others to show you favor regardless of where you are. Joseph was sold into slavery but God gave him success even in that. He was put in charge of Potiphar's household and eventually everything that Potiphar owned.

God can show favor to you and bless you right where you are. If you work in an environment where others intend you harm, God can make it good for you. No matter what undesirable situation you may be in today, have faith that God sees you and can give you success in the messiest circumstances.

Prayer for Today: Heavenly Father, thank You for being sovereign. Thank You for being such an awesome God! Thank You for Your unconditional love. I am thankful that You can and will bless me right where I am. Help me to remain faithful to You. In Jesus' name, Amen.

Additional Scripture reading: Genesis 39:1-6

~Day of Reflection~

Faithful during temptation

Read: 1 Peter 1:6-7

Meditate: Do you believe that you can remain faithful to God when you are tempted? Do you believe that you are strengthened when tested?

Apply: What will you do to ensure that you remain faithful to God and His ways when you are being tested?

Temporary Satisfaction

"No one here has more authority than I do. He has held back nothing from me except you, because you are his wife. How could I do such a wicked thing? It would be a great sin against God." (Genesis 39:9 NLT)

"God gave this to me, I don't want to mess things up!" We would all be much better off if we thought like this every time the temptation to sin and disappoint God came up!

This is exactly what Joseph's line of thinking was when Potiphar's wife wanted to sleep with him. He considered how God blessed him through Potiphar and he considered how great a sin against God it would be to sleep with her. It would have been a slap in God's face! Joseph understood that his position and favor came from the Lord and he would not act as if it was meaningless or as if he did not appreciate God's favor.

Let's think like Joseph today. When temptation arises, consider all that God has done for you and choose not to mess it up for temporary satisfaction. Nothing the enemy can offer you is worth giving up your blessings and favor!

Prayer for Today: Heavenly Father, give me the mentality of Joseph when it comes to sin. Let me consider all that You have blessed me with and remember that it can all be taken away in an instant. Let me not submit to temporary satisfaction and give up eternal blessings. In Jesus' name, Amen.

Additional Scripture reading: Genesis 39:8-9 and Psalm 112

Just say no

She kept putting pressure on Joseph day after day, but he refused to sleep with her, and he kept out of her way as much as possible. (Genesis 39:10 NLT)

When you know the people and types of situations that constantly tempt you, avoid them. Joseph was determined not to sin by sleeping with Potiphar's wife, so he avoided her as much as he could. We have to be the same way when we are aware of tempting situations. Sometimes, people won't take no for an answer and will continue to ask and present the temptation to us. *The enemy is persistent.* We have to take charge and commit to being faithful to God and true to our own convictions.

As you go throughout your day, be mindful of the obvious temptations and go in a different direction. No one knows you better than you do so take charge and stay on the path to righteousness.

Prayer for Today: Heavenly Father, help me to stay away from situations and people that tempt me to sin. Give me the courage to say no and walk away. In Jesus' name, Amen.

Additional Scripture reading: Genesis 39:10-18 and Matthew 26:41

Moments of destiny

"But don't be upset, and don't be angry with yourselves for selling me to this place. It was God who sent me here ahead of you to preserve your lives." (Genesis 45:5 NLT)

Have you ever been at a place in your life where you wondered, *"How did I get here?"* or *"What am I doing here?"* Did it occur to you that God had you there for a specific purpose?

Everything that God allows to happen to you or for you is not always about you. God often uses us to help someone else. Have you ever thought, *"Maybe that's why I came here today"* or *"I needed to see and talk to this person in this moment."* These are moments of divine destiny. Consider the moment in today's Scripture when Joseph revealed who he was and why God brought him there (to preserve his family members' lives).

We don't always know how God will take care of us. But we can trust and believe that all things truly do work together for the good of those who love God and are called according to His purpose. Wherever God has you now, have faith that it is part of His plan.

Prayer for Today: Heavenly Father, thank You for the plans You have for my life. Thank You for moments of divine destiny. I trust that all things are working together in my life for my good and Your purpose. In Jesus' name, Amen.

Additional Scripture reading: Genesis 45:1-15 and Romans 8:28

Not Without You

Use what you have

"The master was full of praise. 'Well done, my good and faithful servant. You have been faithful in handling this small amount, so now I will give you many more responsibilities. Let's celebrate together!'" (Matthew 25:21 NLT)

What are you doing with that which God has already given to you? What are you doing with the talents, gifts, resources, visions and dreams? Have you buried them? Are you using them in ways to glorify the Giver (God)? Are you using them to fulfill your assignments?

Before you ask God to give you more, consider what you are doing with what you already have. God gives to each of us according to His will and our abilities. He desires that we use what He's given us to glorify Him and uplift His people. We were given everything we needed to complete our assignments before we were even aware of them. The issue is that we haven't even began to use or tap into those things so we do not know what we have.

Today, spend some time thinking about what you are doing with what you already have. If you haven't been faithful, start over, commit and move forward.

Prayer for Today: Heavenly Father, help me to be wise with what You've already given me. Teach me to be faithful with what I already have so that I may honor You and bring Your name glory. In Jesus' name, Amen.

Additional Scripture reading: 25:14-30

Not Without You

A willing vessel

"And the King will say, 'I tell you the truth, when you did it to one of the least of these my brothers and sisters, you were doing it to me!'" *(Matthew 25:40 NLT)*

As a Christian, your actions and deeds are a reflection of your relationship with Christ. The way you treat others should be a manifestation of the love Christ has for you and vice versa. We are to love our neighbors as ourselves. How do we love ourselves? We take care of all of our needs.

How do you know if you love others as God intended? Reflect on these things:

- What was your response the last time someone asked you to pray for or with them regarding a specific thing?
- Were you in a position to do more than just pray but to help? Did you help?

We are to allow God to work through us so that others may experience His love. Pay attention to the needs of those around you and seek to be of assistance when you are able.

Prayer for Today: Heavenly Father, teach me to bestow upon others an outpouring of love and kindness as if I'm doing it to You. Help me to be a vessel that honors You and love others with the same heart in which You love me. In Jesus' name, Amen.

Additional Scripture reading: Matthew 25:31-46

Multiply your faith

But the more the Egyptians oppressed them, the more the Israelites multiplied and spread, and the more alarmed the Egyptians became. (Exodus 1:12 NLT)

In the Scripture text, the Egyptians were trying to crush the spirit of the Israelites. The Israelites began to outnumber the Egyptians, which frightened them. The Egyptians feared that the Israelites would become allies with their enemies and revolt against them. To keep this from happening, the Egyptians tried to wear them down by increasing their labor. However, the more the Egyptians oppressed them, the more the Israelites multiplied.

This is just like the enemy. He fears what you will do when you realize who you are and how much strength you have. However, you must not allow his tactics to keep you from being faithful, to keep you from growing or to keep you from learning.

When the enemy attempts to keep you down, use that as an opportunity to increase in faith.

Prayer for Today: Heavenly Father, thank You for the power to overcome adversity. Give me strength to use opposition as an opportunity increase my faith. In Jesus' name, Amen.

Additional Scripture reading: Exodus 1:1-14

~Day of Reflection~

Feeling like giving up

Read: Joshua 23:10; 1 Corinthians 1:8; Galatians 6:9

Meditate: Think of something that you felt like giving up on. Why did you want to give up?

Apply: Choose at least one project that you're working on, consider why you're motivated to finish it, and write down all of the reasons why you need to see it through to the end. Place your list in a place where you will see it daily to keep you motivated when you feel like giving up or begin to feel defeated.

Holy direction

But because the midwives feared God, they refused to obey the king's orders. They allowed the boys to live, too. (Exodus 1:17 NLT)

Whose voice do you listen to? Do you listen to God's voice? The voice of the enemy? Voices of friends? Know that your life is a direct reflection of the voices you listen to.

Take a moment to assess your place in life. Assess your personal life, family life, professional life, finances, etc. What drives your behavior? What are your rules for living?

Many voices give direction and instruction but you should only be listening to those that are in alignment with the Holy Spirit. Look at the midwives in today's text. They feared the Lord more than Pharaoh and did what was right in God's sight. They chose not to listen to Pharaoh when he decreed that newborn Israelite boys should be killed.

Like the midwives, choose the path that gives God glory; that is how you'll know you're listening to God's voice and living according to His will.

Prayer for Today: Heavenly Father, I want to live according to Your purpose and will. Quiet all other voices but Yours so that I may hear clearly and follow You. In Jesus' name, Amen.

Additional Scripture reading: Exodus 1:15-22

Peacemakers needed

Similarly, a family splintered by feuding will fall apart. (Mark 3:25 NLT)

Division exists in our government, churches and sometimes, families. Constant feuding and bickering hinders productivity. We must learn to work together to achieve the common goal. God desires that we work together to accomplish His will. The word of God tells us that there is blessing when we work together in harmony.

We cannot do much about the division in our government other than cast our vote and pray that our leaders work together for the greater good. However, we can do plenty about the division in our churches and families. Consider your roles in your church community and in your family. Are you working to bring people together or are you at the center of the division? What can you do to bring peace in divisive situations? The first thing you can do is consider the common goal. What are you working toward? You can also challenge yourself to be the peacemaker.

In order to accomplish God's will for the church and family, you have to put your selfish desires aside and put the needs of others first. Choose to love and not allow differences to get in the way of God's will.

Prayer for Today: Heavenly Father, help me to be the peacemaker in troubled situations so that nothing gets in the way of me doing Your will. I realize that Your will is most important; I desire Your will and not my own. In Jesus' name, Amen.

Additional Scripture reading: Mark 3:23-27 and Psalm 133

Love is glue

Let no one split apart what God has joined together. (Mark 10:9 NLT)

Divorce is very real in our society. Statistics show that up to half of all marriages end in divorce. This is heartbreaking. We don't value relationships or the person that we enter into relationship with. We must learn to take them seriously and treat others the way that God would have us treat them. This is not the easiest thing to do but it is the best thing to do to save relationships.

Before I got married, one of my mentors shared this with me. He said that being married is a sacrifice and that each day I have to die to myself, put the needs of my spouse before mine and do what's right for the relationship. The longer I stay married, the more I understand what he meant. If each person in the relationship seeks to love the other and treat them as God would have you treat them, then it will work. I can attest to the fact that things are more peaceful and loving in my marriage when I treat my husband in a way that pleases God and vice versa.

Whether or not you're married, this piece of advice is valuable in any relationship: avoid selfishness and love people the way God wants you to love them. A relationship can only work if both parties want it to work. Consider your behavior in your relationships. Are you putting the needs of others before yours? Do you love them as Christ would have you love them?

Prayer for Today: Heavenly Father, thank You for the relationships that You've blessed me with. Help me to cover each person with love and to give selflessly to the relationship. In Jesus' name, Amen.

Additional Scripture reading: Mark 10:1-12; Proverbs 16:24 and 1 Corinthians 13:4-7

Blessed is she that believed

And blessed is she that believed: for there shall be a performance of those things which we were told her from the Lord. (Luke 1:45 NJKV)

Those who believe and have faith are blessed! In this text, Mary had just been told that she would be impregnated by the Holy Spirit and give birth to Jesus. She received the angel's message with joy and acknowledged that nothing is impossible with God. She believed that God would do what He said He would do! Unlike Zechariah, she didn't need proof. Knowing God's character and the angel appearing to her were proof enough to believe God.

Many times, we are like Zechariah. After all that God has done in our lives, all the sermons we've heard and the Scriptures we've read, we still don't believe that God will move in our lives one more time. We have to have unwavering faith! God's word is enough and we have to believe that it is enough. We must learn to declare the word of God over our life and believe that it is done. Nothing is impossible when we believe God without doubt!

Today, I encourage you to release every bit of doubt that you may be holding on to. Believe God with every fiber of your being because if He said it, then it is so. When doubt creeps into your heart, combat it with the word of God. Blessed are you when you believe!

Prayer for Today: Heavenly Father, I choose to obey and believe in Your Word! Today, I declare that I am blessed because I believe You. I am blessed because I have faith. I ask that You help me to keep doubt out of my heart and mind and replace it with Your word. With You, all things are possible. In Jesus' name, Amen.

Additional Scripture reading: Luke 1

Not Without You

Attention please

"This is amazing," Moses said to himself. "Why isn't that bush burning up? I must go see it." (Exodus 3:3 NLT)

The Lord used the burning bush to get Moses' attention. Usually, when the Lord gets our attention, He does so to give us an assignment.

Has the Lord been trying to get your attention? Have you taken a moment to stop and listen? The assignment may have nothing to do with your current occupation or skillset. The assignment is to glorify God and not yourself. Don't be afraid to accept the assignment because you feel like you're unqualified. Whatever tools you need to complete the assignment, you either already have them or God is going to make sure you get them.

Today, take some time to think about what the Lord wants you to do. Operate in faith and accept it. God's plan and purpose for you is far greater than you can imagine.

Prayer for Today: Heavenly Father, thank You for the plan You have for my life. I choose to trust You by accepting and pursuing it. Help me to walk in faith not fear. In Jesus' name, Amen.

Additional Scripture reading: Exodus 3 and Acts 26:13-16

The Golden rule

Do to others as you would like them to do to you. (Luke 6:31 NLT)

The Golden Rule! This simple statement was plastered all over my grade school classrooms. We teach this to our children but sometimes forget this rule when we become adults. There are no exceptions to this rule. For example, it doesn't mean to only treat those who you love in the same manner as you would like to be treated. You are to deal with everyone in the same way you desire to be regarded.

It is easy to love those who love you in return. The challenge is being kind to the person who doesn't like you, despises you or wants nothing to do with you. Consider the coworker who never greets you in return or the nasty retail associate; you should apply the golden rule to them as well. This is how you truly let the love of God shine through you.

It doesn't matter whether you know someone personally or if you even like them, you should always treat them the way you want to be treated. The love you show them just may be the love that they need. Some people don't know how to deal with personal problems so everyone they come into contact with suffers.

As you go throughout your day today, choose to be kind to all who you come into contact with regardless of their disposition. God desires that you love everyone, even the unlovable.

Prayer for Today: Heavenly Father, sometimes it is hard for me to treat others the same way I want to be treated. Help me to look past the nasty behavior of difficult people and show them the same level of love and courtesy that I desire. In Jesus' name, Amen.

Additional Scripture reading: Luke 6:27-36

~Day of Reflection~

Insulted

Read: Proverbs 12:16 and 1 Peter 3:9

Meditate: How do you respond when others insult you? Do you allow your emotions to rule over you?

Apply: How can you avoid being led by your emotions when someone insults you? Will you choose God's way and not repay others when they offend you?

Act like you know Him

"So why do you keep calling me 'Lord, Lord!' when you don't do what I say?" (Luke 6:46 NLT)

When we know how the Lord wants us to live and choose to do the opposite, we are denying that we know Him. When we don't do what the Lord says, we cannot fully experience the abundant life that He has promised. Here are some of the consequences of disobedience:

- We aren't using the authority and power given to us by the Holy Spirit.
- We aren't as blessed as we could be.
- We are destroying our spirit and giving more power to our flesh.
- We draw further away from God making it more difficult to hear His voice.

None of us desires to be out of God's holy presence and unable to hear his voice. As Christians, we desire to be close to Him and experience the joy of our salvation.

Ask the Lord to search your heart and show you areas where you need to be obedient and turnaround to follow Him.

Prayer for Today: Heavenly Father, I want to be all that You have created me to be and I want to experience life that way You intended. Forgive me for not doing as Your word says and cleanse my heart. Let me consider how my disobedience affects my relationship with You before I choose the wrong path. In Jesus' name, Amen.

Additional Scripture reading: Luke 6:46-49

Remove the lampshade

"No one lights a lamp and then covers it with a bowl or hides it under a bed. A lamp is placed on a stand where its light can be seen by all who enter the house." (Luke 8:16 NLT)

As Christians, the "light" is the word of God that has been planted in our hearts. We must not cover it up but let it shine brightly. How? We allow the light to shine through our deeds. Our deeds should reflect what we know in Christ to be true. Our hearts have been changed and everything we do must be an example of this truth.

Our light to the world is to demonstrate the love of God in how we live, love God, love ourselves and one another.

Keep your light powered by constantly refueling on the word of God. Keep your light shining by living according to God's word so that others may see it and be drawn closer to Him.

Are you letting your light shine today?

Prayer for Today: Heavenly Father, thank You for Your word that is a light unto my path. Help me allow my light to shine so that You will be glorified in all that I do. Let me not be afraid to walk in Your path. In Jesus' name, Amen.

Additional Scripture reading: Luke 8:16-18 and Psalm 119:105-112

Not Without You

The Father's love

So if you sinful people know how to give good gifts to your children, how much more will your heavenly Father give the Holy Spirit to those who ask Him. (Luke 11:13 NLT)

Becoming a parent helps put things in perspective when it comes to love. The love that parents have for their children is immeasurable. Parents love their children so much that they will do anything for them and provide the best for them. Parents desire to give children everything they need and even the things they want when suitable.

You may be able to understand or identify with the love of a parent either because you are a parent or you have experienced a parent's love. Now consider our Father in Heaven. He is much greater and powerful than we are. His love for us far exceeds the love that we have for our own children. When I consider how much I love my children, I am overwhelmed thinking about how much more God loves me!

The Holy Spirit is the best gift that God gives us next to salvation. God gives us what we need and all that we need is wrapped up in the Holy Spirit. The Holy Spirit gives us direction, comfort, peace and so much more. Through the Holy Spirit, God gives what we ask when it is in our best interest and in alignment with His will.

Trust and know today that God provides His best for you as a parent does for his child and that His way is perfect.

Prayer for Today: Heavenly Father, thank You for being the ultimate parent. Thank You for loving me beyond measure and doing what's in my best interest at all times. In Jesus' name, Amen.

Additional Scripture reading: Luke 11:9-13

Deep cleaning

"When an evil spirit leaves a person, it goes into the desert, searching for rest. But when it finds none, it says, 'I will return to the person I came from.'" (Luke 11:24 NLT)

Sweeping only cleans surface dirt while washing cleanses the cracks and crevices. If you attempt to cleanse yourself, you are sweeping the surface. When you ask Christ to wash you of your sins, you are truly cleansed. When you do not allow Christ to cleanse you, you allow room for the sin to return – leaving you worse off than before.

Only the word and power of God can truly cleanse you and make you righteous in the eyes of God. Nothing else will do. When a person tries to rid themselves of their sin on their own, they only sweep the surface by removing the sin seen by others but not the secret sins of the heart. Christ comes to purify our hearts, which is where sin is conceived. Once the inside is clean, then the outside can be cleansed.

If you're struggling with any specific sin, perhaps you have not given it over to God to get to the root of the problem – your heart. Allow God to create within you a clean heart and renew within you the right spirit.

Prayer for Today: Heavenly Father, thank You for having the power and the will to clean my heart. I submit my heart to You so that You may cleanse me of the sins I struggle with. I don't want to be surface cleansed but deeply cleansed. In Jesus' name, Amen.

Additional Scripture reading: Luke 11:24-28

Stir up the gift

Therefore I remind you to stir up the gift of God which is in you through the laying on of my hands. For God has not given us a spirit of fear, but of power and of love and of a sound mind. (2 Timothy 1:6-7 NKJV)

God has given each of us a divine set of assignments to accomplish during our lifetime for His glory (our purpose). In the Scripture reference above, the Bible teaches us that we should stir up the gift of God within us. You see, before we were even born, God had a plan for our lives. When we became believers, the gift of God was placed within us. Now that we are believers, it is our duty to carry out what God has already pre-destined:

- We should preserve and protect the gift(s) that God has given us. We will walk in true destiny and purpose if we use our gifts correctly.
- We should not be afraid to use our gifts.
- God gave us the power we needed when He placed the gift(s) in us; we don't have to be timid or apprehensive about using our gifts.

True peace and fulfillment comes when we're walking in purpose to fulfill our God-given assignments.

Prayer for Today: Heavenly Father, thank You for the gifts that You've given me. Help me not to walk in fear but in the power and love that you've given me. In Jesus' name, Amen.

Additional Scripture reading: 2 Timothy 1:5-11

Fulfilling the Requirements

But someone who does not know, and then does something wrong, will be punished only lightly. When someone has been given much, much will be required in return; and when someone has been entrusted with much, even more will be required. (Luke 12:48 NLT)

Have you ever been at a place in your life where God has constantly blessed you to achieve success after success? Or, have you ever been in the opposite place? A place where you've felt like you've worked and worked but have not experienced the reward of your hard work? Have you found yourself longing for the moment where you can chill, but at the same time you have so much that you need and want to accomplish? Are you always *grinding*?

There may come a time in your life where the temptation comes to want to slow down and chill. The reason you aren't relaxing is because God has placed so much in you that He needs to get out. You may find yourself wanting to take a short cut at work, in your personal life, in your spiritual life or even trying to get to your destiny. Remember, God requires so much more of you. He requires that you give your very best.

In order to determine what is required of you, you need to know what you're trying to accomplish and why. Think of two students matriculating through college who are studying two different programs. The courses that are required of each student are different and each student must meet the requirements of their own respective programs in order to earn their degrees. Remember that everyone is not on the same "degree plan" as you are in life so resist the temptation to do the same thing your neighbor is doing. Fulfill the assignments given to you.

Prayer for Today: Heavenly Father, thank You for the plan that You have set for me. I choose to follow You and seek after Your will. Help me not to get sidetracked by attempting to follow the plan that you have for someone else. In Jesus' name, Amen. *Additional Scripture reading*: Micah 6:8, Genesis 26:4-6 and Deuteronomy 10:11-13

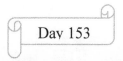

Day 153

~Day of Reflection~

Laziness

Read: Proverbs 6:6-11; 10:4-5; 12:24; 22:13; 26:14; 1 Thessalonians 5:14 and 2 Thessalonians 3:10

Meditate: Are you lazy? Can you identify areas in your life where you have been lazy?

Apply: What can you do to avoid being lazy? How will you avoid being lazy in the future?

Not Without You

Who is He to you?

But Jesus remained silent and gave no answer. Again the high priest asked him, "Are you the Messiah, the Son of the Blessed One?" "I am," said Jesus. "And you will see the Son of Man sitting at the right hand of the Mighty One and coming on the clouds of heaven." (Mark 14:61-62 NIV)

Mark 14 and 15 lead up to and through Jesus' death on the cross. Before His death, the priests were trying to find something (anything) to accuse Jesus of to justify their killing Him. In today's Scripture passage, the priest asked and revealed who Jesus is. They all knew the Scriptures so they knew that the Messiah was coming. Jesus performed all of those miracles, lived a life that was holy and perfect and spoke with such wisdom, yet they refused to believe that He could be who He said that He was. Because of their hardened hearts, they missed out on having a relationship with Jesus and everything that He taught. They killed the Messiah! With all that Jesus had done during His ministry and the way He lived His life, I wonder why they didn't believe. Just who were they expecting?

This brings me to the question: Who is He to you? Are you missing out on having a genuine relationship with Him because He isn't answering your prayers as you expect? Are you putting Him on trial and expecting Him to meet all your desires and whims, or do you see that *He* is the judge and has a right to decide what is right or wrong even if it doesn't align with your expectations?

Today, choose to see Jesus for who He is: mighty, powerful, forgiving and loving. Don't allow your heart to be hardened, missing out on a relationship that will change your life forever.

Prayer for Today: Heavenly Father, thank You for being a holy and sovereign God! Thank You for the life of Jesus' Christ that demonstrates how You want me to live. Let me not live a life filled with unbelief but of faith in You. In Jesus' name, Amen.

Additional Scripture reading: Mark 14:53-15:15

Life-giving Word

The Word gave life to everything that was created, and his life brought light to everyone. (John 1:4 NLT)

Do you know that feeling you get after you drink a tall glass of cold water when you're thirsty? Or how you feel when you eat after you've been hungry all day? That satisfying moment. That is how our spirits feel when we receive a word from God because the word of God is refreshing and gives life to us!

Consider how God's word created the heavens and the earth. How powerful is that? That same power of His word gives life to our souls and renews us. The power of His word has not and will not change. God has not changed. All it takes is a word from God to transform you and your life.

Is your spirit hungry or thirsty? If so, you need to hear the word of God. God's word is meant to empower us, teach us, correct us and direct us. Do not neglect the opportunity to hear a word from God. Whether you attend church service, listen to a sermon CD or watch online, you need the Word of God to live an abundant life.

Prayer for Today: Heavenly Father, my soul thirsts for You. I need the power and the life that Your word provides to my spirit. Thank You for Your Word. In Jesus' name, Amen.

Additional Scripture reading: Genesis 1 and John 1

Not Without You

An invitation for Jesus

And Jesus and his disciples were also invited to the celebration. (John 2:2 NLT)

Jesus was invited to a wedding celebration. During the festivities, the hosts ran out of wine. An interesting thing to note is that Jesus was invited into the situation before there was a problem (no more wine). There was also someone at the party who knew Him and knew that He could fix the problem.

We can learn plenty from this situation. As Christians, if we learn to invite the Lord into our lives before we encounter problems, we don't have to run looking for Him after there are issues. Oftentimes, we place the Lord and our relationship with Him on the backburner until our wine runs out. Then we attend church or begin praying and studying the Bible when these are things that we should have been doing anyway.

Challenge yourself to spend time with God even when things are going well in your life. Invite the Lord into your life now by praying and studying the word of God so that when trials come, you are prepared because the Lord is already with you. You don't have to go searching for Him because you already invited Him into your life. You won't be anxious or worried because you will already know what His word says about your situation.

Prayer for Today: Heavenly Father, thank You for Your Word. I invite You into my life today to grow closer to You and seek your will. In Jesus' name, Amen.

Additional Scripture reading: John 2:1-12

Exposure

"All who do evil hate the light and refuse to go near it for fear their sins will be exposed. But those who do what is right come to the light so others can see that they are doing what God wants." (John 3:20-21 NLT)

Think about your actions when you know that you're doing something wrong. Generally, you want to cover it up so you stay away from any light that may expose your wrongdoing. Perhaps you stop praying, attending church, studying your Bible or checking in with your accountability partner because doing any of these things will expose you. Your flesh is enjoying the sin, and to keep from feeling guilty, you cease doing all the things you need to do to strengthen your spiritual life.

When you feel like you're doing things well by praying, studying God's word and listening to His voice, you have no problem being in His presence. You feel like you're being transparent so you do not resist being in the light. You aren't ashamed when others see you.

This is human nature. We want others to see us doing the right thing but not the wrong thing. However, we cannot straddle the fence. We must choose God's way and keep it. We must not cover up our sin but confess it and turn away from it and allow the Lord to cleanse us. Accept His love and cleansing today.

Prayer for Today: Heavenly Father, thank You for eternal life. Thank You for Your love and compassion. Help me to confess all of my sin to You and no longer live in darkness but in the light. In Jesus' name, Amen.

Additional Scripture reading: John 3:1-21

Not Without You

Backseat drivers

"My thoughts are nothing like your thoughts," says the Lord. "And my ways are far beyond anything you could imagine." (Isaiah 55:8 NLT)

Backseat drivers. Aren't they annoying? You know who they are. They are the people who sit in the passenger seat of the car giving directions or instructions on how to drive. This person may not know where you're going or even how to get there, yet they have so much advice to give. When the driver knows that the person is wrong and has no idea what they're talking about, it can be very irritating.

When it comes to God's plans for our lives, we often become backseat drivers as well. God sees the big picture when we can only see the present situation. We become backseat drivers when we attempt to navigate our lives without consulting Him or create our own plans and expect God to go along with them.

God tells us in His word that His thoughts and ways are nothing like ours. We must submit to His will for our lives and allow Him to direct our paths instead of attempting to do things our own way.

Today, allow God to be your navigator by listening to His voice to determine when to turn, stop or go. It's best to listen to the one who created the path for your life.

Prayer for Today: Heavenly Father, thank You for the plans You have for my life. I thank You that Your thoughts and ways are much greater than mine. Thank You for having a plan for my life far greater than I could imagine. I submit my will to Yours today. In Jesus' name, Amen.

Additional Scripture reading: Isaiah 55:8-9 and Proverbs 16:9

Not Without You

Now I know

Then the father realized that that was the very time Jesus had told him, "Your son will live." And he and his entire household believed in Jesus. (John 4:53 NLT)

You have heard it said that "hindsight is 20/20." Essentially, we have greater vision and clarity when we view or think about things of the past, specifically the Lord at work in our lives. You can probably think about certain past situations and say, "Now I know it was the Lord who did this for me."

When the father in the scriptural text realized that Jesus healed his son just as He said, he moved from believing Christ's words to believing in Him. Just like the father in the text, when we look back over our lives, we have enough evidence of God's power at work. We must move from just believing in His words to believing in Him. Our belief in Him and the sharing of our belief in Him will move those around us to believe. Take the father in the text: because of all that happened, he began to believe in Christ and so did his household.

We are living testimonies of God's work. We should always be willing to share this with others and live in a manner that reflects Christ. Today, I encourage you to live like the living testimony that you really are!

Prayer for Today: Heavenly Father, thank You for Your word at work in my life. I have enough proof of the power of Your word that not only do I now believe Your word but I believe in You. I trust that You have my best interest at heart and that Your love towards me is unconditional. In Jesus' name, Amen.

Additional Scripture reading: John 4:43-54

~Day of Reflection~

Love

Read: John 13:34; Romans 12:9; 1 Corinthians 13:4-8; 1 Peter 4:8;   2 John 1:5

Meditate: How do you express your love for others? Do you have trouble expressing love to others God's way?

Apply: Think of someone in your life who needs to receive an expression of love from you, whether it is forgiveness, listening ear, mercy or a tangible gift. Allow God to lead you to show love to that person today.

Sin Less

But afterward Jesus found him in the Temple and told him, "Now you are well; so stop sinning, or something even worse may happen to you." (John 5:14 NLT)

Jesus made this statement to the man whom he had just healed and given the ability to walk. We can learn a very important lesson from this passage of Scripture. We should live righteously every day and not just because we are seeking something from the Lord. The Lord requires that we seek him, love him, praise him, worship him and pray to him in obedience and not simply because we want something. If anything, we should already be doing these things and they should be magnified even more when we need the Lord to move on our behalf.

Once we receive what we've been seeking, we should continue to live righteously. We shouldn't go back to living any kind of way but continue to walk in obedience to the Lord. Getting what we asked for is not a license to return to our old ways. After all, something even worse may happen and we may find ourselves in an even bigger mess than before.

Prayer for Today: Heavenly Father, thank You for Your word. I pray that You help me to not only become obedient when I want something from You but to make obedience part of who I am. Let me be mindful of Your love for me and help me to sin less. In Jesus' name, Amen.

Additional Scripture reading: John 5:1-15

Not Without You

God is always working

But Jesus replied, "My Father is always working and so am I." (John 5:17 NLT)

In the Scripture text, the Jewish leaders persecuted Jesus because He worked on the Sabbath day by healing a man. In their eyes, nothing should be done on the Sabbath day, including making people whole. However, we should rejoice in the fact that God is always working.

Take comfort in knowing that our Father in Heaven is always working on our behalf. Jesus' power is always at work within us. God is always saving, always forgiving, always loving, always providing, always listening, always comforting, always showing mercy, always giving grace and always being God!

It doesn't matter what day of the week it is, God is making things work together for your good and His glory. Whatever it is that you seek from the Lord today, know that God is already on it! He is not limited to any specific time of the day or week. He will complete the good work that He began within you.

Prayer for Today: Heavenly Father, thank You for always being at work in my life. My soul rejoices in knowing that You are not limited to a specific time to be all that I need You to be. In Jesus' name, Amen.

Additional Scripture reading: John 5:16-30

Let Him in the boat

Then they were eager to let him in the boat, and immediately they arrived at their destination. (John 6:21 NLT)

The disciples were in a boat headed to Capernaum in the middle of the storm when Christ appeared walking on the water. We learn from the preceding verses that the absence of Christ in our lives causes us to fear. We also learn Jesus Christ has power even over natural forces like storms and time; the disciples learned to fear and trust Him, and so can we.

Though we may not be encountering a natural storm as the disciples were, we do experience many storms in life. We should learn to invite Jesus into our lives before we enter into a storm because His presence in our lives gives us peace, comfort and guidance. The Lord is more concerned about being in the boat with us than the storm that we're in; so whether you're entering a storm, in a storm or coming out of one, invite Jesus into your *boat* today. Learn to trust in Him to provide the peace that only He can give.

Prayer for Today: Heavenly Father, You're always invited into my boat. Thank You for the peace and calm You give in the midst of my storms. In Jesus' name, Amen.

Additional Scripture reading: John 6:16-21

Not Without You

Don't listen to naysayers

They replied, "Are you from Galilee, too? Search the Scriptures and see for yourself - no prophet ever comes from Galilee!" (John 7:52 NLT)

The Pharisees were trying to arrest Jesus but had no charges to bring against Him. Nicodemus spoke up and challenged them by asking if it was legal to convict Jesus without first giving Him a hearing. Their rebuttal was that no prophet ever came from Galilee.

The Pharisees attempted to discount Jesus because of where He came from, but they didn't know God's plan for Jesus and refused to believe in who Jesus really is. Remember that Jesus is much greater than we are and God's plan for His life far exceeded the plans He has for ours, so if people discounted Jesus, they will surely do the same to us.

At times people will try to discount you because of your background, your looks, your walk, your talk or other discriminatory factors. However, not everyone knows, neither will they understand, the plans that God has for your life. No one can stop God's plan; they may delay the plan but never can they keep God's plans from going forward.

Stay in faith and don't allow the negativity of anyone to keep you from your purpose. God's way always prevails.

Prayer for Today: Heavenly Father, thank You for the plans that You have for my life. Give me courage and strength to ignore those who try to distract me from carrying out Your will. Thank You for the Holy Spirit who leads and directs me. In Jesus' name, Amen.

Additional Scripture reading: John 7:40-53

God's power at work

"It was not because of his sins or his parents' sins" Jesus answered. "This happened so the power of God could be seen in him." (John 9:3 NLT)

We don't always learn spiritual lessons by going through tests but sometimes we learn by the testimonies of others. God will use other people to get a message through to you. Sometimes your life will be used so that someone else may learn more about God's power.

At times in each of our lives we will experience difficulties that are not consequences of our sins but so that God's power can be demonstrated in our lives. The faith of those around us will be strengthened and others will be drawn to Christ. When our neighbors witness the way we go through these trials, they will be empowered to seek and trust Christ even more than before.

God chooses those whom He trusts to go through these kinds of trials because He knows that these saints will honor and magnify Him throughout it all. So don't be discouraged when you find yourself going through something that you feel isn't warranted. Instead, rejoice! Don't rejoice in the trial but rejoice in the fact that God chose you. God's plan is perfect and God will use you to accomplish His purpose.

Prayer for Today: Heavenly Father, thank You for Your purpose and Your power. Though it may not feel right, I thank You for choosing me to demonstrate Your power. I am Your vessel and I trust You. In Jesus' name, Amen.

Additional Scripture reading: John 9:1-34

His voice

After he has gathered his own flock, he walks ahead of them, and they follow him because they know his voice. (John 10:4 NLT)

Just as sheep follow the shepherd, so we should also follow God's voice. The word of God says that sheep do not follow the voice of a stranger. In order to follow His voice, we must know what it sounds like. To know what God's voice sounds like, we must study His Word. Studying and living God's word is essential in Christian life. When we live in this way, we experience the satisfying and abundant life that God promises.

The shepherd goes before the sheep and marks the path that the sheep must follow. When we follow the shepherd, we stay along the path that God intended for us. God desires that we live according to His word and follow along the path that He created for each of us.

Assess the path that you're on. Are you following Christ? We may not always be sure where we're going but we can be certain that we're going in the right direction when we're following Christ. Commit to following Christ so that you may experience life as God intended.

Prayer for Today: Heavenly Father, thank You for being my shepherd. Today, I choose to turn around and follow You wholeheartedly. Thank You for the path and purpose that You've created for me. In Jesus' name, Amen.

Additional Scripture reading: John 10:1-21

~Day of Reflection~

Lust

Read: Matthew 5:28; Colossians 3:5; 1 Thessalonians 4:3-5

Meditate: Do you have trouble overcoming lust? What problems has this caused you?

Apply: What actions can you take to combat the lustful spirit?

Not Without You

God's deliverance

So Moses told the people of Israel what the Lord had said, but they refused to listen anymore. They had become too discouraged by the brutality of their slavery. (Exodus 6:9 NLT)

Our trials and difficulties are not meant to discourage us but to empower us. In Exodus 1, the Israelites didn't allow their slavery to keep them down. Instead, they continued to multiply in numbers and strength. As time continued on, they became discouraged even after hearing the promises of God's deliverance through Moses.

Life's problems can cause us to grow weary and tired. However, we must hold on to God's promises. We don't always know when we will be delivered, but we can trust that it will happen. That alone should serve as our strength and help us to remain encouraged. God will come through on our behalf; we just have to do our part and remain faithful and patient.

No matter what you're facing today, know that it is coming to an end. There is an expiration date on your problems, whether in this life or the next. I challenge you today to hold fast to God's promises of deliverance. In the meantime, focus on God and His faithfulness and not your problems.

Prayer for Today: Heavenly Father, thank You for deliverance. I know that current problems are no different than past problems because You are just as You were yesterday. Thank You for being almighty and sovereign. In Jesus' name, Amen.

Additional Scripture reading: Exodus 6:1-13

Spiritual death

For the wages of sin is death, but the free gift of God is eternal life through Christ Jesus our Lord. (Romans 6:23 NLT)

In the book of Exodus, Moses and Aaron went to Pharaoh numerous times requesting that he let the Israelites go to worship the Lord. The Lord performed miracles through Moses and Aaron to demonstrate His mighty power to Pharaoh so that Pharaoh would know that God is God! After seeing the miraculous signs, Pharaoh's magicians used their magic and did the same things. Because of this, Pharaoh's heart was hardened and he did not believe that the Lord sent Moses and Aaron. His stubbornness caused him, his officials and the Egyptians to experience plagues at the hand of the Lord. The Lord allowed multiple plagues to come upon them until Pharaoh did what God wanted him to do - let the Israelites go.

As a consequence of sin, the Lord will allow different things to happen to us until we return unto Him. Is something dying in your life as a consequence of sin? Have you been ignoring the Holy Spirit's conviction? Don't get to a place where your heart is hardened and you're ignoring all the signs that God is showing you to alert you that you've gotten off the right path. Don't get to a place where your spirit has to be broken in order for you to return to the Lord. Seek and accept the Lord's forgiveness today and return to Him. He is waiting to receive you.

Prayer for Today: Heavenly Father, thank You for Your love and gift of eternal life. Let me not ignore Your warnings when I'm wrong. Help me to hold on to Your word and Your way. In Jesus' name, Amen.

Additional Scripture reading: Exodus 10 and 11

Not Without You

Faithful at all times

But when Pharaoh saw that the rain, hail, and thunder had stopped, he and his officials sinned again, and Pharaoh again became stubborn. (Exodus 9:34 NLT)

Do you ever pray prayers that sound like this? "Lord, if You will please bless me with this, then I will stop doing that. I promise not to do that again if only You will give me this one request." The Lord grants your request and you keep your promise for a while, but then you return to what you gave up. Does this sound familiar? I think we've all been here before. However, we shouldn't be using our sin as a bargaining chip with God in exchange for blessings. This is not what God desires.

First, the Lord wants true repentance from us, meaning that we ask forgiveness, allow the Lord to cleanse our heart and completely turn away from our sin. Second, we should keep our vows to God. When God blesses us, He deserves our praise and gratitude, not betrayal. Once we receive the Lord's blessings, we should not forget where the blessings came from. We are not supposed to return to our stubborn, sinful ways because we think that we no longer need anything from God.

Today, I encourage you to release the bargaining spirit. Choose to be faithful and obedient whether or not you receive what you have been asking.

Prayer for Today: Heavenly Father, thank You for your faithfulness and kindness. I am truly grateful for all that You have blessed me with and for the blessings of not giving me what I asked for because You know what's best for me. Keep me encouraged to be faithful and obedient. In Jesus' name, Amen.

Additional Scripture reading: Exodus 9

No good thing

For the Lord God is our sun and our shield. He gives us grace and glory. The Lord will withhold no good thing from those who do what is right. (Psalm 84:11 NLT)

The Bible tells us that the Lord is our sun. The sun illuminates our path and gives us direction. The Lord is also our shield which protects us from the evils of this world. He gives us what we do not deserve when He gives us grace.

He seeks to give us good things when we are blameless before Him. Our belief in Christ's death and resurrection is what makes us righteous. We cannot be righteous on our own. We will not always do what is right but God is merciful. When we slip and fall, we should get back up and try again. God in all of His infinite wisdom knows what is good for us and will give it to us.

As you go throughout your day today, remember that God gives direction, protection, grace and glory. He will also give you good things in due season. So if you desire something from God today, know that He doesn't withhold any good thing from His children. Be patient and wait on Him.

Prayer for Today: Heavenly Father, thank You for being who You are: faithful and powerful. Thank You for not withholding any good thing from me. I trust that all that You give to me is good and I only want Your good gifts. In Jesus' name, Amen.

Additional Scripture reading: Psalm 84

Don't Compromise

Then Nebuchadnezzar said, "Praise to the God of Shadrach, Meshach, and Abednego! He sent his angel to rescue his servants who trusted in him. They defied the king's command and were willing to die rather than serve or worship any god except their own God. (Daniel 3:28 NLT)

How do you handle tough situations? Do you handle them in the same manner as Shadrach, Meshach and Abednego? In this familiar passage, King Nebuchadnezzar created a gold statue and ordered everyone to bow down and worship it at the sound of the instruments. Shadrach, Meshach and Abednego refused to bow down and worship any god besides the Most High God. They were thrown into a fiery furnace that was heated 10 times its normal temperature because of the king's fury with their disobedience to his decree. We learn that the heat of the furnace was no comparison to God's power. We also know that it was really hot because the soldiers who threw them into the fire were killed. Once the king saw the three of them, and who I believe was God inside the furnace, the king ordered them out and noticed that they were not burned. Their hair didn't even smell of smoke. King Nebuchadnezzar acknowledged that God is the Most High God and that no god can rescue like Him. The king became a believer because of their obedience.

This passage teaches us to remain faithful to God regardless of our circumstances. God's power is much greater than the power of anyone in the heavens or earth. Second, even if we find ourselves in a "hot" situation, God is faithful and just to save and deliver (rescue) us. Third, being faithful and acknowledging God will elevate us. God used the king, who tried to kill them, to promote them. Our promotion will come from our faithfulness. Continue to walk in destiny regardless of your present circumstances.

Prayer for Today: Oh most Holy and gracious God, I come into your presence with praise! Thank you for being faithful. Help me to remain steadfast regardless of my circumstance. In Jesus' name, Amen.

Additional Scripture reading: Daniel 3

Rest in God

Those who live in the shelter of the Most High will find rest in the shadow of the Almighty. (Psalm 91:1 NLT)

To live in the shelter of God is to live in intimacy with God, which is to find joy in being in God's presence. When we have a close relationship with the Lord and make Him our spiritual dwelling place, we receive all that we need. Psalm 91 lays out many promises that we are to receive when we trust and find our rest, peace and identity in God.

Some of the promises we find here are:

- Protection
- Not to be conquered by evil
- Victory over enemies
- Answered prayers
- Deliverance
- Long life
- Salvation

Find peace and rest in God today. Trust him with your worries and cares. Choose to live in intimacy with Him so that you may experience the fruit of His promises.

Prayer for Today: Heavenly Father, I am thankful that I can find serenity and peace in You. Thank You for Your word that promises all that I need if I dwell in You. I choose to live under Your covering today. In Jesus' name, Amen.

Additional Scripture reading: Psalm 91

~Day of Reflection~

Don't forget

Read: Psalm 103

Meditate: When you think about God's unfailing love and mercy does it bring you joy?

Apply: How can you show God that you appreciate His love, forgiveness, mercy and grace? Think about all of His good deeds towards you and let that drive your actions.

Be consumed by His light

Jesus replied, "My light will shine for you just a little longer. Walk in the light while you can, so the darkness will not overtake you. Those who walk in the darkness cannot see where they are going." (John 12:35 NLT)

Jesus is the light that we should walk in. We walk in the light when we live according to His word and under the direction of the Holy Spirit. It is impossible for us to live the way God desires for us to live if we don't study the word of God for knowledge of His ways. When we are not walking in the light, we are walking in darkness, the path of the enemy.

The enemy desires to keep you busy so that you are too tired to even study the word of God. The less time you spend studying the Bible, the less you are renewing your mind to become like Christ. The less you are like Christ, the more you are walking in darkness with no direction from the Holy Spirit.

We have to get to a place where we realize that spending time in God's presence is a necessity like our bodies need food and water. The word of God is food and water for our spirit. Are you spiritually malnourished?

Prayer for Today: Heavenly Father, forgive me for not spending time in Your presence as I should. My spirit craves the nourishment Your Holy Spirit provides. Help me to keep my spirit fed so that I may walk in light under your direction. In Jesus' name, Amen.

Additional Scripture reading: John 12:20-36

Not Without You

No more people pleasing

For they loved human praise more than the praise of God. (John 12:43 NLT)

God's thoughts toward us are more important than those of our friends, family, church members and coworkers. Far too often, we downplay our faith because of fear of what others may say, do or think when this should not be our focus. Our focus should be centered on pleasing God and doing His will.

We will never please God if we choose to please people, because God's thoughts are far different and greater than our thoughts. If we continue to live trying to meet the standards of anyone other than God, then we fail. We miss the mark. We aren't living the abundant life that God has predestined us to live because we are, in essence, putting our light under the table or hiding our faith.

We should be open Christians. It's time for us to come out of the closet and live boldly for Christ and what we believe in. Remember that Jesus died boldly for us.

Seek the praise of God today and not the praise of anyone else because God desires all of you.

Prayer for Today: Heavenly Father, forgive me for the times that I desired the praise of others more than praise from You. I choose to please You today. In Jesus' name, Amen.

Additional Scripture reading: John 12:37-50

Fear and foundation

Fear of the Lord is the foundation of wisdom. Knowledge of the Holy One results in good judgment. (Proverbs 9:10 NLT)

What happens when we fear the Lord? The word of God tells us that fear is the foundation of wisdom. Fearing God is having a reverence for Him and acknowledging who He is in all of His power. Fearing God is knowing what He is capable of, grasping His sovereignty and knowing that it is He who made us. We belong to him, everything on this Earth belongs to Him (Psalms 24:1) and He can do whatever He pleases. It is also knowing that we need Him, and without Him, we can do nothing.

When we fear the Lord, we think differently; recognizing that the Lord is Holy and that we must praise and worship Him. We began to rely on Him for every single thing, thinking about the consequences of our actions before we act to make certain we are pleasing God.

When we fear the Lord, we act differently. Our actions are an outward manifestation of our thoughts and heart. We change the way we talk because we don't want to bring shame to the name of the Lord. We change the places we go, the people we surround ourselves with and many of the things we do.

When we think and act differently, we walk in wisdom, becoming the person who God has called us to be. Commit to living a life filled with wisdom.

Prayer for Today: Heavenly Father, thank You for the wisdom that You give. Help me choose wisdom daily so that I may be pleasing to You. In Jesus' name, Amen.

Additional Scripture reading: Romans 12:2; 12-14

Not Without You

Remember when

Just believe that I am in the Father and the Father is in me. Or at least believe because of the work you have seen me do. (John 14:11 NLT)

Some of us have amnesia when it comes to remembering what God has done in our lives. The moment we're in trouble, we forget God's promises and His previous works. All we need to do is take a deep breath and remember. Remember all the answered prayers, the things He delivered us from and His love for us.

Life can sometimes make it difficult to believe in the promises of God. Circumstances can be so tough to the point that it makes us wonder if God is present and if He has heard any of our prayers. It is in these moments when we find it hard to believe that God wants us to believe based on what we already know to be true.

Search your memory bank to see God at work in your life. The God who moved in your life before is the same God who can move in your life today. Don't allow life's ups and downs to discourage you or cause you to forget God's faithfulness. Remain faithful because of who God is.

Prayer for Today: Father in Heaven, thank You for my memory! Because of all that You have been to me, I can trust in You. I know that You never change and that You are faithful. I am grateful that I can always believe in You because of the work that I have seen You do. In Jesus' name, Amen.

Additional Scripture reading: John 14:1-14

Not Without You

Show Your Love

Those who accept my commandments and obey them are the ones who love me. And because they love me, my Father will love them. And I will love them and reveal myself to each of them. (John 14:21 NLT)

When we are obedient to God's word, we draw closer to Him and He draws closer to us. He reveals more about Himself to us, therefore giving us more wisdom and understanding into who He is and what He requires of us. If we want to know more about God and His purpose for our lives, we must start by accepting and obeying His commandments.

Not all of God's commandments are easy, but we should live by them out of love for Christ. We should love Him because He first loved us. Our love for God is measured by our actions. Are we following Him? Are we allowing the Holy Spirit to lead our lives?

In order to develop a greater intimacy in your relationship with Christ, you must begin by getting in alignment with His will and being obedient. God wants to have a deeper and more meaningful relationship with you. Decide to walk in His will today.

Prayer for Today: Heavenly Father, thank You for Your Holy Spirit. Thank You for loving me and wanting a better relationship with me. Today, I choose to draw closer to You by submitting to Your word. In Jesus' name, Amen.

Additional Scripture reading: John 14:15-31

Remain in Jesus

Remain in me, and I will remain in you. For a branch cannot produce fruit if it is severed from the vine, and you cannot be fruitful unless you remain in me. (John 15:4 NLT)

Take a moment and think of a grapevine. The fruit is connected to the vine, which is connected to the branch. The fruits can only continue to grow if they are connected to the vine. Once they are severed, they cease growing and become rotten and withered. They are no longer any good.

As children of God, we are the same way. When we are separated from Christ, we cannot do anything that God has called us to do. We are rendered useless in the kingdom of God because we are not doing the work that we have been called to do, which is producing the fruit of the Spirit and spreading the gospel of Jesus Christ. When we stay connected to Jesus, we can accomplish all that Jesus has placed in our hearts. All things are possible when we remain in Him.

If you find yourself disconnected, the good news is that you can become connected again unlike fruit that is severed from a vine. Jesus loves you and wants a relationship with you, so accept His open invitation of unconditional love today.

Prayer for Today: Heavenly Father, thank You for Your unconditional love. I recognize that apart from You, I cannot accomplish Your will. I want to be all that You have called me to be so I choose to stay connected to You. In Jesus' name, Amen.

Additional Scripture reading: John 15:1-8

~Day of Reflection~

Harmony

Read: Psalm 133

Meditate: Are you living in harmony with your friends, family, coworkers and church members?

Apply: What can you do to live in harmony with the people involved in each of these relationships?

Chosen

You didn't choose me. I chose you. I appointed you to go and produce lasting fruit, so that the Father will give you whatever you ask for, using my name. (John 15:16 NLT)

This Scripture is loaded with awesome truths:

- We did not choose God, He chose us!
- We are appointed to do His will.
- The Lord trusts us to produce lasting fruit.
- If we do the Lord's will, we will receive whatever we ask for in Jesus' name.

If you have ever been in a place of uncertainty, I hope that you are now convinced. God chose you for His purpose! He chose you because He knows that you can do all things through Him. You don't have to do any of it alone. Trust in God to lead you along the path that He has chosen for you.

When God chose you, He gave you a number of assignments. He trusts you to go out and be fruitful. Accept these facts and walk in the Lord's will today. He will give you all that you need to do what He has called you to do.

Prayer for Today: Heavenly Father, thank You for choosing me to be Your vessel. Give me strength and courage to boldly do what You have called me to do. In Jesus' name, Amen.

Additional Scripture reading: John 15:9-17

Not Without You

Guidance from the Holy Spirit

When the Spirit of truth comes, he will guide you into all truth. He will not speak on his own but will tell you what he has heard. He will tell you about the future. (John 16:13 NLT)

The Holy Spirit is our connection to Christ and God the Father. The Holy Spirit communicates with us, comforts us and intercedes for us. That small voice that we often hear is God speaking to us through His Holy Spirit. We often identify it by saying something like this: "Something told me to go this way or to do this or that." That something may be the Holy Spirit nudging us in the direction that God would have us to go.

God wants to be a part of our daily lives through prayer and providing direction. We should not ignore God's voice; instead we should ask the Lord to make us more sensitive to His voice so that we can be more confident in doing what He has called us to do.

When the Holy Spirit communicates with you today, do not ignore Him. Choose to say "Yes, Lord," and move in the direction in which you are being led. God wants to lead you and draw you closer to Him, so be obedient to His voice today.

Prayer for Today: Heavenly Father, thank You for Your Holy Spirit who leads, guides and intercedes for me even when I don't know what to pray for. I choose to listen to the voice of the Holy Spirit and follow You today. In Jesus' name, Amen.

Additional Scripture reading: John 16:1-15

Not Without You

Jesus prays for us

I'm not asking you to take them out of the world, but to keep them safe from the evil one. (John 17:15 NLT)

Before Jesus was betrayed, He prayed to God the Father concerning His disciples. In his prayer, Jesus asked God to protect them, make them holy and teach them His word. He also asked God to protect them from the evil one.

Jesus knew that Satan would attempt to attack us at every turn. He knew that we would endure many difficult times. We won't always be shielded from experiencing difficulties, but God will see us through them. Though the enemy may come to attack us, he will not win. We have already been given victory over the enemy because Jesus conquered the world and we are more than conquerors through Him. By His strength and power, we can get through anything.

Whatever you're going through today, know that Jesus has already prayed to the Father for your safety and your victory. You are protected from the evil one. He cannot do anything more to you than God allows. Remember Job? The enemy has to get permission to mess with you and even then, you still win.

Prayer for Today: Heavenly Father, thank You for Your word that gives me strength and encouragement. I thank You because Jesus continues to intercede on my behalf. Thank You for protecting me from the evil one. In Jesus' name, Amen.

Additional Scripture reading: John 17

Fellowship

All the believers devoted themselves to the apostles' teaching, and to fellowship, and to sharing in meals (including the Lord's Supper), and to prayer. (Acts 2:42 NLT)

We are strengthened when we spend time encouraging and uplifting one another. We have an example of this in today's meditational Scripture. The disciples spent time together each day over food, fellowship, worship and prayer. As they continued to do this, they were able to perform many miracles in Jesus' name.

The enemy knows that we are strengthened when we spend time together in God's word and sharpening one another. For this very reason, he causes confusion and dissension among the Christian community and in our churches. We have become so caught up in things that do not matter that we neglect what does matter - being who God has called us to be and spreading His word, joy and love to others.

We can be much more effective if we come together in fellowship with one another. Commit to coming together with other believers, strengthening and empowering one another to do God's will.

Prayer for Today: Heavenly Father, give me opportunities to fellowship with other believers. Give me a willing heart to become part of the community that You desire Your people to have. In Jesus' name, Amen.

Additional Scripture reading: Acts 2:42-47 and Proverbs 27:17

Not Without You

Corporate worship

He jumped up, stood on his feet, and began to walk! Then, walking, leaping, and praising God, he went into the Temple with them. (Acts 3:8 NLT)

Peter had just healed a man who had been crippled since birth. Once the man was healed, he began praising God and went into the Temple to worship with Peter and John. Going to church does not save us or give us eternal life but it is a way of showing our gratitude and obedience. The word of God says that we should not forsake the fellowship of believers.

We should consider our behavior now that we have been delivered from our many sins. How do we show our gratitude? Do we go to worship services? I've read many articles regarding reasons that many people do not attend church services anymore, and all of the reasons are simply distractions from the real reason why we should be in service. We should be attending worship services to worship the Lord corporately, receive a message from God through the pastor and uplift our brothers and sisters in Christ.

When we stay away from church, the enemy wins. He wants to keep us away from church for any reason. When we feel like we don't need to go, we need to be there all the more. Let's express our praise and gratitude to God in corporate worship.

Prayer for Today: Heavenly Father, strengthen me so that I will not be tricked by the enemy to stay away from Your house of worship. I want to be obedient to You by not forsaking the fellowship with other believers. While I attend service, help me to stay focused on You. In Jesus' name, Amen.

Additional Scripture reading: Acts 3:1-11

Share your story

*Peter saw his opportunity and addressed the crowd. "People of Israel,"
he said, "what is so surprising about this? And why stare at us as though
we had made this man walk by our own power or godliness?" (Acts 3:12
NLT)*

Every time God does something in our lives, we have an
opportunity to be a witness for Him. It is our time to tell others about our
faith in Him and how that faith has worked in our lives. All that God does
for us is for His glory. We must be mindful to give Him the glory and
point others toward Him.

I can think of many missed opportunities to share my faith but I
will not dwell on past failures. You shouldn't dwell on them either.
Instead look for chances to tell others about how God has comforted,
healed, protected, promoted, encouraged, lifted, transformed and loved
you.

Someone needs to hear your story. They need to hear what God
has done for you and how your faith in Him has strengthened you. You are
the only one who can share your testimony. Your testimony will help
someone else overcome so don't miss another opportunity to share it.

Prayer for Today: Heavenly Father, forgive me for missed opportunities to
point others toward You. Help me to recognize and take advantage of
every occasion to share my testimony. In Jesus' name, Amen.

Additional Scripture reading: Acts 3:12-26

Not Without You

~Day of Reflection~

Guard my lips

Read: Psalm 141:3

Meditate: Do you have issues controlling what you say?

Apply: Ask God to help you control your lips. In addition to prayer, what can you do to ensure your words are pleasing to God and helpful to others?

Time with Jesus

The members of the council were amazed when they saw the boldness of Peter and John, for they could see that they were ordinary men with no special training in the Scriptures. They also recognized them as men who had been with Jesus. (Acts 4:13 NLT)

We are not required to have biblical training to lead others to Christ or to tell others about the gospel. Our confidence and training comes from spending time with God through prayer and His word. God's word equips us to tell others about Him.

When we spend time in God's word, people will know it because our lives will be transformed and our minds will be renewed. We begin to live differently because, by faith, we begin to live a life that pleases God. We are empowered and strengthened when we spend time in God's word. Our faith is also increased and we are able to walk in the authority that Jesus gave us through His Holy Spirit.

As you go throughout your day today, know that you have all the training you need to be a witness for Christ. Your time spent studying His word and what He has done in your life should give you all the boldness that you need.

Prayer for Today: Heavenly Father, help me to walk in boldness as I share Your love with others. Thank You for giving me all that I need to be all that You have called me to be. In Jesus' name, Amen.

Additional Scripture reading: Acts 4:1-22

Not Without You

God's plans can't be thwarted

"But if it is from God, you will not be able to overthrow them. You may even find yourselves fighting against God!" (Acts 5:39 NLT)

God's plan will be carried out no matter what! No one can stop it. The high council did not want Peter and the apostles preaching about Jesus. They were planning to kill them but one member of the council spoke up and advised them to leave them alone. He recognized that if they were doing anything by their own power, it would not last and would be overthrown; but if they were working by the power of God, nothing would be able to stand against them.

When God gives you an assignment, opposition will likely come to distract you and keep you from carrying it out. The good news is that nothing can thwart God's plans. God will put people in place to assist you, and those against you may delay you but won't stop you.

Today, remember that you are victorious! God will accomplish all that He has started in you so continue to be faithful and do all that God has called you to do.

Prayer for Today: Heavenly Father, thank You for what You have started within me. I am thankful that Your plans always prevail. Thank You for being sovereign and all powerful. Let me be encouraged to continue on in faith into my destiny. In Jesus' name, Amen.

Additional Scripture reading: Acts 5:17-42

Not Without You

Appointed anyway

But the Lord said, "Go, for Saul is my chosen instrument to take my message to the Gentiles and to kings, as well as to the people of Israel." (Acts 9:15 NLT)

Saul was one of the biggest persecutors of the church. He agreed to the stoning of Stephen, one of the disciples (*he was not one of the original twelve*), and he threw many of God's followers into prison. However, the Lord chose Saul to take his message to many parts of the world. As terrible a person as Saul was to Christians, the Lord still chose to use him for the good of the kingdom of God.

Just as the Lord converted Saul and used him to preach the gospel in many places, the Lord can use you regardless of your past. When God chooses you, it doesn't matter what you have done in the past, you have been chosen. God doesn't make errors when choosing people to carry out His will. The more messed up you are, the greater the testimony your life will be to those with whom you share the message. Those who knew the person you were before your conversion will be able to see God's power and will be drawn to Christ as well. That is what it's all about - Christ!

Don't allow your past to keep you from doing what God wants you to do in the present.

Prayer for Today: Heavenly Father, it is an honor to be chosen by You in spite of my past. Thank You for choosing and entrusting me with such a task as this. Thank You for Your love and faithfulness. Keep me strengthened and encouraged to do Your will. In Jesus' name, Amen.

Additional Scripture reading: Acts 9:1-31

Pray and Believe

"You're out of your mind!" they said. When she insisted, they decided, "It must be his angel." (Acts 12:15 NLT)

Do you actually believe that God will answer your prayer by giving you what you asked for? In this passage of Scripture, many Christians had gathered together praying for Peter's release from prison. While they were still praying, the Lord answered their prayer by sending an angel to get Peter out of prison. When Peter arrived, no one believed that he was really there. They didn't believe that God had answered their prayers so quickly.

How many times do we show our lack of faith in God by praying for something and not believing that God will actually do it? God responds to our faith; so we need to make sure that when we pray, we have faith in God's power to do that which we request. Pray with expectancy.

God wants us to believe in Him wholeheartedly. He wants us to have unwavering faith, trusting that He can do even the impossible. Know that God has the power to do all that you ask and more.

Prayer for Today: Heavenly Father, forgive me for not having total faith in You when things look gray. Thank You for being faithful even when I am faithless. Thank You for the power of Your love and Your Holy Spirit. In Jesus' name, Amen.

Additional Scripture reading: Acts 12:1-19

Not Without You

Give God His glory

Instantly, an angel of the Lord struck Herod with a sickness, because he accepted the people's worship instead of giving the glory to God. So he was consumed with worms and died. (Acts 12:23 NLT)

God uses each of us to carry out His will for our lives. Although God uses us in different ways, the will of God for each of us is to draw others to Him. We must not get carried away by thinking that we are in control or that we deserve the praise. When others praise you, give it right back to the Lord.

There is nothing wrong with doing things well and being acknowledged for it. However, the issue is not acknowledging that God works within you. We have to remember that all things are made possible through Him; without Him, we are useless to the kingdom of God. We must also remember that it is not our kingdom that we are working for, but for His kingdom and His glory.

Do not allow anyone to shift their worship or praise to you, because it is not yours to receive. It is all about that Lord. So whatever you do for Him, make sure that everyone else knows it as well.

Prayer for Today: Heavenly Father, I give You all the glory, honor and praise. Without You, I cannot do anything. All things are possible through You and I pray that all that I do in Your name brings You glory. Let me always be careful to give You all of the worship and praise. In Jesus' name, Amen.

Additional Scripture reading: Acts 12:20-25

Not Without You

Freedom to choose

"In the past he permitted all the nations to go their own ways, but he never left them without evidence of himself and his goodness. For instance, he sends you rain and good crops and gives you food and joyful hearts." (Acts 14:16-17 NLT)

Serving God is a choice. Each day we awaken, we get to make the choice all over again. We choose whether or not we will be obedient, pray, praise, worship or live our lives according to His will. We each have free will. God has laid out His instructions for us and even given us His love but it is our choice whether or not we will accept it.

God has proven how much He loves us by sacrificing His only Son to restore us back unto Him. He has provided us with His unfailing love, mercy and grace that are new to us each morning. He blesses us with all that we need and many of our wants. We are blessed far beyond anything that we could ever measure. Yet, God does not force His love upon us but gives us a choice.

You have the freedom to choose whether or not you will follow Christ today or any other day. As much as He has done for us, being obedient is the least that we can do to show our gratitude.

Prayer for Today: Heavenly Father, thank You for Your unconditional love. Thank You for being who You are in all of Your glory - holy, righteous, faithful and merciful. Today, I choose to be faithful to You and live according to Your word. In Jesus' name, Amen.

Additional Scripture reading: Acts 14:8-20 and 2 Corinthians 3:17

~Day of Reflection~

Honesty

Read: Psalm 51:6; proverbs 6:16-17; 19:1; Ephesians 4:25

Meditate: Do you have a problem with being honest? Do you fear what others will think of you if you tell the truth? Remember that God desires honesty in all circumstances.

Apply: Consider why you tell lies. Pray and ask God to empower you and resolve to tell the truth. Think of someone that you may have been lying to; tell them the truth, ask their forgiveness and begin repairing the relationship.

Power of praise

Suddenly, there was a massive earthquake, and the prison was shaken to its foundations. All the doors immediately flew open, and the chains of every prisoner fell off! (Acts 16:26 NLT)

Our praise has the power to change our situations, affect the situations of those around us and draw others close to the Lord! Consider what Paul and Silas' praise did for them and those around them. They had been thrown into prison and instead of complaining about their situation or allowing it to discourage them, they chose to praise God by praying and singing hymns unto Him.

Their praying and singing moved God to break their chains and open their prison cells. Not only did God move for them but for everyone around them. All of the prisoners experienced the same grace! Their praise also caused the jailer and his family to believe in Christ after the jailer saw what God had done.

Praying and singing unto the Lord has the power to move God to bless you and those around you. It doesn't matter what kind of situation you're facing today, choose to focus on God and not your problems. God would much rather hear your praise than your issues. Set the atmosphere for God to move in your life today by praying, praising and singing unto the Lord.

Prayer for Today: Heavenly Father, You are so worthy of all of my praise. I choose to set my heart and mind on You today and not my problems. You are sovereign and much greater than any problem that I could ever have. I praise and trust You today. In Jesus' name, Amen.

Additional Scripture reading: Acts 16:16-40

Not Without You

Intercession is a serious matter

But one time when they tried it, the evil spirit replied, "I know Jesus, and I know Paul, but who are you?" (Acts 19:15 NLT)

In this passage, there were Jewish brothers attempting to cast out evil spirits in the name of Jesus. However, they lacked the power of the Holy Spirit because they were disobedient to the Lord. They had no communion or covenant with the Lord and even the evil spirit knew it.

Earlier in this chapter, the Bible tells us that God gave Paul the power to perform unusual miracles. In fact, if fabric touched his skin and then touched sick people, they were healed and evil spirits were cast out!

Use caution when allowing others to pray with you or for you. Not everyone walks in obedience to God or can call upon His name to pray against the evil that comes up against you. We must also be sure to walk in faith and obedience so that we may be able to operate in the power given to us by the Holy Spirit. We cannot possess and use the power when we aren't connected to the power source.

Prayer for Today: Heavenly Father, thank You for the power of Your Holy Spirit. Let me be mindful that I am powerless against the evils in this world without Your Holy Spirit. I choose to stay connected to You so that I can walk in the power that You've given me through Your Holy Spirit. In Jesus' name, Amen.

Additional Scripture reading: Acts 19:8-22

Not Without You

Finishing the assignment

But my life is worth nothing to me unless I use it for finishing the work assigned me by the Lord Jesus-the work of telling others the Good News about the wonderful grace of God. (Acts 20:24 NLT)

Christian life is all worshiping God. As part of our worship to God, each one of us has been given assignments. In essence, the assignments are the same but the way we are to carry them out is different. We have all been given gifts so that we may edify the kingdom of God and point others toward our Lord, Jesus Christ.

Everything we do should be pleasing to God and leading others to Him. This is why it is so important to live according to His will. The Bible encourages us to do everything as if we're doing it unto the Lord; when we approach life this way, our behavior changes. We treat people with respect and love; we honor those in authority and we give the best of ourselves. People will then see Christ in us and want to know more about Him.

Regardless of the way you are to fulfill the assignments, do it with love and unto the Lord so that He may receive all the glory and praise due to Him. Remember that your life is all about glorifying Him.

Prayer for Today: Heavenly Father, thank You for choosing me as a vessel to do Your will. Help me carry out my assignments with courage and wisdom. I pray that my life will be pleasing unto You. In Jesus' name, Amen.

Additional Scripture reading: Acts 20:13-38

Not Without You

Salvation is for everyone

And I will rescue you from both your own people and the Gentiles. Yes, I am sending you to the Gentiles to open their eyes, so they may turn from darkness to light and from the power of Satan to God. Then they will receive forgiveness for their sins and be given a place among God's people, who are set apart by faith in me. (Acts 26:17-18 NLT)

The Gentiles were considered sinful and unworthy of receiving God's grace according to Jews. In fact, Jews were constantly in an uproar because Paul was preaching the Good News to them, converting them into followers of Christ. The Jews despised this so much so that they plotted to kill Paul. The problem here is that God is not a respecter of persons and His message is to be given to everyone.

We are not at liberty to decide who gets to hear God's word. We shouldn't decide who deserves hope based on gender, race, background or sin. That is not our job. We were called to love and tell others about the Lord, not judge them. Everyone needs to hear the joy of the Lord's salvation. Do not discriminate against anyone because they don't fit the profile that you think Christians should fall into.

As you go throughout your day today, show love to everyone because we all need it. Let others see the light of the Lord within you.

Prayer for Today: Heavenly Father, thank You for Your word. I am thankful that You did not disregard me because of my past sins and failures. Thank You for unconditional love, grace and mercy. Help me to extend that same love to others. In Jesus' name, Amen.

Additional Scripture reading: Acts 21, 23 and 26

Day 200

Not Without You

Refresh others

When we get together, I want to encourage you in your faith, but I also want to be encouraged by yours. (Romans 1:12 NLT)

It feels good to know that you can be refreshed by others in the faith as you are refreshing them. It can be spiritually draining to always pray, encourage and uplift others if you're never being refilled. Paul heard about the Romans' faith and longed for the moment that he would get to share the Good News with them. Not only did he want to share the Good News, he also wanted to be encouraged by the strength of their faith. Iron sharpens iron and Paul needed to be sharpened.

Encouragers also need to be encouraged. Surround yourself with people who can pour back into you, strengthening your faith by their testimonies. Make sure your circle includes people who can pray and uplift you. As you continue your journey in Christ, you will need to be refreshed from time to time. Take time to learn how someone else's faith in God has propelled them to reach greater heights.

Be encouraged and encourage someone else today.

Prayer for Today: Heavenly Father, thank You for those You've placed in my life to encourage me. Thank You that I can be encouraging to them as well. I am thankful that You understand that I need refreshing to be all that You have called me to be. Thank You for putting the right people in my life. In Jesus' name, Amen.

Additional Scripture reading: Romans 1:1-15

Not Without You

Nothing before Him

They traded the truth about God for a lie. So they worshiped and served the things God created instead of the Creator himself, who is worthy of eternal praise! Amen. (Romans 1:25 NLT)

When the Lord gave the Ten Commandments to Moses as noted in Exodus 20, He instructed that we should not have any other gods before Him and that we should not have idols. The people of Israel disobeyed Him and constantly created and worshiped idols in place of the Lord. They knew who the Lord was and what He required of them, yet they chose to do as they wished.

We may not worship statues or created images, but what we allow to take God's place in our lives is idolatry as well. Those things that we give our time, heart and money to when we should be giving those things to God become idols. God is a jealous God so we shouldn't put anything before Him. Whenever we begin putting things in God's place, we create distance between ourselves and God, our relationship with Him is weakened and He will destroy what we have made idols. We must worship Him in spirit and truth with pure hearts.

Let nothing that the Lord created take His place in your life. Be careful to honor God and worship Him alone because only He is worthy of worship.

Prayer for Today: Heavenly Father, thank You for Your love. Examine my heart and show me anything that I may have placed before You. Please remove it from me because I only want to worship You. In Jesus' name, Amen.

Additional Scripture reading: Romans 1:18-32 and Exodus 20: 1-17

~Day of Reflection~

Stressed out

Read: Exodus 18:13-26; Psalm 62:1-8; Psalm 69:1-36; 2 Corinthians 4:8-12

Meditate: What causes stress in your life? Trying to do things alone? Although you may be capable of doing things alone, delegating tasks can alleviate stress. Stress also causes worry and sometimes illness.

Apply: How do you deal with stress? Get organized and remove unnecessary and unproductive tasks from your *to do* list. Take time to pray and release your cares to God. What can you do to prevent stress in your life?

Not Without You

Life-changing word

For merely listening to the law doesn't make us right with God. It is obeying the law that makes us right in his sight. (Romans 2:13 NLT)

What do you do with the sermons that you hear during the week or the biblical knowledge that you receive from Bible study?

We can attend church or listen to sermons every night of the week but if we do not allow the message to change us, then it is useless. Simply hearing the word of God will not make us right with Him. God wants to see our faith in action! He wants us to be moved by what we hear from Him. We have to allow the word to become hidden in our hearts so much so that we let it change our lives.

There must be an outward manifestation of our belief in Christ. Since we profess to believe in Him and all that He did while walking this earth, our lives should emulate His love and kindness towards others. We should be God's heart and hands here on earth. What good is it to hear the word if we're not going to do anything with it?

Prayer for Today: Heavenly Father, thank You for Your word that changes my heart and my life. Let me not harden my heart against Your word but receive and apply it to my life with joy and understanding. In Jesus' name, Amen.

Additional Scripture reading: Romans 2:1-16

Follow to Lead

You are so proud of knowing the law, but you dishonor God by breaking it. No wonder the Scriptures say, "The Gentiles blaspheme the name of God because of you." (Romans 2:23-24 NLT)

At times, Christians can be the worst example of Christianity. We can be the most damaging thing to our faith. Why? Because we know what the word of God says and we choose to do the opposite. We cannot lead others to Christ when we are not following Him. They will be able to see it and we already know this. God is not pleased when we live double lives - saying one thing and doing another.

We have to get to a place where we honor God in our walk and our talk. People need to see God in us. They need to see us living out the Scriptures. They need to see us loving our neighbors, praising God, being patient, not worrying, being kind, being peacemakers and exuding the light that is Jesus Christ. We miss the mark and the point of Christianity when we live any other way.

Let's commit to proving that we know the Scriptures by following them, no matter the circumstance. God rewards faithfulness.

Prayer for Today: Heavenly Father, thank You for your faithfulness and kindness. Help me to live out Your word and let Your light shine through me. I want to be a Christian that You can be proud of. In Jesus' name, Amen.

Additional Scripture reading: Romans 2:17-29

Forever faithful

True, some of them were unfaithful; but just because they were unfaithful, does that mean God will be unfaithful? (Romans3:3 NLT)

God is the only constant. He never changes. Isn't it comforting to know that God's character is not based upon how good or bad we are or how much our lives are filled with sin? God's love is unconditional and He desires that we understand and have faith in this truth.

No one knows us like we know ourselves; therefore, we should be able to attest to the mercy and grace of God. We know how unfaithful and ungrateful we can be towards God and yet He continues to bless us. He lavishes His love on us so that we may turn to Him, trust Him and live according to His will.

In response to God's faithfulness towards you, be faithful to Him today in all that you do. Serve Him wholeheartedly with joy. Be obedient to what He has called you to do. Although He is faithful and merciful, there are consequences for disobedience.

Prayer for Today: Heavenly Father, thank You for being faithful even when I am unfaithful. Teach me to live according to Your will at all times so that I may be who You have called me to be. In Jesus' name, Amen.

Additional Scripture reading: Romans 3:1-8

Not Without You

Change while you have time

"O Israel, can I not do to you as this potter has done to his clay? As the clay is in the potter's hand, so are you in my hand. (Jeremiah 18:6 NLT)

In the previous chapters, the Lord repeatedly speaks about destroying His people for constantly disobeying Him, ignoring Him and worshiping idols. Verse 8 states that if his people would turn from their evil ways and follow Him, He would not destroy them as planned. He also says that if He says that He will build up a nation and the nation turns away from Him, and disobeys, He will no longer bless them.

Consider whether or not you are on the right path. Remember, your goal is to please God, complete your assignments and walk in destiny. Remember, the enemy's goal is just the opposite – to keep you from pleasing God, completing your assignments and out of your destiny. If you are not on the right path, there is still time to get on track. It is never too late to do what you have been called to do. It is your calling! It is your destiny! If you turn around and follow God, He will bless you and lead you. God is faithful, merciful and kind. He welcomes His children back to Him. Seek Him with your whole heart today and get back on track to complete your assignments.

One may ask the question, how do I get on the right path? Consider how you got off the path chosen for you. Retrace your steps. Do the opposite of what you've been doing. Repent to the Lord and turn away from the path that doesn't please God. Ask God for direction and spend time in His word. God answers prayers. Continue to seek him. He will certainly show you the way that you should go.

Prayer for Today: Heavenly Father, thank You for the plans You designed for me. Thank you for keeping me on the right path and accepting me back to You when I turned from Your path and walked in my own way. Thank you for your goodness, In Jesus' name, Amen.

Additional Scripture reading: Jeremiah 18 and Galatians 1:15-16

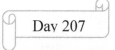

Not Without You

Lesson from the ants

Take a lesson from the ants, you lazybones. Learn from their ways and become wise! (Proverbs 6:6 NLT)

Ants work really hard and we can learn plenty from their habits. First, ants have a preparation and planning spirit. In the summer they gather food for the winter, preparing two seasons ahead of time for what they will need. Here we learn: Always plan ahead and prepare for what is going to happen next.

Second, the ants do not need to be micromanaged. They don't need someone to rule or watch over them to make sure the task is getting accomplished (v.7). Likewise, when you're at work each day, take initiative. Be proactive by making a list of the tasks that need to be completed for each day and set out to complete them without needing to be told to do so. "Own your work." When you take initiative, see projects through to the end and do more than what's expected, promotion and success are inevitable.

Lastly, ants do not work alone. When you see ants, they are always working with other ants. Very seldom will you only see one ant. Like the ants, you should have someone helping you accomplish your goals. Working with someone who has already accomplished what you're trying to accomplish is even better. Surround yourself with other people who have goals. If not, you just may find yourself being sidetracked or being a "lazybone"—not accomplishing anything. 1 Corinthians 15:33 says "Do not be misled: Bad company corrupts good character."

Prayer for Today: Heavenly Father, help me to be a person who plans, works hard and works well with others to accomplish the purpose for which You have created me. Help me overcome laziness and procrastination so that I may walk in wisdom. In Jesus' name, Amen.

Additional Scripture reading: Psalm 33:10-12 and Psalm 40:4-6

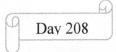

Day 208

Falling short

For everyone has sinned; we all fall short of God's glorious standard. (Romans 3:23 NLT)

We are all sinful but the good news is that we don't have to continue living in sin. Jesus' shedding His blood on the cross for everyone is how we are reconciled to the Lord. We are made righteous unto the Lord when we believe in Jesus' death and resurrection.

Following God's commandments does not save us. We must believe in Jesus Christ. We must believe that He is the Messiah sent by the Lord and that He died for our sins. To demonstrate our faith in Him, we then live according to God's word. In verse 31, we learn that it is only when we have faith that we truly fulfill the law.

No matter where you are in life today, God's word still stands. Jesus died for all of us and acceptance of this truth is what reconciles you to God. Though you will still sin, you should strive to sin less because of your faith in God washing away your sin. It is by faith that you should choose to trust and live by God's holy Word. It is then that you will be able to walk in destiny and live the life that God has predestined for you to live.

Prayer for Today: Heavenly Father, thank You for sending Jesus Christ to die for my sins. As I live a life of faith, help me to be pleasing to You as I strive to obey Your Holy Word. In Jesus' name, Amen.

Additional Scripture reading: Romans 3:21-31

Not Without You

~Day of Reflection~

Thankful

Read: Colossians 3:15-17; 1 Thessalonians 5:16-18

Meditate: Do you have a countenance of thanksgiving?

Apply: How do you express your appreciation to God? What are other ways that you can show thanksgiving to God for who He is and all that He has done?

Unwavering faith

Abraham never wavered in believing God's promise. In fact, his faith grew stronger, and in this he brought glory to God. (Romans 4:20 NLT)

Abraham is known as the Father of Faith because of the way He trusted God. When God promised Abraham that he would have a child and that he would be the father of many nations, Abraham never wavered in his faith, although what God promised seemed impossible. Abraham's faith teaches us that:

- Our faith in God is what makes us righteous.
- Our faith in God brings Him glory.
- Our faith in God is what sustains us.

Faith is the foundation of our relationship with God. If we do not have faith, we do not have a true relationship with Him. To have the type of intimate relationship that God wants with us, we must fully trust and believe in His word, without hesitation. Our faith in Him is what causes Him to move in our life.

God is always faithful so do not allow any circumstance to undermine or cast doubt on your faith in Him. He will do all that He has promised; don't stop believing.

Prayer for Today: Heavenly Father, thank You for being faithful. Thank You for being true to Your promises. Let me not waver in my faith so that I may bring Your name glory. In Jesus' name, Amen.

Additional Scripture reading: Romans 4

Developmental problems

We can rejoice, too, when we run into problems and trials, for we know that they help us develop endurance. And endurance develops strength of character, and character strengthens our confident hope of salvation. (Romans 5:3-4 NLT)

Problems are not meant to tear us down and discourage us, but they are meant to make us stronger. We often hear this but it certainly doesn't feel like the truth while we going through trials. Trials strengthen us, teach us more about ourselves and help build our faith and trust in God.

We are strengthened by trials when we learn from them. Problems have a way of teaching us lasting lessons and giving direction. If the problem was self-inflicted, we learn what works and doesn't work. If the trouble occurred because of something beyond our control, we still learn how to deal with future issues.

Problems teach us about ourselves in that we learn whether or not we have integrity, where our faith lies in God and if we're as strong as we thought we were. Our character and our faith are strengthened as a result of struggles.

When we encounter problems, if we haven't been fully trusting in God, we will have to wholeheartedly trust Him. We have to believe that He will see us through and that He is working things out for our good and His glory. So when we're going through tough times, we know that we can truly rejoice because we will come out better people.

Prayer for Today: Heavenly Father, thank You for sharpening and strengthening my spirit as I go through trials. I thank You that You want the best from me and sometimes trials are the way to bring that out. I trust that You have my best interest in mind and I can put all of my faith in You. In Jesus' name, Amen.

Additional Scripture reading: Romans 5:1-11

Not Without You

It only takes one

Because one person disobeyed God, many became sinners. But because one other person obeyed God, many will be made righteous. (Romans 5:19 NLT)

When I was in grade school, one of my teachers often said, "The good will have to suffer with the bad." This was terrible because this often happened when another student misbehaved and as a result, the entire class had a shortened recess or no recess at all. We would have to sit in the classroom quietly, with our heads down, for about 30 minutes or so.

It is amazing how the behavior of one person, whether done secretly or openly, can have consequences on everyone around them. It doesn't matter whether or not everyone participated in the behavior; our behavior can result in blessings or curses, draw people to or away from God, and give or not give God glory. For example, Adam sinned and brought condemnation on everyone and Christ's death gives eternal life to everyone who believes in Him! Thank God for Jesus Christ!

We need to be mindful that we now have direct access to God and it is all because of Jesus Christ. His one act of obedience reconciled us back to God and made us heirs to His throne of grace. Because of Christ, we are made whole, righteous and free. Commit to seeking after God and enjoying the abundant life that Jesus Christ's death richly gives us.

Prayer for Today: Heavenly Father, thank You for the obedience of Jesus Christ that restores me unto You. I thank You that I am made righteous because of His obedience and my belief in His obedience. Help me to daily make the choice to serve You and bring Your name honor and glory. In Jesus' name, Amen.

Additional Scripture reading: Romans 5:12-21

It is not okay

Well then, since God's grace has set us free from the law, does that mean we can go on sinning? Of course not! (Romans 6:15 NLT)

Here are some truths about sin:

- It is in our nature to sin.
- God does not condemn us for our sin when we accept Christ but we should not continue in sin.
- We have a choice in whether or not we sin.
- We have been given the power over sin through Christ's death.
- Sin destroys our intimacy with God.

Although God is a forgiving God, we should not willingly continue in sin. Because of our faith in God and what Jesus did for us, we should desire to live a life that is holy and acceptable unto God. There will be times when we sin but we should not have an attitude that sin is okay to engage in.

We have been given the power to overcome sin, so we must make the choice to do what is right in God's sight. We have been chosen to do God's work and we cannot be wholeheartedly committed to doing His will and allowing sin to control us. No sin is worth it.

Prayer for Today: Heavenly Father, thank You for the power that You've given me over sin. I am free from the sin that entraps me and tries to get in the way of my relationship with You. In Jesus' name, Amen.

Additional Scripture reading: Romans 6

Struggle or Surrender

I have discovered this principle of life - that when I want to do what is right, I inevitably do what is wrong. (Romans 7:21 NLT)

We often have the desire to do what is right and pleasing to God, but many times we fail at actually doing the right thing. Sin will be a constant struggle in our lives until Jesus returns. However, there is a difference between struggling with sin and surrendering to sin.

When we struggle with sin, there is a war within us. We know that it's wrong and we desire not to do it; we have internal conflict. When we surrender to it, we have given up. There is no struggle but acceptance.

To deal with the struggle of sin, what the spirit wants versus what the flesh wants, we must stay in constant communion with God. We must pray often, study the word of God continuously and be mindful of what we feed our spirit by what we watch, listen and surround ourselves with. We must also have a conquering spirit - knowing that we can overcome sin by the power of Christ that lives in us.

Prayer for Today: Heavenly Father, thank You for the power of Your Holy Spirit that gives me strength to overcome sin. Although I may struggle, I know that You are with me giving me strength to live a life that is pleasing to You. In Jesus' name, Amen.

Additional Scripture reading: Romans 7

Dominant thoughts

Those who are dominated by the sinful nature think about sinful things, but those who are controlled by the Holy Spirit think about things that please the Spirit. (Romans 8:5 NLT)

What's on your mind? What are your dominant thoughts? Our thoughts are manifested in our actions. Whatever we spend our time thinking about, that is what we eventually do; this is why it is important to think about things that please God if that is what we truly desire. If we think about things that are pleasing to ourselves, those are the things that we will act upon.

To live according to what the Spirit desires, we need to meditate on those things. To meditate on those things, we have to know what they are. We can only hide these things in our heart if we study God's word. We need to fill our minds with thoughts of what God considers holy and pleasing to Him. We will be forever dominated by our sinful nature if sin is all we think about.

Whatever sin dominates your thoughts, combat it with what God's word says about it. We have to be able to battle against our sinful thoughts with holy thoughts. To live by the Spirit, we have to start by meditating on what pleases the Spirit, because our thoughts become our actions.

Prayer for Today: Heavenly Father, thank You for Your Word that cleanses my thoughts and my heart. Purify me so that my thoughts and actions may please You today. In Jesus' name, Amen.

Additional Scripture reading: Romans 8:1-17

~Day of Reflection~

Too big for God

Read: Isaiah 1:18

Meditate: Have you ever felt like your sins were too great to be forgiven?

Apply: Seek God in prayer and turn your sin over to Him. He is faithful and wants to reconcile you back to Him. No sin is too great or small to receive God's forgiveness.

Help of the Holy Spirit

And the Holy Spirit helps us in our weakness. For example, we don't know what God wants us to pray for. But the Holy Spirit prays for us with groanings that cannot be expressed in words. (Romans 8:26 NLT)

We cannot see the big picture. We don't know what's going to happen tomorrow, next week, next month or next year. However, God knows all and therefore the Holy Spirit intercedes on our behalf when we pray, petitioning God for what we really need and for what He really desires to give us. This is one of the privileges of being a child of God.

The Holy Spirit is in tune with God's will for our lives and knows that God's will is perfect. The Holy Spirit also knows that whatever God does, it is for our good and His glory. Because of this, we have faith that the intercession of the Holy Spirit strengthens our prayers to God.

Though we don't always know what to pray for, this should not hinder us from praying. Instead this should encourage us to pray even more so that we can stay in alignment with God's perfect will for our lives.

Prayer for Today: Heavenly Father, thank You for Your Holy Spirit who helps me every day and intercedes for me. Let me always be receptive to the Holy Spirit at work in my life. In Jesus' name, Amen.

Additional Scripture reading: Romans 8:18-30

Not Without You

Victory is mine

No, despite all these things, overwhelming victory is ours through Christ, who loved us. (Romans 8:37 NLT)

The Bible assures us that nothing can separate us from God's love. Though we may encounter many ups and downs, none of those things will stand in the way of God's love for us. God did not promise that our conditions would be perfect and that we would not have hard times but He did promise that He would never leave us or forsake us.

There may be times when it feels like God isn't there and He has shut us out, but this cannot be further from the truth. No matter what is going on, God cares. Everything can seem to be going wrong in your life but remember that it is temporary and you have already been given the victory. All you have to do is go through it.

The love that God has shown through Jesus is too great for Him to leave you or separate Himself from you. He wants you to trust and lean on Him in all things. Allow the love of the cross to convince you of the magnitude of God's love and the victory that you have been given. Whenever you feel that things are unbearable, remember the ultimate sacrifice. If God would do that for you, surely He will see you through anything you have to endure on this earth.

Prayer for Today: Heavenly Father, thank You for the victory that You have given me to overcome anything that I may be faced with. Thank You for the love You have shown and continue to show me daily. I trust that You are always with me and that You will never leave or forsake me. In Jesus' name, Amen.

Additional Scripture reading: Romans 8:31-39

Not Without You

Before you were born

But before they were born, before they had done anything good or bad, she received a message from God. (This message shows that God chooses people according to his own purposes; he calls people, but not according to their good or bad works.) She was told "Your older son will serve your younger son." (Romans 9:11-12 NLT)

Before you were born, God had a plan and a purpose for your life. He chose you for a specific reason and this reason has nothing to do with how much or how little you sin. Your assignment was given to you before you could even go after it. There is nothing that you can do to change the destiny that God has for you. You just have to accept it and pursue it.

Since God's plan for your life has been predetermined, you have to seek Him. Seek Him for guidance regarding what you should be doing and the wisdom to determine when you need to do it. God already has the right people and opportunities in place to get you to where you need to be; you just need to commit to being His vessel.

You have been chosen for greatness - to help carry out God's perfect will. Don't allow anything to get in your way because someone is waiting on you to do what God has called you to do. Your obedience will bless someone else.

Prayer for Today: Heavenly Father, thank You for choosing me to be Your vessel. Speak to my heart and give me direction regarding what You will have me do for Your glory and the empowerment of Your people. In Jesus' name, Amen.

Additional Scripture reading: Romans 9

Not Without You

Be transformed

Don't copy the behavior and customs of this world, but let God transform you into a new person by changing the way you think. Then you will learn to know God's will for you, which is good and pleasing and perfect. (Romans 12:2 NLT)

As children of God, we should want to learn and live God's will for our lives. However, we cannot accomplish this if we continue to straddle the fence and desire to live as though we do not know God. We shouldn't talk like people of the world, treat our enemies like people of the world or even attempt to blend in with people of the world. We should be different because God has set us apart. People should be able to look at God's children and take note that something is peculiar about them.

To live a changed life, we must first transform our thoughts. We cannot do this on our own; therefore, we must allow God to change our thought patterns. God can only do this through His word and prayer. We have to consistently spend time in His word because what we put into our spirit is what we will get out. If we're constantly feeding our spirit things that are holy and pure, our thoughts will become the same, which is what God desires.

Once our thoughts are transformed, then we will be able to learn God's will for us. Only then will we live the life that God has called us to live, pleasing Him and doing His will. God's will propels us into destiny, gives Him glory and elevates His people. Let the Lord transform your mind today so that you can do what you have been created to do.

Prayer for Today: Heavenly Father, thank You for Your will that has been predetermined for me. Today, I commit to allowing You to change my mind and my thoughts so that they may be pleasing to You. In Jesus' name, Amen.

Additional Scripture reading: Romans 12:1-2 and Philippians 4:8-9

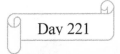

Day 221

Parts of one body

Just as our bodies have many parts and each part has a special function, so it is with Christ's body. We are many parts of one body, and we all belong to each other. (Romans 12:4-5 NLT)

In every relationship, each person has a different role or function. Whenever either person in the relationship isn't doing all that they should do, the relationship suffers and isn't operating at its fullest potential. Just as this is true in all our relationships, it is true in the body of Christ.

We have all been given different gifts, and if we don't use them like we should at the level that we're supposed to, then we aren't contributing to the kingdom like God intended and God's people are the ones who suffer. Not giving our best is disobedience because we aren't giving of ourselves as God desires. Our disobedience cheats someone else of their blessing because we are God's instruments. He uses us to serve, teach, encourage, give to and bless His people.

No matter what gift God has given you, use that gift well to glorify God and serve His people. Do it to the best of your ability, not cheating yourself or others of the gift. No gift is too small or greater than another; they are all needed to accomplish God's will. Find joy in doing what you do well.

Prayer for Today: Heavenly Father, thank You for the gifts that You have placed within me. I recognize that they are a blessing from You to bless others. Help me to use my gifts well in ways that glorify You. May You receive all the glory and praise! In Jesus' name, Amen.

Additional Scripture reading: Romans 12:4-13

Do good

Don't let evil conquer you, but conquer evil by doing good. (Romans 12:21 NLT)

God's word says that vengeance belongs to Him, but in our human nature, we desire to get revenge and get it sooner rather than later. We don't want to wait on God to do what He said He will do in His word. We want offenders to suffer and we want to be the ones to make them suffer. Not only that, we want to watch them suffer.

However, this is not God's way and we must trust in Him to repay the wrong doer. We must learn to forgive and let the Lord have His way in hurtful situations. Instead of trying to get payback, we are supposed to show them love in return for their misdeeds. If we can get to a place where we can truly turn the other cheek and love those who do us wrong, God will be glorified.

Not only will God be glorified but the enemy loses. In fact, enemies will begin receiving their payback when you're not returning their evil gestures. Oftentimes, offenders will be more upset if you're nice to them instead of bowing down to their level of evil. But when others see you handling the situation the way God wants you to, God gets the glory. You pass the test. You move to the next level in your relationship with the Lord. You get the victory. You win.

Prayer for Today: Heavenly Father, give me strength to overcome evil by doing good. It is difficult for me to wait on You to get vengeance. Let Your Holy Spirit heal my heart so that I won't be troubled or discouraged. Teach me to treat others the way You desire regardless of how they treat me. In Jesus' name, Amen.

Additional Scripture reading: Romans 12:17-21; Deuteronomy 32:35 and Proverbs 25:21-22

~Day of Reflection~

Authority

Read: John 19:11; Romans 13:1-2

Meditate: Do you have problems with people who have been placed in authoritative positions? Church, government, work?

Apply: Respect those who have been placed in authoritative positions. What actions can you take to show that you respect the authority that God has placed in your life?

Not Without You

God gives authority

Everyone must submit to governing authorities. For all authority comes from God, and those in positions of authority have been placed there by God. (Romans 13:1 NLT)

We have been given authority figures in our government, churches, workplaces and homes. God has given us governing authorities in each of these places to keep order and honor Him. He has chosen those whom He desires to be authority figures, and as children of God, we must respect that. We often have issues with the way the president runs the country, the pastor and elders lead the church, our managers supervise their employees and husbands lead their households. However, we should not allow our issues with authorities to cause us to disrespect them.

Sometimes, issues arise because leaders aren't doing what we think they should do or because we aren't doing what's right so we're in conflict. We must respect those in authority as God's leaders and treat them the way that God wants us to treat them, with love and obedience. When we submit to proper authority, we are able to have a clear mind because we have done what we're supposed to do.

In any area of life where you have an issue with those in authority, do not allow your issues to cause you to sin by being disrespectful. The Bible warns us that when we rebel against authority, we are rebelling against God because He has placed them in those positions.

Prayer for Today: Heavenly Father, thank You for the governing authorities that You've given us in every area of life to help keep peace. Let me treat them with love and respect as you have said in your Word. I know that You will hold them accountable when they are in the wrong. Help me hold on to that truth. In Jesus' name, Amen.

Additional Scripture reading: Romans 13:1-7

Day 225

Learn to love

Love does no wrong to others, so love fulfills the requirements of God's law. (Romans 13:10 NLT)

The Bible repeatedly admonishes us to love one another as we love ourselves. This is the greatest commandment that God has given us. When we love one another the way God intends, everything else is in alignment. Love keeps us from hurting one another. Love keeps us from stealing, killing and cheating one another.

We cannot love the way God wants us to love if we do not love God and accept the love that He has so freely given to us. We have to understand the magnitude of God's love and how that love should be manifested in our lives one to another. God loved us so much that He gave His only Son to die on the cross for our sins so that we may be redeemed back unto Him. Imagine the amount of love it would take for you to give up your only child so that everyone else could be saved.

When we understand God's love, we must ask Him to teach us to love others. We have to look at our lives to see how God loves us and the amount of mercy, grace and forgiveness that He constantly gives. In that same way, we must extend the same mercy, grace, forgiveness and love to another. Only then will we love one another the way God desires.

Prayer for Today: Heavenly Father, thank You for Your love. It is so great and powerful. Teach me to love others in the way that You desire. I cannot love others without You. In Jesus' name, Amen.

Additional Scripture reading: Romans 13:8-14

Not Without You

Live to lead others to Jesus

So let's stop condemning each other. Decide instead to live in such a way that you will not cause another believer to stumble and fall. (*Romans 14:13 NLT*)

We have to monitor our behavior at all times: in public and in private. All of our actions have consequences, and sometimes cause others to sin. For example, take the question about whether or not it is a sin to drink alcohol. The Bible doesn't speak against having a drink but it does speak against being drunk. However, if there is a babe in Christ with drinking issues, and the babe witnesses the mature Christian having a drink, they are bound to think it is okay. The result may be the babe going against his/her own convictions and drinking as well, therefore sinning, because the Bible says that we sin when we do not follow our own convictions.

There will always be debates regarding many issues that the Bible doesn't speak specifically about. As children of God, we should encourage and build up one another and not lead another person into sin. Therefore, if engaging in any act will lead another person to sin, we should not do it. We must remember that this life isn't about us, but it is about drawing others closer to God. Simply put, our lives should lead people to Christ and not away from Him.

Prayer for Today: Heavenly Father, help me to live in a way that brings people closer to You and not push them away. Help me to be mindful of my actions so that I may not lead another person into sin. In Jesus' name, Amen.

Additional Scripture reading: Romans 14

Mind of Christ

No one can know a person's thoughts except that person's own spirit, and no one can know God's thoughts except God's own Spirit. (1 Corinthians 2:11 NLT)

The Holy Spirit is our connection to God. The Holy Spirit guides us and gives us godly wisdom. When Jesus said that He would not leave us comfortless, He told us that we would receive the Holy Spirit. In order to understand God's plans and thoughts, we cannot use our natural mind. God is spirit so we must use spirit to understand spiritual things that He wishes to reveal to us.

The Holy Spirit gives us the mind of Christ. A Christ-like mindset begins with a clean mind, pure heart and willing spirit. We have to commune with the Holy Spirit and invite Him into our daily lives. It is impossible to develop the mind of Christ if we don't spend time in His presence.

Begin each day with prayer and the word of God to invite the Holy Spirit into your daily life. Make room for Him so that you may be able to hear His voice, follow His direction and walk in spiritual truths. It is then that you will begin to have a Christ-like mind and live as God desires.

Prayer for Today: Heavenly Father, thank You for Your Holy Spirit who gives wisdom and guidance. I want the mind of Christ so that I can live according to Your will so I invite You into my life today. In Jesus' name, Amen.

Additional Scripture reading: 1 Corinthians 2

Not Without You

Spiritual maturity

I had to feed you with milk, not with solid food, because you weren't ready for anything stronger. And you still aren't ready, for you are still controlled by your sinful nature. You are jealous of one another and quarrel with each other. Doesn't that prove you are controlled by your sinful nature? Aren't you living like the people of the world?

(1 Corinthians 3:2-3 NLT)

In this passage of Scripture, Paul isn't talking about the food that we eat but he is speaking of spiritual food. He is explaining that he cannot talk to the Corinthians about the deeper things of God because they are still disobeying the word of God that they have been given.

We may be like the Corinthians. We want to experience God on new levels but we still allow sin to control us. We hear the same messages about loving one another and getting rid of sin from our lives, and yet we continue to live according to what we want as opposed to what the Spirit wants. In order to take our relationship with God to greater heights and deeper intimacy, we must first begin to fully obey His word. We have to put into practice all of the things we've been taught from the beginning.

God desires to draw closer to us and reveal more of Himself to us but we have to be able to handle what we've been given. Think about babies. We don't give them solid food until their stomachs are developed and we know that they can handle it. In the same way, we have to become spiritually mature by following God's greatest commandment of loving one another and living a life that is pleasing to Him.

Prayer for Today: Heavenly Father, I desire more of You. Give me strength as I strive toward spiritual maturity. Help me to put away spiritually childish things and live according to Your Word. In Jesus' name, Amen.

Additional Scripture reading: 1 Corinthians 3

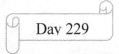
Day 229

Get moving

Then the Lord said to Moses, "Why are you crying out to me? Tell the people to get moving!" (Exodus 14:15 NLT)

We should always spend time in God's presence consulting Him before we make decisions. However, sometimes we can be fearful and use this as a crutch to not move forward. When we've spent enough time in God's presence, we'll realize that he has given us all that we need to accomplish His will.

Consider the Israelites in today's text. They were crying out to God and ready to turn around because they were fearful. They were about to miss their blessing by allowing fear to engulf them. Everything that they needed to cross the Red Sea was already in their possession - God's power represented by Moses' staff! Once the Lord revealed this to Moses' their problem was solved.

As you spend time seeking God for direction, make sure that you aren't doing it out of fear. God always gives us what we need to complete His assignments. What has God placed in your hand? Are you using it? Ask God to reveal to you what He has given you to get the job done instead of crying out in fear.

Prayer for Today: Heavenly Father, thank You for giving me all that I need to move forward to do what You have called me to do. Don't let me be paralyzed by fear but encouraged because You are with me and have already gone before me. In Jesus' name, Amen.

Additional Scripture reading: Exodus 14

~Day of Reflection~

Greed

Read: Proverbs 28:25; Ephesians 5:3

Meditate: How has greed played a part in your life?

Apply: What causes you to lose contentment? What can you do to make sure greed doesn't ruin you, your relationships or cause you to sin?

Is your job too big?

"You're going to wear yourself out - and the people, too. This job is too heavy a burden for you to handle all by yourself." (Exodus 18:18 NLT)

There are times when the task you've been given will be too great for you to handle alone. In these times, ask the Lord to give you people who can assist you. These people should have a heart for the Lord's will, availability and a willingness to serve.

God's work is not meant to be a burden on anyone. God desires that His will be done with joy. Assignments from God are always to bring His people closer to Him and not further away. They are also to bring Him glory and not glory to ourselves.

Spend a moment assessing the tasks that God has given you. Are they becoming burdensome? Are you trying to handle your job alone? We all need trustworthy people in our corner to help us carry out the Lord's plan. In Exodus 18, Moses appointed leaders to help him with settling disputes between the Israelites. This eased Moses' burden and helped him become even more effective. The same is true for us. We are more effective when we are less burdened. If you need help, ask for it. It will be a blessing to your soul.

Prayer for Today: Thank You for the people in my circle whom You have appointed to help me carry out my assignment. Help us to remember that it is all for Your glory and not ours so that we may remain focused on the true reason that we are working. In Jesus' name, Amen.

Additional Scripture reading: Exodus 18

Not Without You

Who do you serve?

You must serve only the Lord your God. If you do, I will bless you with food and water, and I will protect you from illness. (Exodus 23:25 NLT)

The Lord promises many things to us if we serve only Him. Some of these promises are:

- Protection
- Guidance along our journey
- He will be an enemy to our enemies
- Food and water
- Long full life
- He will go ahead of us and prepare the way

We need the Lord to provide all these things and so much more .The Lord promises to give us everything that we need if we love and serve only Him; and He is faithful to do all that He says He will do. We can trust Him. Besides, one of the Lord's commandments is to not have any other gods; serving anyone or anything else should not be an option.

Whatever you need from the Lord, it all begins with you serving Him and making sure that He is first in your life. Serve Him by obeying His word, praying and loving others. Serve Him by giving your time and resources to build His kingdom. Remember that only what you do for the Lord will last; everything else is meaningless.

Prayer for Today: Heavenly Father, I choose to serve You today in all that I do. I pray that my thoughts and my servitude be pleasing to You. As I serve You by serving others, I pray that it brings You joy. In Jesus' name, Amen.

Additional Scripture reading: Exodus 23:20-33

Not Without You

Time in His presence

Then Moses disappeared into the cloud as he climbed higher up the mountain. He remained on the mountain forty days and forty nights. (Exodus 24:18 NLT)

The higher we go in our relationship with God, the less there is of us. Take Moses for example. As he went farther up the mountain into the Lord's presence, the Israelites saw less and less of him. Those at the foot of the mountain saw the glory of the Lord. As we spend more and more time in God's presence, others should see more of God in us.

The more time we spend in God's presence, the more we began to look like Him in our speech and actions. In fact, when we spend time at length with anyone, we begin to take on some of their habits. They rub off on us. We began speaking and acting like them and those around us take note of it. Can you recall a time when someone said, "you two are just alike" or "this person acts just like you" or vice versa. When we spend a lot of time with anyone, good influence or bad, one of two things happen: we began to act like them or they began to act like us.

We know that God doesn't change, so spending time in His presence is a safe bet. When we spend time with Him, we will become more like Him. We will begin to see people and circumstances the way He sees them: with eyes of love. Draw closer to the Lord today so that you may become more like Him.

Prayer for Today: Heavenly Father, as I strive to be more like You, I commit to spending more time in Your presence. I want my life to be a reflection of the time I spend with You. In Jesus' name, Amen.

Additional Scripture reading: Exodus 24

Who's blocking you?

"Why did you beat your donkey those three times?" the angel of the Lord demanded. "Look, I have come to block your way because you are stubbornly resisting me." (Numbers 22:32 NLT)

In the text, Balak sent for Balaam because he wanted him to curse the Israelites. There are two issues here: 1) No one can curse what the Lord has already blessed and 2) The Lord did not want Balaam to go with them. Balak was persistent until finally the Lord allowed Balaam to go. However, the Lord was angry with Balaam for going to see Balak and sent an angel to block his path.

There are times when the Lord will allow us to move forward in doing something that He has not called us to do. When this happens, we will meet resistance. However, we can also meet resistance when the Lord has given His blessing for us to move. We must seek Him to know the difference. We need to be so in tune with God to the point where we know when He wants us to move and when He wants us to be still. We have to get to a place where we can discern whether the Lord is blocking us or the enemy is trying to keep us from completing our assignment.

We all need discernment to navigate these situations. We have to spend enough time in God's presence to know what He is calling us to do and what He is not calling us to do. Are you experiencing resistance today? Seek the Lord to make sure that you're on the right path.

Prayer for Today: Heavenly Father, give me discernment so that I may know when I am getting in the way of Your plan for my life and when the enemy is getting in the way of me doing Your will. In Jesus' name, Amen.

Additional Scripture reading: Numbers 22

The enemy is powerless

But how can I curse those whom God has not cursed? How can I condemn those whom the Lord has not condemned? (Numbers 23:8 NLT)

Balak saw how mighty the Israelites were and how they defeated the Amorites, and he became terrified. He thought that he could get Balaam to put a curse on them to keep them from destroying Moab. The issue here is that the Lord had already blessed Israel; they were His chosen people. No one can put a curse on what the Lord has already blessed. It just cannot happen.

The same thing is true today. When God blesses you, no one can take your blessing away or reverse your blessing to curse you. No matter how hard the enemy tries, he cannot make it happen. The most that he can do is distract you to keep you from walking in the fullness of your blessing. Consider how Balak took Balaam to different places to see Israel from various angles. He figured if Balaam could just curse some part of them, then he would be satisfied. That is how the enemy works. He attacks you in different areas of your life trying to convince you that you aren't blessed or chosen. For example, the enemy attacks your finances, relationships and health all in an attempt to make you feel less than who you were called to be. Remember that when God blesses you, the enemy cannot curse you. You are all that God says you are!

Prayer for Today: Heavenly Father, thank You for your blessings that can withstand anything that the enemy brings my way. I will hold fast to Your truths today so I may continue to live victoriously in You. In Jesus' name, Amen.

Additional Scripture reading: Numbers 23 and 24

Day 236

Repetition

Repeat them again and again to your children. Talk about them when you are at home and when you are on the road, when you are going to bed and when you are getting up. (Deuteronomy 6:7 NLT)

Our obedience to God's word is what moves God to bless us. The word of God says that we will enjoy long life, success and all that God has promised when we keep His word in our hearts and obey it. How do we keep His word hidden in our hearts so that it may come to our remembrance when we need it? Repetition!

We have to continuously keep the word of God before us. The word of God says to talk about it all the time, day and night, at home and away from home and to our children. It is so easy to slip into unholy conversation so we should strive to keep the word of God in our mouths strengthening ourselves and those around us. The word of God is refreshing and life changing. It's like holding up a mirror so that one can see himself just as He is and submit to God for cleansing.

Choose to talk about the word of God and His promises today. Give Him praise and keep your heart and mind focused on Him so that you can be sure to do all that He has called you to do. Be intentional in serving God wholeheartedly today!

Prayer for Today: Heavenly Father, thank You for Your word that gives my spirit life. Keep Your word on my mind today so that my focus may remain on You. Keep Your word in my mouth today so that I may encourage others and myself to walk along the path that You have designed. In Jesus' name, Amen.

Additional Scripture reading: Deuteronomy 6

~Day of Reflection~

More like Jesus

Read: 1 John 1:5-2:6

Meditate: Think of one area in your life that you know doesn't reflect the light of Jesus.

Apply: Write down things you can change in this area to help you live a more pleasing life to God.

Not Without You

Hand-picked because of love

The Lord did not set his heart on you and choose you because you were more numerous than other nations, for you were the smallest of all nations! (Deuteronomy 7:7 NLT)

God wasn't concerned with your exterior when He chose you. He didn't choose you because you fit a certain profile or you acted a certain way. He didn't choose you because you were perfect; He chose you because He loves you!

God loves you so much that He chose you before you were born to carry out His will. He made a promise to Abraham that He would give him numerous descendants and that they would be blessed. God chose you because of His faithfulness and promise to Abraham. Because of this, you can rest assured that God chose you and has a plan for you.

Think of all the things that you have been through and how God has preserved you. You have been preserved for a purpose and it's up to you to live out that purpose. Don't allow the voice of the enemy to keep you from walking into your destiny. Instead, let the voice of the enemy remind you that you are chosen by God to achieve greatness.

Prayer for Today: Heavenly Father, thank You for choosing me in spite of my shortcomings. Thank You for choosing to lavish Your love and grace upon me. Thank You for choosing me to carry out Your will. Lead me into the paths of righteousness for your name's sake. In Jesus' name, Amen.

Additional Scripture reading: Deuteronomy 7

Lifestyle of obedience

"But that is the time to be careful! Beware that in your plenty you do not forget the Lord your God and disobey his commands, regulations, and decrees that I am giving you today." (Deuteronomy 8:11 NLT)

When things are going well in our lives and we are enjoying the many blessings of God, we often forget the Blessor! We become lazy about praising God, praying, attending worship services and acknowledging God. We allow the blessings to take center stage of our lives and neglect spending much needed time alone with God until something happens. When there is a glitch, we run to God trying to make up for the time away, but God doesn't want us live this way.

God wants us to remember all that He has done for us. He wants us to praise Him and spend time in His presence when things are going well and when things are going not so well. God desires that we keep His mighty deeds in the forefront of our minds. When we stay focused on God and all that He has done, we won't forget Him when we have plenty because we never stopped thinking about Him.

Whether you're currently in a place of plenty or not, spend time in God's presence. Don't let your blessings dictate when, where and how often you're obedient. Let obedience become your lifestyle.

Prayer for Today: Heavenly Father, thank You for your blessings. I choose to praise and keep You in my thoughts at all times. Let Your praises continually be in my mouth. In Jesus' name, Amen.

Additional Scripture reading: Deuteronomy 8

Sin spreads

Your boasting about this is terrible. Don't you realize that this sin is like a little yeast that spreads through the whole batch of dough? (1 Corinthians 5:6 NLT)

Sin is like a disease. Though only one part of the body may be infected, it is damaging to the entire body. When we allow ourselves to hold on to sin, we are weakening our spirit. That sin is eating away at us, causing us to lose our power. We are not as strong and courageous when we hold on to sin, because we are afraid to live boldly due to the hidden sin.

When we choose to continue living in sin, we become more accepting of others' sin when we should be helping others come out of their sin. We live in fear that others may see us as judgmental because we have sin in our lives as well. However, we must get to the place where God wants us to be; that is to live boldly by the power of the Holy Spirit. We must decide to reject sin and choose Christ.

If you're holding on to something today that you know doesn't please God, make the healthy decision to let it go so that it won't destroy you. Get rid of the dead weight. The enemy enjoys seeing you hold on to sin because He knows that you aren't as effective as you could be without it. He knows that you aren't experiencing the abundant life that God promised. Choose to disappoint the enemy today by choosing Christ and not your crutch.

Prayer for Today: Heavenly Father, thank You for Your powerful word. Today I choose to cling to You and release my sin. I choose to live the abundant life that You freely give. In Jesus' name, Amen.

Additional Scripture reading: 1 Corinthians 5

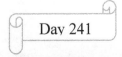

Not everything is good for you

You say, "I am allowed to do anything"—but not everything is good for you. And even though "I am allowed to do anything," I must not become a slave to anything. (1 Corinthians 6:12 NLT)

Although God's word gives instructions on what we should and should not do, we have the freedom to choose. We can do whatever we want to do, but that doesn't mean that we should. We must use this liberty wisely.

We cannot allow this freedom to cause us to slip into sin or live recklessly. Instead, we should show the world that even though we have liberty, we choose God. We choose to live according to His word. God doesn't force anyone to keep His commandments, believe in Him or choose Him. We must come to God willingly and wholeheartedly.

What are you doing with the freedom that you have? Are you using it to indulge your sinful desires, or are you using it to grow closer to the Lord? Whatever you choose, choose wisely.

Prayer for Today: Heavenly Father, thank You for the liberty that I have found in You. I pray that my choices please You and draw others closer to You. I submit my will to Your will so that I may serve You completely. In Jesus' name, Amen.

Additional Scripture reading: 1 Corinthians 6:9-14

A clean temple

Don't you realize that your body is the temple of the Holy Spirit, who lives in you and was given to you by God? You do not belong to yourself, for God bought you with a high price. So you must honor God with your body. (1 Corinthians 6:19-20 NLT)

We neglect our bodies in many ways, both physically and spiritually. Our bodies are temples of the Holy Spirit which means that the Holy Spirit dwells within our bodies. We must be cognizant that the Holy Spirit is *holy* and we should honor God with our bodies by keeping our temples clean.

In order to take better care of our temples, we must understand that the Holy Spirit is a gift from the Most High God! God Himself gave us the Holy Spirit. He chose to allow His Spirit to live in us. When we truly understand how important this is, we will desire to keep our temples clean; we will keep filth from entering our bodies and carefully manage what we do with them.

Today, decide not to commit sins with your body: sexual sins, gluttony or any other impurities. Choose to keep your temple clean and healthy so that the Holy Spirit may dwell within a clean temple. Honor God with your body today.

Prayer for Today: Heavenly Father, I choose to honor You with my body. Let Your Holy Spirit convict me before I choose to do something that would disrespect or dishonor Your temple. In Jesus' name, Amen.

Additional Scripture reading: 1 Corinthians 6:15-20

Pleasant Thoughts

May all my thoughts be pleasing to him, for I rejoice in the Lord. (Psalm 104:34 NLT)

As Christians, we should desire to please God with our thoughts, honor Him with our life and become more like Him each day. To have thoughts that please Him, we must first change the way we think. What we meditate on determines the direction of our life.

How do we get to the point where we have pleasing thoughts? The first thing we must do is be careful about what we watch. Psalm 101:3 NLT states "I will refuse to look at anything vile and vulgar." The NKJV states, "I will set no wicked thing before my eyes." We have to be very careful about what we set our sight on. Think about it. How many times have you saw something, thought about it, and then took some sort of action based on what you saw? What you see drives your thoughts and your thoughts drive your actions.

Next, we must train our thoughts. We cannot get to this place over night. We must continue to work at it and be intentional. Philippians 4:8b says "Fix your thoughts on what is true, and honorable, and right and pure, and lovely, and admirable. Think about things that are excellent and worthy of praise."

Lastly, we must be careful about what we listen to. James 1:21 NLT says "So get rid of all the filth and evil in your lives, and humbly accept the word God has planted in your hearts, for it has the power to save your souls." God's word cannot be planted in our heart unless we listen to it and meditate on it. We must listen to God's word, meditate on it and do what it says.

Prayer for Today: Heavenly Father, give me the desire to honor You with my thoughts. Let me be mindful that I need to guard my ears and eyes from things that are not pleasing to You. In Jesus' name, Amen.

Additional Scripture reading: Luke 11:34-36 and Psalm 104

~Day of Reflection~

Taking His place

Read: 1 John 5:21

Meditate: Is there anything in your life that might take God's place in your heart?

Apply: What can you do to ensure things stay in their proper place? God first, then other things.

Run with purpose

So I run with purpose in every step. I am not just shadowboxing. (1 Corinthians 9:26 NLT)

In the previous verses, Paul discussed how he did whatever possible to bring others to Christ. When he was with the Jews, he lived like them. When he was with the Gentiles, he lived like them. When he was with those who were weak, he shared in their weakness. He did these things because he wanted to find common ground with them. Once he found common ground, he received their trust and found an opening to share Christ with them.

God has given each of us purpose. We must share His love with others. People will not know about Christ and what He has done for us if we do not tell them. We have to be intentional about sharing Christ with others. We can begin by the way we love them. Others have to not only hear what we're saying but they have to see us living it.

We have to constantly and consistently study God's word. This puts us in a place where we can confidently run the race that is before us. Not only will we run with confidence but we will be able to run so that we may win souls to Christ.

Prayer for Today: Heavenly Father, thank You for the purpose that You have given me. Help me to be consistent with studying and living Your word so that I may be the vessel that You have chosen me to be. In Jesus' name, Amen.

Additional Scripture reading: 1 Corinthians 9:19-27

Not Without You

Look for the window

The temptations in your life are no different from what others experience. And God is faithful. He will not allow the temptation to be more than you can stand. When you are tempted, he will show you a way out so that you can endure. (1 Corinthians 10:13 NLT)

We can take comfort in knowing that: 1) God is faithful, 2) Others are experiencing the same temptations, 3) God will not allow us to be tempted beyond what we can bear and 4) God always provides a way out.

Knowing that others are experiencing the same temptations provides comfort; we know that we can get through it because someone else has. It also gives comfort that we are not alone.

It is important to know that God is aware of the temptation and of your abilities. He knows what you can and cannot take. When you are tempted, trust in the power of Christ within you to handle the situation in the way that God expects. You are much stronger than you think you are! It is also imperative that you recognize the "out" that God gives you when you are tempted. If you take a moment to think about it, something always happens while you're being tempted to give you a moment to think about what you're considering doing and give you a chance to say no. Use wisdom by refusing to give in to temptation.

When you are tempted, look for the way out because God always presents it to you, often more than once. Look for God in all circumstances and you will be sure to find Him.

Prayer for Today: Heavenly Father, thank You for not allowing me to be tempted beyond what I can stand. I thank You even more for showing me a way out so that I don't give in to temptation. In Jesus' name, thank You, Amen.

Additional Scripture reading: 1 Corinthians 10:12-13

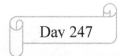

Love is the greatest gift

Three things will last forever – faith, hope, and love – and the greatest of these is love. (1 Corinthians 13:13 NLT)

God has given each one of us spiritual gifts. God gave us spiritual gifts to help and encourage one another. Using our spiritual gifts alone is not what pleases God, but using them in love does. Love is the greatest commandment, and when we love others the way God intended, we give glory to God. People respect and value the gifts, but God values love.

No matter how good you are at executing your spiritual gifts, doing so without love is meaningless. We miss the purpose of having spiritual gifts when we put the emphasis on the gifts and not on the love needed to fully function in the gift.

We cannot forget that in everything, love is most important. Love is what moved God to save us. Love is how God saved us. Love is what keeps God faithful when we are unfaithful. Love is the foundation of our faith.

Having spiritual gifts is great but having love is greater. Choose today to love God's people just as He desires.

Prayer for Today: Heavenly Father, thank You for loving me. I understand that I can have all the spiritual gifts in the world and be the best at using them, but if I don't have love, then I am useless in Your kingdom. Teach me to use them in love as You desire. In Jesus' name, Amen.

Additional Scripture reading: 1 Corinthians 12 and 13

Guilty by association

Don't be fooled by those who say such things, for "bad company corrupts good character." (1 Corinthians 15:33 NLT)

When I was an undergraduate, I was accused of treating someone unkindly. When I was confronted by an authority figure, I told her that I was not to blame but it was some of the people in my circle. I actually had no contact with the accuser. After explaining this, her response to me was "birds of a feather flock together." Although common, the expression has some truth to it. I wasn't involved in the situation but because I was associated with those who were, my name was included.

We must be mindful of whom we allow in our inner circle because either their behavior will rub off on us or we become guilty by association. Don't get trapped into thinking that the immoral behavior of those closest to you will not affect you. If you spend enough time with them, you will begin to pick up their bad habits. In the event that you do not pick up their bad habits, you will be perceived as being just as they are because you hang out with them.

Assess your inner circle. Is it reflective of who you are? Is it reflective of who God has called you to be?

Prayer for Today: Heavenly Father, thank You for those You have placed in my life. Allow me to be the light in my circle so that others will be drawn to You. Help me to be mindful of the company that I keep. Let my choice of associations reflect who You have called me to be. In Jesus' name, Amen.

Additional Scripture reading: 1 Corinthians 15:33-34 and Proverbs 22:24-25

The Lord's requirements

And now, Israel, what does the LORD your God require of you? He requires only that you fear the LORD your God, and live in a way that pleases him, and love him and serve him with all your heart and soul. And you must always obey the LORD's commands and decrees that I am giving you today for your own good. (Deuteronomy 10:12-13 NLT)

The word of God is pretty clear regarding what the Lord requires of us. Moses gave these requirements to the Israelites while in the wilderness. The requirements have not changed. God still desires that we live in a way that pleases Him, love him, serve Him and obey His commandments. God wants us to serve Him wholeheartedly and revere His Holy name.

We must change our hearts to want what God requires of us. We have to remember all that God has done for us and how sovereign He is. When we reflect on God's character, living the way He desires should not be an issue.

Part of the reason we do not live according to God's word is that we don't consider His holiness or His grace and mercy towards us. He has been so awesome to us and the least we could do is to love Him and obey His word. Choose love and obedience today.

Prayer for Today: Heavenly Father, today I choose to give You what You require of me. I choose to revere Your Holy name, live a life pleasing to You, love you, serve You and obey Your word. Give me the strength and wisdom as I strive to live as You command. In Jesus' name, Amen.

Additional Scripture reading: Deuteronomy 10:12-22

Not Without You

Trust Him at all times

"But even after all he did, you refused to trust the Lord your God."
(Deuteronomy 1:32 NLT)

The Lord did many wonderful and miraculous things for the Israelites on their journey from Egypt, through the wilderness and into the Promised Land. Even after witnessing the Lord's mighty power in their lives, they still refused to trust in Him. They continued to complain, disobey and doubt Him.

Every time I read about the Israelites, I say a little prayer asking God to not let me be like them. However, the truth is that oftentimes, we are a lot like the Israelites. God continues to bless us and show us favor and yet when issues arise, we question His presence, His plan and His purpose for us.

We can be very ungrateful when one little thing doesn't go the way we think it should go. We begin to doubt God and often veer off the right path when we think God's way isn't working. We cannot allow difficulties to shake our faith. We have to remain faithful and trust in the Lord even in the wilderness.

Today, take a moment to reflect over your life. Every time you thought that God wasn't there, He was. His way and His timing proved perfect. Because you have experience with His faithfulness, you should trust Him at all times.

Prayer for Today: Heavenly Father, thank You for being faithful even when I am not faithful. Thank You for not changing and turning Your back on me when I doubt You. I choose to rely on Your plan today even when I don't know what it is. I trust You. In Jesus' name, Amen.

Additional Scripture reading: Deuteronomy 1:26-46

Not Without You

Build each other up

Read: Jude 17-23

Meditate: Do you build up and encourage others or do you tear them down? How do people encourage you?

Apply: Write down ways you can encourage others to remain strong and faithful to what God has called them to do.

Obedience gives strength

"Therefore, be careful to obey every command I am giving you today, so you may have strength to go in and take over the land you are about to enter." (Deuteronomy 11:8 NLT)

In order to take possession of what God has promised us, we have to be obedient to His word. How would we be able to get what God has promised if we don't listen to His instructions on how to get it? We all want every blessing that God has for us, but we don't always do what needs to be done to receive them. Many of the promises of God, as written in the Bible, have an if/then clause, meaning that if we do what God says, He will bless us in certain ways.

God often blesses us in spite of our disobedience, but how much more will we be blessed if we only do what He says?

Find joy in being obedient. Spend some quiet time alone with God studying His holy word so that you can learn His promises and do what God requires to receive them. God loves us and He wants to bless us but even more than that, He wants us to obey His holy word.

Prayer for Today: Heavenly Father, thank You for Your promises. Lead me in the paths of righteousness for Your name's sake. Help me to be obedient to Your word so that I may experience fullness in you. In Jesus' name, Amen.

Additional Scripture reading: Deuteronomy 11:8-32

Not Without You

Giving back to the Lord

"You must set aside a tithe of your crops - one-tenth of all the crops you harvest each year." (Deuteronomy 14:22)

The word of God requires that we set aside a tenth of all of our earnings and present it back to the Lord. We should tithe out of obedience and fear of the Lord, to honor the Lord and receive the Lord's blessings. Tithing reminds us that our blessings come from God. It is also our way of saying "thank you" and giving God praise.

We often have an issue with talking about giving money to the church or worrying about how the church uses the funds. However, we cannot dwell on these things. All we can do is give out of obedience to God's word and let the Lord handle how His money is being used.

We have to remember that God blesses us even more when we are obedient with our finances by tithing. If you have an issue with tithing, pray and ask God to soften your heart or even send you to a ministry that will use the funds appropriately. Whatever your issues are, don't let them stand in the way of you receiving your blessings.

Prayer for Today: Heavenly Father, thank You for blessing me with income so that I can tithe. I thank You that I am able to help support Your ministries. Remove anything from me that hinders me from giving as You require in Your Word. In Jesus' name, Amen.

Additional Scripture reading: Deuteronomy 14:22-29; Malachi 3:6-12 and Luke 6:38

Not Without You

Give the same to others

He comforts us in all our troubles so that we can comfort others. When they are troubled, we will be able to give them the same comfort God has given us. (2 Corinthians 1:4 NLT)

Every ounce of love and compassion that God gives to us is to show us that He cares for us and so that we can demonstrate that same love towards others. The way He demonstrates His love towards us is an example of how He expects us to love our brothers and sisters in Christ.

For example, when you're hurting, God comforts you. When you're in need, He provides for you. When you need someone to talk to, He is there with a listening ear. When you need love, He gives it to you. In the same way, we are to allow God's love and light to work through us to be the same thing to others. People need to see God in us. They need us to love, give, listen and help them as God would want us to.

Think about how great God is to you. Are you extending that same love to others?

Prayer for Today: Heavenly Father, thank You for being a God of sovereignty, mercy, love, grace, forgiveness and comfort. Thank You for all that You are in my life. Help me to extend the same level of love and kindness to others.

Additional Scripture reading: 2 Corinthians 1:3-11

Not Without You

Familiarity with the enemy's patterns

So that Satan will not outsmart us. For we are familiar with his evil schemes. (2 Corinthians 2:11 NLT)

In this passage of Scripture, Paul was speaking of forgiving the sinner. He urged the Corinthians to forgive the sinner so that Satan will not outsmart us. He knows that when we hold unforgiveness in our hearts, we are not living as God has called us to live. Satan uses this as a tool to keep us from becoming all that we should be. However, we are familiar with all of Satan's schemes; they haven't changed.

Satan does the same things time and time again to trick us. We are aware of his tactics and yet we continue to allow them to trip us up. We fall for the same things over and over again. We find ourselves praying and asking for forgiveness for the same stuff. Since we are familiar with Satan's trickery, why do we continue to allow him to lure us into his trap of deceit?

We have to be smarter in our walk with Christ. We know what God requires of us and we must commit to doing what God wants us to do. Be mindful that all of the enemy's offers are temporary and are meant to keep you from living a godly life. God offers eternal life, love and abundance. Which will you choose?

Prayer for Today: Heavenly Father, thank You for the wisdom to know when the enemy is attempting to trick me. Give me the wisdom and courage to choose You and Your way when the enemy offers temporary satisfaction and solutions. In Jesus' name, Amen.

Additional Scripture reading: 2 Corinthians 2:5-13

Prequalified

It is not that we think we are qualified to do anything on our own. Our qualification comes from God. (2 Corinthians 3:5 NLT)

Whatever it is that God has called you to do; He has already qualified you for it! God chose each one of us for a specific purpose. It doesn't matter what you do or what you have done, God doesn't care about your resume. God only wants you to make yourself available to Him.

I began writing my first book three years before I published it. I struggled with whether or not I should complete it and publish it because of my occupation. I wasn't a pastor or ordained minister so I had doubt. I thought other people would question my qualifications. It took me three years to learn that my qualification and calling came from God.

When God calls you to do something, you don't have to worry about what other people will think. Your calling is for His purpose and will touch and encourage others' lives as He chooses. All of that is already worked out; you just need to be obedient. So whatever it is God called you to do in His kingdom, He has already prequalified you to do it!

Prayer for Today: Heavenly Father, thank You for qualifying me for my calling. I trust that You will lead me and help me to accomplish Your will. In Jesus' name, Amen.

Additional Scripture reading: 2 Corinthians 3:1-6

How Are You Conducting Your Life?

Good comes to those who lend money generously and conduct their business fairly. Such people will not be overcome by evil. Those who are righteous will be long remembered." (Psalm 112:5-6 NLT)

Have you ever worked at a company where lying, cheating and manipulating others to get ahead is rampant? Perhaps you're working at a place like that right now. Rest assured that you don't have to do any of those things to get ahead and progress in your career. You also don't have to do any of those things to get to your destiny.

One of the most difficult places to live out our faith consistently is probably the workplace. That is probably where we experience the most hell: gossiping, backbiting, adultery, jealously and lying. However, we must rise above all of these things and daily put on the whole armor of God (Ephesians 6:13-17).

No matter where you spend your time each day, you are always being watched because you bear the name of Christ as Christian. You should not let the behavior of others affect the way you behave. Instead, what you do should affect others. You should live your life in such a way that glorifies God and causes those around you to do the same.

Today I want to encourage you to remain faithful to God. Treat people fairly. Be honest in your work. Be trustworthy. Evil will not overcome you. Continue to do well and seek after God. You will prosper and you will not have to step on anyone's toes to do it. Just stay the course and remain faithful.

Prayer for Today: Heavenly Father, thank You for keeping me grounded in Your word. Teach me to conduct business fairly with everyone that I come into contact with. Your word says that I would be long remembered if I did so. I believe that I will not be looked over but I will receive the best from You for my life. In Jesus' name, Amen.

Additional Scripture reading: Deuteronomy 6 and Ephesians 6:10-20

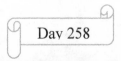

~Day of Reflection~

Helper and Shield

Read: Psalm 115

Meditate: Are you careful to give God His glory?

Apply: Write a list of things you are thankful for today. Then write a prayer of thanksgiving to God. Reflect on it throughout the day to shift your focus to God and give Him glory.

Turn your back

My child, if sinners entice you, turn your back on them! (Proverbs 1:10 NLT)

The enemy uses people to carry out his dirty deeds. He knows what your flesh desires and uses people to tempt you with that very thing. The Bible warns us to stay away from people who tempt us to sin. The person who leads you into sin is not your friend. A friend is one who will lead you towards Christ.

We must also know ourselves. We know if we go to certain places, hang around certain people, watch certain things, listen to certain things or think about certain things, we will be led into sin. When we truly understand and accept our weaknesses, we can begin to ask for strength and stay away from things and people that will bring those weaknesses out of us.

The goal is to be like Christ and live a life that is pleasing to God; therefore, we have to put today's Scripture into practice and turn our back on people who entice us to sin. We have to separate ourselves from them because we desire to please God. We cannot flirt with sin; we have to make up our minds to follow God wholeheartedly.

Prayer for Today: Heavenly Father, thank You for Your Word. I desire to honor You with my ways so I ask that You give me discernment when it comes to things or people that lead me into sin. In Jesus' name, Amen.

Additional Scripture reading: Proverbs 1:10-19

Benefits of wisdom

Tune your ears to wisdom, and concentrate on understanding. (Proverbs 2:2 NLT)

In Proverbs 2, the Bible teaches us to gain wisdom because living a wisdom filled life leads us down the path that God desires. We are to search for wisdom as if we were searching for treasures and continue to search for and apply it to our everyday lives. Here are a few benefits to us when we use wisdom:

- We learn to fear the Lord.
- The Lord is our shield.
- The Lord guards our paths.
- The Lord protects those who are faithful.
- We will know the right path to take.
- We will know which people to allow in our lives.

When we use wisdom, we learn how we are supposed to live because God is the giver of wisdom. He gives wisdom to those who ask for it. Not only must we continuously ask for wisdom, but we must hide it in our hearts and use it.

When we ignore wisdom, we do foolish things and get into trouble. Not using wisdom leads down a path of destruction and brokenness. Don't live defeated and discouraged but live the abundant life God has promised by using the wisdom that He freely gives to those who ask.

Prayer for Today: Heavenly Father, I ask You for wisdom today. Help me to hide it in my heart and live by it. I want to please You with my life and I know that starts with using wisdom. In Jesus' name, Amen.

Additional Scripture reading: Proverbs 1:20- Proverbs 2:22

Not Without You

A promise to show you the way

Trust in the Lord with all your heart; do not depend on your own understanding. Seek his will in all you do, and he will show you which path to take. (Proverbs 3:5-6 NLT)

Here, we have one of God's many promises: a promise to direct our path! In order for God to direct our path, we must trust in Him. We learn here that we should trust the Lord wholeheartedly, not rely on self-guidance, and seek His will in everything. After we submit to God, we open our hearts up to be led by Him.

One key thing to note here is that we must do this in *everything*! We cannot pick and choose when we want to submit to God and allow Him to direct our paths. We must come to a place where we trust in Him and His plan completely, because if we do not, we will always battle with our will versus His will.

To trust in the Lord is to know Him. Do you know Him well enough to trust Him? To choose His will over yours? To submit to His plan?

Whatever you may be dealing with today, give it over to God so that He can lead you in the right direction. From finances to relationships through career changes to His plan for you in His kingdom – allow Him to direct your path.

Prayer for Today: Heavenly Father, today I choose to acknowledge Your sovereignty and power in my life. I choose to trust You wholeheartedly and seek Your will. I ask that You direct my path so that my walk may be pleasing to You. In Jesus' name, Amen.

Additional Scripture reading: Proverbs 3:1-26

Help when you can

Do not withhold good from those who deserve it when it's in your power to help them. (Proverbs 3:27 NLT)

Sometimes our friends, coworkers or church members divulge personal information to us that reveal that they may be in need of something. It is great to take a moment to pray with them but it is even better to help them if it is in our power to do so. I believe that God impresses upon their hearts to share certain things with people who can help in some way. So, we shouldn't send people away with a prayer and a hug when we can do more for them.

As children of God, sometimes we are excellent with the prayers and "God bless you" sentiments, but God desires that we do much more than that. Even if you cannot help, you may know someone who can help. We are a body of believers who should take care of the *entire* body. When parts of the body are neglected, the body isn't as effective as it could be.

Be intentional about helping others. Strive to be a vessel that God can use to bless His people. Has someone come to you lately needing help? Were you able to help? Did you do so?

Prayer for Today: Heavenly Father, forgive me for not helping others when it has been in my power to do so. Help me not make that mistake again because I desire to let Your love live in me. In Jesus' name, Amen.

Additional Scripture reading: Proverbs 3:27-35 and 2 Corinthians 8:11-14

Let your words be pleasing to God

Avoid all perverse talk; stay away from corrupt speech. (Proverbs 4:24 NLT)

Are you familiar with the gum commercial with the tagline that says, "Do you have a dirty mouth? Well clean it up!" The actor then smiles after chewing the gum portraying a clean mouth. Well, the word of God is our gum. We need to chew on it as much as possible to clean our hearts so that we can clean our mouths.

Many things may bring the dirty words out of our mouths: terrible traffic and careless drivers; hot water; smashing fingers; stubbing toes, bad news, wild children, rude people and the list goes on. We shouldn't allow any of these things to rob us of our peace or sanity and result to using words that are not representative of God. A foul mouth can be a tough habit to break but first you have to want to change. Once you decide that you don't want to praise and curse out of the same mouth, then begin working on it by studying God's word and allowing Him to transform your heart and your words.

Prayer for Today: Heavenly Father, I desire to be like You in all of my ways. Cleanse my heart so that even my speech may be pleasing to You. Let the words out of my mouth be a reflection of Your holiness within me. In Jesus' name, Amen.

Additional Scripture reading: James 3:9-12

Joy and Faithfulness

Praise the Lord! How joyful are those who fear the Lord and delight in obeying his commands. (Psalm 112:1)

Think about a time when you were faced with a difficult choice and you made the right decision—one pleasing to God? When you realized that you made the right decision, didn't that bring joy to your heart? (Now if you've never made the right decision, today is a great day to start!) Our key verse says those who delight in obeying God's commands are joyful people.

Now think about a time when you made a choice not to follow God but to sin and do things your own way? Didn't that feel terrible? (Even if it did feel good in the beginning.) Were you faced with "should haves, could haves and would haves?" Didn't that road lead to destruction? (More problems than you started with.)

As you are faced with decisions (daily) remember the joy of following God's commands. Listen to that gentle, small voice that steers you in the right direction. Seek God with your whole heart. Commit yourself to His will for *every* area of your life. Your obedience stores up blessings for your children as well. Psalm 112:2 states, "Their children will be blessed." We all want the best for our children don't we? Even if you do not have children, your obedience or disobedience affects those around you. So let's continue to walk in the path that God has set before us.

Prayer for Today: Heavenly Father, I want to make decisions that please You. I trust in You and commit my mind, body and spirit to You today. In Jesus' name, Amen.

Additional Scripture reading: Isaiah 56:3-5 and Proverbs 21:3

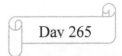

~Day of Reflection~

Joyful

Read: Psalm 112

Meditate: Do you take pleasure in obeying the Lord?

Apply: Highlight each scripture in this Psalm that encourages you to be obedient. Write out a prayer asking God to help you to be more obedient so that you will experience the life God wants you to have.

Troubles won't last

For our present troubles are small and won't last very long. Yet they produce for us a glory that vastly outweighs them and will last forever! (2 Corinthians 4:17 NLT)

What an awesome truth! Our troubles are temporary! They pale in comparison to what we gain and in comparison to what's to come! As we go through troubles, they may seem big and overwhelming but that is only the lie that the enemy wants you to believe.

Your troubles are going to make you spiritually stronger and push you in the direction that God wants you to go. Your troubles are only meant to bring out the best in you and not crush your spirit. Don't allow the lies of the enemy or the hurt from the troubles to drag you down. Instead, allow your troubles to strengthen you, knowing that they won't last and you have victory.

Remember that God knows the end when you can only see the present. Trust that God will not let you endure more than you can bear. Trust His purpose, plan and process. Even when the enemy does something to hurt you, God will make it work out for your good and His glory.

Prayer for Today: Heavenly Father, thank You for the promise that my present troubles are temporary! I thank You that my troubles produce a glory that far outweighs the actual troubles. Thank You for my destiny and giving me the encouragement to not allow anything to keep me from getting there. In Jesus' name, Amen.

Additional Scripture reading: 2 Corinthians 4:17-18

Ambassador for Christ

So we are Christ's ambassadors; God is making his appeal through us. We speak for Christ when we plead, "Come back to God!" (2 Corinthians 5:20 NLT)

An ambassador is a representative. If you've ever been a part of any organization (work, civil, social, community), then you should be aware that while you're representing that organization, your behavior is a reflection of the entire organization. So if you did something that could possibly bring shame to the organization, people considered the entire organization to be just like the representative.

Like it or not, you are an ambassador for every organization in which you hold a membership including, the body of Christ. Think about it: When you do something unsavory, people associate you with the organization and that gives the organization a bad reputation. Likewise, if your behavior is not reflective of Christ, you give the entire Christian community a bad reputation. When one Christian does something wrong, people tend to generalize that behavior about all Christians.

We have to remember that we are Christ's ambassadors and we should be trying to win others to Christ and not run them away. Once we decided to follow Him, we became His and we bear His name. Our desire should be for His purpose alone; we have to give up our old ways in hopes that others may see Christ through us and be drawn to Him.

Prayer for Today: Heavenly Father, as an ambassador for Christ, help me to live a life pleasing and acceptable to You so that I may help draw others into Your kingdom. In Jesus' name, Amen.

Additional Scripture reading: 2 Corinthians 5:11-21

Moved to repentance

For the kind of sorrow God wants us to experience leads us away from sin and results in salvation. There's no regret for that kind of sorrow. But worldly sorrow, which lacks repentance, results in spiritual death. (2 Corinthians 7:10 NLT)

When we go to God with feelings of regret or we hear messages in church that cause us to be filled with sorrow because of our sin and disobedience, God wants us to be moved to repentance. He doesn't want us to experience temporary sadness in which we want forgiveness in that moment only to return to our sin. God desires that we fully return to Him and repent.

Godly sorrow helps us to see our sin for what it is, moves us to true repentance and pushes us closer into God's loving arms. We are moved to live godly lives and turn our back on our wrongs. This is the kind of sorrow that God desires from us – sorrow that moves us towards Him. God cannot be fooled; He knows our hearts. He knows when we truly regret our actions and desire to follow Him wholeheartedly. He also knows when we do not sincerely regret our sin and still want to hold on to it. This surface regret hinders our relationship with God and keeps us from growing closer to Him.

When you repent, do you really want forgiveness and to turn away from your sin? Or do you want to hold on to your sin and repeatedly ask for forgiveness for the same thing? You cannot have it both ways; you must choose.

Prayer for Today: Heavenly Father, thank You for forgiveness. Thank You for being a loving, kind and merciful God. Give me the kind of conviction that will make me turn away from my sin and grow closer to You. In Jesus' name, Amen.

Additional Scripture reading: 2 Corinthians 7:5-16

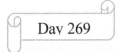

Help them fight

During all this time you have not deserted the other tribes. You have been careful to obey the commands of the Lord your God right up to the present day. (Joshua 22:3 NLT)

Of the twelve tribes of Israel, two and a half of them received their promised land before the others. However, they did not return to their land to rest until every tribe received its allotment of land. They remained faithful to God and helped the remaining tribes conquer their land.

Far too often, we become satisfied when we receive our blessings and forget about others. We have to get to a place where we do not rest until we help those around us get what the Lord has promised them. We have to be encouragers and help our fellow brothers and sisters fight to obtain their *land*. We should not feel comfortable enjoying our land when our friends and family are still striving to get theirs.

Commit to giving back by helping your friends and family get into college, find a job, connect to resources, etc. Become a bridge to someone who needs it. Share your knowledge. Empower others. God doesn't want us to desert one another but help others achieve their goals as well.

Prayer for Today: Heavenly Father, thank You for sending people in my life to help me along my journey. Help me extend that same level of assistance to someone else who needs help getting to where You have called them to go. Thank You for Your faithfulness and resources. In Jesus' name, Amen.

Additional Scripture reading: Joshua 22:1-9

Not Without You

The Lord is with you

The angel of the Lord appeared to him and said, "Mighty hero, the Lord is with you!" (Judges 6:12 NLT)

In this passage of Scripture, the people of Israel cried out to the Lord for help after He handed them over to the Midianites. The Israelites were disobedient but the Lord had compassion on them and decided to give them a judge, Gideon. When the angel of the Lord appeared to Gideon, and told him to rescue Israel, Gideon had a couple of excuses as to why he was not fit for the task: his clan was the weakest and he was the least in his entire family. However, the Lord didn't care about any of that. His response to Gideon's excuses was simply, "I will be with you!"

No matter how many excuses you can come up with as to why you cannot do what God has called you to do, they are useless. God is still the same and He will be with you just as He has always been. God will not give you an assignment only to walk away from you while you're carrying out the task. He chose you so of course He wouldn't just leave you hanging!

As you go throughout your day today, remember that the Lord will be with you. Fear cannot conquer you and faith will sustain you! No more excuses as to why you cannot begin walking in your destiny! God is with you and that is all that you need.

Prayer for Today: Heavenly Father, forgive me for making excuses and using them to keep me from doing Your will. I trust that You are with me and I will find security and comfort in that truth. In Jesus' name, Amen.

Additional Scripture reading: Judges 6

God rewards hard work

Lazy people want much but get little, but those who work hard will prosper. (Proverbs 13:4 NLT)

Lazy people are slackers. In general, they don't work or even desire to work. They prefer for others to do the work for them or to engage in get-rich-quick schemes. They are always looking for shortcuts instead of putting in the required amount of work to get things done. Another characteristic of lazy people is that they are talkers. They spend plenty of time talking about what they want and how much wealth they desire and yet they do nothing to make progress towards these dreams.

It is not God's will for us to be lazy. In fact, God speaks against laziness in several passages throughout the Bible. God wants us to be diligent in all things. He has many promises of success for us in His word but they are conditional; we have to do our part.

If you have dreams or goals, only talking about them will not bring them to pass. Proverbs 14:23 NLT says that "Work brings profit, but mere talk leads to poverty." Be bold and courageous by taking action to get to where you want to be in life. You have the power to accomplish all the plans that God has placed in your heart; but you must work hard to attain them!

Prayer for Today: Heavenly Father, forgive me if I have been lazy about accomplishing my goals. Keep me encouraged so that I may experience the abundant life that You have promised in Your holy word. Give me an attitude of expectancy and a spirit of diligence. In Jesus' name, Amen.

Additional Scripture reading: Proverbs 10:4, 26; Proverbs 12:24, 27; Proverbs 13:11 and Proverbs 15:19

Not Without You

What can you offer?

Read: Psalm 116

Meditate: Think back over the past week and take note of all that God has done for you.

Apply: There is no way that we can repay God for His goodness to us so spend a moment writing down your reflections of God's presence in your life over the past week. Write down a prayer of praise.

The way to speak

A gentle answer deflects anger, but harsh words make tempers flare. (Proverbs 15:1 NLT)

The way in which we use our words and tone of voice in conversation can spark conflict or keep the peace. As children of God, we are called to be peacemakers, so we must be mindful of how we talk to others, regardless of how they talk to us. Sure, it can be difficult to remain calm and polite when someone is being disrespectful. However, I have found that you can either put a fire out or increase the flames with what you say and how you say it.

You have the power to speak words of encouragement, inspiration, kindness, gentleness and love. You also have a choice. When you choose to speak words that promote peace and harmony, you change the course of a heated conversation to one that could possibly salvage a relationship. You don't have to be in a heated conversation but you could be simply having a bad day. If you make the decision to think before you speak and choose to speak kind words, you avoid crushing someone's spirit and/or the relationship.

Remember to speak gentle and kind words to others. We never know what kind of day someone else is having. Our kindness may be just what is needed to uplift someone else. Choose to let the love of God reflect in your words today.

Prayer for Today: Heavenly Father, thank You for Your goodness. Let Your goodness work in me so that I can be a reflection of You in words and deeds. In Jesus' name, Amen.

Additional Scripture reading: Proverbs 15:1-10, 23, 28

Enemy disguises

But I am not surprised! Even Satan disguises himself as an angel of light. So it is no wonder that his servants also disguise themselves as servants of righteousness. In the end they will get the punishment their wicked deeds deserve. (2 Corinthians 11:14-15 NLT)

The enemy is subtle. Those whom he uses won't always have a blaring red flag on their foreheads alerting you that they are being used by the enemy. Most times, the enemy is among you trying to fit in to win you over. He learns what your secret desires are and uses them against you to tempt you into sin.

You have to be aware that the enemy wears a disguise. You have to pray and use discernment in everything that you do. The enemy is smart and quick but you have to be smarter. I am reminded of the insurance commercial where the agent is using a fishing pole to dangle a dollar over the head of one of his customers. He says, "You have to be quicker than that." In the same way, we have to be quicker than the enemy. The enemy will often dangle lies, temptation and deceit over our heads but we have to be quick to discern his tricks.

God freely gives wisdom and discernment to those who ask for it. Although God knows what we need, we are still required to ask for it. I encourage you to petition His throne daily so that you will not be outsmarted by the enemy.

Prayer for Today: Heavenly Father, give me the right amount of wisdom, knowledge, understanding and discernment that I need for today. Help me to see the enemy for who he is and reject his advances. In Jesus' name, Amen.

Additional Scripture reading: 2 Corinthians 11: 1-15

Sufficient grace

Three different times I begged the Lord to take it away. Each time he said, "My grace is all you need. My power works best in weakness." So now I am glad to boast about my weaknesses, so that the power of Christ can work through me. (2 Corinthians 12:8-9 NLT)

There are times when we go through troubles, pray to God to remove the troubles, and He does not. When He doesn't take the troubles out of our lives, He gives us the strength, courage and wisdom to deal with them. It is when we are weak that we are able to truly see God's power at work in our lives. If God always answered our prayers by removing the pain, heartache and troubles, we wouldn't experience the magnitude of His grace. We would never experience God's power in adversity.

Take a moment to recall times when you prayed and asked the Lord to remove some trouble from you and He did not. You made it through it by the power of God's grace. Because you made it through it, you are now able to attest to God's mighty power at work within your life. You now have a testimony to share with someone else about how the Lord brought you through your troubles, how He gave you strength and comforted you.

God will not always remove the *thorn from your side* but He will give you what you need to endure it. He will answer your prayer for help but just not in the way that you would like. It should be comforting to know that God is with us and gives us sufficient grace to overcome adversity.

Prayer for Today: Heavenly Father, thank You for Your grace that is sufficient for me at all times. Thank You for displaying Your power and strength in my life. Let me offer up praises and not complaints when You give Your grace instead of taking me out of my troubles. In Jesus' name, Amen.

Additional Scripture reading: 2 Corinthians 12:1-10

Not Without You

Servitude and love

For you have been called to live in freedom, my brothers and sisters. But don't use your freedom to satisfy your sinful nature. Instead, use your freedom to serve one another in love. (Galatians 5:13 NLT)

Salvation does not come from obeying the law but it comes through Jesus' death and resurrection. Our belief in Jesus Christ is what gives us salvation and freedom from the law. Although we are free from the curse of the law, we are still obligated to follow God's commandments. Jesus did not come to destroy the law but to fulfill it. Jesus lived according to God's word and since we believe in Him, so should we.

As the Scripture says, we shouldn't use our freedom to please our sinful desires but we should use our freedom to demonstrate God's love in our lives by loving one another. When we love one another, we serve and treat each other the way God wants us to. God desires that we love our neighbor as ourselves and not destroy one another.

How are you using your freedom? Are you using it to live according to God's word or are you using it as an excuse to do what you desire to do?

Prayer for Today: Heavenly Father, thank You for the freedom that I have in You. Help me to live a life that is pleasing to You by obeying Your Word. In Jesus' name, Amen.

Additional Scripture reading: Galatians5:1-15

Not Without You

The life your spirit craves

So I say, let the Holy Spirit guide your lives. Then you won't be doing what your sinful nature craves. (Galatians 5:16 NLT)

When we accept Jesus Christ as Lord of our lives and receive the Holy Spirit, a war begins within us. The Spirit within us desires to be like Christ but our flesh desires to continue in sin. We have to choose to be led by the Holy Spirit in order to do what the Spirit craves and not what our sinful nature craves.

When we allow the Holy Spirit to guide us, we live like God desires us to live. Since we have accepted Christ, this should be the life that we desire to live as well. We have evidence of the Holy Spirit guiding us, because we will produce the fruit of the Spirit and draw others near to God. When we decide to be led by our sinful desires, the result is sin. The more we sin, the less the Holy Spirit is at work within our lives and the weaker our relationship with God becomes.

In order to be led by the Holy Spirit, we must decide, commit and obey. The Holy Spirit can give guidance but we must follow. We have to make a decision; there is no other way. We cannot continue to use statements such as, "the devil made me do it" or "God is not through with me yet," when the truth is that we sin because we want to. We have to allow the Holy Spirit to work in our lives so that our desires align with God's will.

Prayer for Today: Heavenly Father, thank You for Your Holy Spirit who guides and connects me to You. I ask that You give me a heart that is receptive to Your Holy Spirit so that I can live the life that my spirit craves. In Jesus' name, Amen.

Additional Scripture reading: Galatians 5:16-26

Finding Favor

My child, never forget the things I have taught you. Store my commands in your heart. If you do this, you will live many years, and your life will be satisfying. Never let loyalty and kindness leave you! Tie them around your neck as a reminder. Write them deep within your heart. Then you will find favor with both God and people, and you will earn a good reputation. (Proverbs 3:1-4 NLT)

What does it mean to find favor? What does favor mean? The dictionary defines favor as "something done or granted out of goodwill, rather than from justice or for remuneration; a kind act." It is also defined as "excessive kindness or unfair partiality; preferential treatment." Finding favor with God has been defined as gaining approval, acceptance, or special benefits or blessings. We all want favor with both God and those around us. We want to have favor wherever we go. In the scripture reference above, Solomon gives instructions on what one must do to find favor.

Throughout chapter two, he instructs the reader to seek wisdom and knowledge. The entire chapter points out the benefits of having wisdom. Some of which are: The Lord is a shield to those who walk with integrity; Wise choices will watch over you; Understanding will keep you safe; Wisdom will save you from evil people.

Next you must never let loyalty and kindness leave you. Wisdom will teach you to consistently treat others with kindness and remain loyal to the Lord. Keep this message before you by constantly living it out each day. Each day, seek wisdom by studying God's word and keeping it close in your heart. When you do these things, the Bible promises that you will find favor with both God and man.

Prayer for Today: Heavenly Father, I want to have favor with You and those around me. Help me to keep Your word in my heart and live it each day. In Jesus' name, Amen.

Additional Scripture reading: Proverbs 2 and Matthew 22:38-40

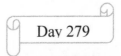

Day 279

~Day of Reflection~

Seeking God

Read: 2 Chronicles 15:2; Deuteronomy 4:29

Meditate: Recall moments when you sought God and He revealed Himself to you.

Apply: Spend time in God's presence today, pouring out your heart to Him. Pray that He gives you guidance where you need it. Write down the areas where you need guidance. Make note of the guidance that you receive.

No need to compare

Pay careful attention to your own work, for then you will get the satisfaction of a job well done, and you won't need to compare yourself to anyone else. (Galatians 6:4 NLT)

When we spend our time focusing on what someone else is doing, we can become jealous. When we're jealous, we begin to compare what we're doing to what they're doing. We then lose focus and neglect the assignments that God has given us.

God knows what He is doing. He knows which person to assign each task to because He knows which gifts each of us has. He is the one who gave us the gifts! Because of this, it is silly to become consumed with what someone else is doing. Don't worry about what ministry someone else is starting or why they're starting it. Don't consume yourself with thoughts of accolades that someone else is receiving because of the great work they're doing with the gifts that God has given them. When we spend time worrying about others in this way, we become disobedient. We are disobedient because we are not doing what God has called us to do (the assignment) and we are doing what God has told us not to do (covet).

If we do what we're supposed to do, we don't have to compare ourselves to others, because we know that we are doing what we have been created to do. If we're diligently and faithfully walking in purpose, we will receive the gratification of a job well done.

Prayer for Today: Heavenly Father, thank You for making me unique. Thank You for the gifts and the assignments that You've given me. Help me to stay focused on what You have called me to do so that I may please You and gain the satisfaction of being obedient. In Jesus' name, Amen.

Additional Scripture reading: Galatians 6:1-5

Harvest time

So let's not get tired of doing what is good. At just the right time we will reap a harvest of blessing if we don't give up. (Galatians 6:9 NLT)

Sometimes it can be challenging to remain encouraged when you're constantly putting your all into something and not getting the results that you hoped for. It can also be difficult to continue working at something when you're not seeing results. However, the Bible encourages us to keep at it and not give up. Whatever we plant, good or bad, plenty or sparingly, we will reap a harvest. We will reap according to the work that we've put in. No seed planted will go unharvested.

God's timing is simply perfect. He has a set time for when we will reap our harvest but we must remain faithful and diligent. Just because we haven't reaped in our timing doesn't mean that we will not reap. Be encouraged to know that any seeds that you have been planting will soon harvest. If you've been planting seeds of love, you will soon receive the harvest. If you've been sowing into the ministry, your career, your family or friends, you will soon experience the fruit of your labor.

Don't become weary but remain in faith, knowing that the time is coming. Think about a farmer. He plants seed and harvests that which he plants. He does not plant a watermelon seed and receive corn and you will not plant seeds for one thing and receive something else. Remember that God is faithful and rewards those who diligently seek Him.

Prayer for Today: Heavenly Father, thank You for Your faithfulness. Help me not to get weary in waiting but to be patient and faithful as I wait for my harvest. In Jesus' name, Amen.

Additional Scripture reading: Galatians 6:7-10

Not Without You

Obedience and Blessings

The Lord appeared to Isaac and said, "Do not go down to Egypt; live in the land where I tell you to live. Stay in this land for a while, and I will be with you and will bless you. For to you and your descendants I will give all these lands and will confirm the oath I swore to your father Abraham. So Isaac stayed in Gerar. (Genesis 26:2-3;6 NIV)

Obedience reaps blessings! This is what we learn in Genesis 26. The Lord told Isaac to stay put where he was. You see, in this particular chapter, there was a famine in the land: little food and water. The Lord wanted to show Isaac his sovereignty and bless him right where he was. God promised him that if he trusted in Him and went where He told him to go, that He would bless him.

Isaac was obedient to what the Lord had asked him to do. Given his current situation, I imagine that Isaac probably wondered to himself why the Lord would want Him to stay there when there was a famine in the land. Nevertheless, Isaac obeyed God. His obedience reaped blessings. Not only were God's promises manifested in his life because of his obedience but he received them in that same year. Not only did God promise to bless him but He also promised to be with Isaac through it all.

No matter what you're facing in life today, be obedient to God. Perhaps you're experiencing a famine-like situation, but remember that God has promised to bless you immeasurably and to never leave you. Today, I encourage you to not take another step until you hear from God. Wait on Him. He can bless you right where you are!

Prayer for Today: Heavenly Father, thank You for Your word that is life changing. Today, I choose to wait on You for guidance. I know that Your power extends far beyond what I can see so I will trust in You. In Jesus' name, Amen.

Additional Scripture reading: Genesis 26

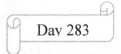

A worthy life

Therefore I, a prisoner for serving the Lord, beg you to lead a life worthy of your calling, for you have been called by God. (Ephesians 4:1 NLT)

Each of us has a calling on our lives. God called us to His ministry before we were born. If we could only understand the power and magnitude of God's calling on our lives, we will receive a glimpse of who we were created to be in Christ. Knowing this would propel us to desire even more to live a worthy life.

To live a life that is worthy of our calling, we must know who we are called to be! When we know who we are called to be and recognize God's holiness, we realize what an honor it is to be chosen by the Lord. Because we are chosen, we should lead lives that demonstrate this. The Bible says that we should be humble, patient and loving. We should have the character of Christ.

As you go throughout your day today and are propositioned at every turn, remember who you belong to. Let your choices reflect that you are chosen by God. You are better than what the enemy has to offer. You are special. You have been set apart for God's purpose!

Prayer for Today: Heavenly Father, thank You for choosing me for Your purpose. Help me to live a life that is worthy of my calling. I desire to bring honor and glory to Your name. In Jesus' name, Amen.

Additional Scripture reading: Ephesians 4:1-16

Not Without You

God's armor

Put on all of God's armor so that you will be able to stand firm against all strategies of the devil. (Ephesians 6:11 NLT)

In this passage of Scripture, Paul gives us instructions on how to fight against the devil. He teaches us that the battle is spiritual and not carnal; we must fight the spiritual battle with spiritual weapons.

In order to resist the enemy we must remember God's truth. The enemy will speak all kinds of lies so it is important that we remember what God's word says. To hide His word in our hearts, we must study. We must also arm ourselves with the Good News of peace with God, ready to tell others of the gospel of Jesus Christ. It is also important to remain faithful because the enemy will do all that he can in an effort to destroy our faith.

It is imperative that we remain in prayer for ourselves and the entire body of Christ. The enemy doesn't just come once per day, week, or month; he is constantly prowling around seeking who he can destroy. We have to be able to fight against him with prayer and the word of God.

Today, remember to pray persistently so that you may remain on guard against the attacks of the enemy. He will be looking for an opening to slither into your life and attack; be sure to wear your armor.

Prayer for Today: Heavenly Father, thank You for providing me what I need to fight against the attacks of the enemy. Let me not forget all that You have given to strengthen me. I ask that You be my shield against the enemy's schemes and help me to recognize him for who he is. Thank You for the victory over the devil. Help me to remember that I am a conqueror because of You. In Jesus' name, Amen.

Additional Scripture reading: Ephesians 6:10-20

What are you searching for?

If you search for good, you will find favor, but if you search for evil, it will find you! Proverbs 11:27 NLT

When I was a child, my mother always warned that if I went looking for trouble, I would find it. It was true then and it's true now. Whatever we set our sights on and seek, that is what we will find. Because of this truth, we need to intentionally seek the good in all things.

We must seek the good in people, circumstances and even in ourselves. When we search for the good in others, we usually see them differently than the way others see them. Seeing the good in them also gives them the opportunity to experience how God sees them. Don't be quick to judge. Seeking the good in circumstances allows us to keep an open mind, remain optimistic and see the up side of things. We shape a positive perspective. When we seek the good in ourselves, we are moved to give the best of ourselves.

As you go through your day, remain positive and look at people and situations through the lens of the Holy Spirit.

Prayer for Today: Heavenly Father, thank You for Your word. Help me to always search for good so that I may find favor. Help me to see life through the lens of the Holy Spirit. In Jesus' name, Amen.

Additional Scripture reading: Proverbs 11

Not Without You

~Day of Reflection~

Salvation

Read: John 3:3-7; 2 Corinthians 5:17, 21; 1 Timothy 2:3-4

Meditate: Recall the moment when you accepted God's salvation.

Apply: In what ways can you share God's message of salvation with others? Can you think of anyone who needs to hear this message?

For God's purpose

The Lord has made everything for his own purposes, even the wicked for a day of disaster. (Proverbs 16:4 NLT)

The Lord created everything, and everything on this earth belongs to Him. Everything has been made for His purposes and we know that all things work together for our good and for His glory.

We can find comfort in knowing that the Lord even uses the wicked for His purposes. Though we may find discomfort in troubles and problems, we can know security in God's sovereignty and His plan. We don't always see the entire plan or why the Lord allows certain things to happen but we know His character. He is faithful, merciful, loving and full of grace. His thoughts are not our thoughts and His ways are nothing like our ways. God doesn't always do things the way we think they should be done, but we have to remember that He does things for a greater purpose – to draw men unto Him.

If you are experiencing troubles today, understand that God is not doing anything to harm you but to carry out His plan. Trust in His process.

Prayer for Today: Heavenly Father, thank You for Your plan that accomplishes the greater good. Help me to find comfort in knowing that all things work out for my good and Your glory no matter what they look like in this moment. In Jesus' name, Amen.

Additional Scripture reading: Proverbs 16

Love and forgiveness

Love prospers when a fault is forgiven, but dwelling on it separates close friends. (Proverbs 17:9 NLT)

Unforgiveness hinders growth in our relationships. When we choose not to forgive one another of wrongs committed in relationships, we essentially decide to give up. Unforgiveness can be viewed as a roadblock. We have to find our way around it in order to move forward and have fruitful relationships.

The type of offense often determines how quickly we forgive or if we even forgive at all. However, we must be mindful that love covers a multitude of sin; if we truly love the offender, we should forgive him. Even if not for the offender's sake, we should forgive because God loves us through our wrongs and is merciful to forgive us.

As the Scripture says, love prospers when we forgive. If we hold grudges and unforgiveness in our hearts, our relationships are destined to end. Take a moment to consider your relationships. Are you harboring unforgiveness or are you protecting your relationships by covering others in love and mercy?

Prayer for Today: Heavenly Father, thank You for forgiving me of my sins. I pray that you help me to be mindful of Your mercy so that I may be merciful and forgiving to others. In Jesus' name, Amen.

Additional Scripture reading: Proverbs 17

Words and wisdom

A truly wise person uses few words; a person with understanding is even-tempered. (Proverbs 17:27 NLT)

When I was an undergraduate, I truly despised being given a word count that had to be fulfilled when writing papers. I just didn't understand why it had to take a certain amount of words to get a point across. In conversation, we sometimes feel like we have to use many words to make a point or seem important, but this can often get us into trouble. King Solomon, one of the wisest persons who ever lived, wrote in proverbs that it is wise for a person to use few words.

The truth is that the more we talk, the more likely we are to find ourselves in trouble. It is wise to listen well and choose our response wisely because when we speak, we have the power to lift people up or tear them down. Our tongues have a lot of power and we must learn how to use them. Just as there are consequences for our actions, there are consequences for our words; and we must be prepared to reap the consequences whether good or bad.

Make sure the words you use are constructive, helpful and life-giving. Be certain that when you're talking that you really are saying something. No one wants to be an empty wagon or listen to one.

Prayer for Today: Heavenly Father, help me to be mindful of my words. Let me speak with wisdom and encouragement. May my words bring joy to others and please You. In Jesus' name, Amen.

Additional Scripture reading: Proverbs 18:4, 6-8, 13 and 17-21

Not Without You

Knowledge and time

Enthusiasm without knowledge is no good; haste makes mistakes. (Proverbs 19:2 NLT)

Have you ever been excited about a new relationship, job or investment opportunity and jumped into it without doing any due diligence first? Most of us have and can attest to the fact that we made a mistake. We weren't using wisdom and probably acted upon what felt right at the time. No matter how good something may feel, we should always take some time to consider all angles and do some research.

Wisdom tells us to get to know someone a little better before entering into a relationship. Wisdom says to research the company and assess our goals with their goals to see if they align. Wisdom says not to invest in every investment opportunity that seems hot at the time. Wisdom is the voice that says, "Wait one minute before you take another step." However, we often ignore that voice.

The Lord wants us to prosper and that is why He gives us wisdom. That is why the Holy Spirit cautions us to take our time. We need to gather as much information as we can before making decisions, and not act on emotion.

Whatever you may be faced with today, take a moment to get as much information as you can before making a decision. If it is a good decision today, it will be a good decision tomorrow as well.

Prayer for Today: Heavenly Father, thank You for wisdom. Help me to use wisdom and seek You in all of my decision making so that I will make fewer mistakes. In Jesus' name, Amen.

Additional Scripture reading: Proverbs 19:20-21 and 27

Be selfless

Don't look out only for your own interests, but take an interest in others, too. (Philippians 2:6 NLT)

When we don't take an interest in others, self is always first. We only care about what we need, what we want, what we have to do, etc. However, God desires that we imitate Christ by not being selfish. Christ was not selfish when He died on the cross for our sins. He prayed and asked God to take the cup away from Him but chose to do the will of God, which was to save us.

When we take an interest in others, we put their needs ahead of ours. This is easier to do when we love one another. We take care of those we love and make sure that they have all that they need. This is what the Lord desires of us when it comes to His kingdom; He wants us to care for one another and love our neighbors as ourselves.

Examine your life and those around you. Have you been selfish? Have you loved others by caring for them? Choose to take an interest in others so that you may demonstrate the love of God that lives in your heart.

Prayer for Today: Heavenly Father, forgive me for being selfish. Help me to be mindful of those around me and how You want me to take an interest in them and love them. In Jesus' name, Amen.

Additional Scripture reading: Philippians 2:1-11

Closer than it appears

No, dear brothers and sisters, I have not achieved it but I focus on this one thing: Forgetting the past and looking forward to what lies ahead, I press on to reach the end of the race and receive the heavenly prize for which God, through Christ Jesus, is calling us. (Philippians 3:13-14 NLT)

Each day our goal should be to grow closer to God and imitate the life of Jesus' while He lived on earth. As children of God, our desire should be to experience God on a deeper level than the day before. Our issue is that we often get distracted by past mistakes and hold them in our heart when God has already forgotten about them. God does not hold on to our sins, so why should we?

As Paul says, we have to forget the past and press toward the future. God has so much in store for us as we experience more and more of Him, but we must stay focused on that. No one has ever moved forward by focusing on what's behind. Think of a car. The rearview mirror is small and the windshield is large because it is important that we focus on what's ahead. There is a message in the side view mirrors that reminds us that the object in our mirror is closer than it appears. What God has for us is closer than it appears; we just have to remain focused and keep pressing toward it.

Prayer for Today: Heavenly Father, thank You for Your Holy word. Thank You for all that you have in store for me. Keep me encouraged as I press toward the goal of becoming all that You have created me to be. In Jesus' name, Amen.

Additional Scripture reading: Philippians 3:12-21

~Day of Reflection~

Righteousness

Read: Psalm 84:11; Psalm 34:10; Proverbs 10:24; Matthew 6:33

Meditate: God promises many blessings to those who walk upright and in obedience to His word.

Apply: What areas of your life do you need to change to live in obedience to God. Write a prayer asking God to give you help and strength in these areas.

Don't worry

Don't worry about anything; instead, pray about everything. Tell God what you need, and thank him for all he has done. (Philippians 4:6 NLT)

As children of God, we are supposed to fully trust Him and His plan for our lives. One translation of this verse says "Be anxious for nothing." Worrying and anxiety are both signs that we aren't trusting God and not trusting Him is sin. Not only is worrying sin, but it is also a distraction.

To combat worrying and distrust, we should pray about everything. Consistent and persistent prayer draws us closer to God. The closer we are to Him, the more we will trust Him and the less we will worry. Prayer is a way to cast our cares upon the Lord and ease our minds. We must pray about everything that bothers us so that we will not give room to worrying. Not only must we pray about things that bother us but we must also pray for direction and desires.

Having a spirit of thanksgiving also prevents us from worrying. We must have an attitude of praise at all times; this keeps our focus on God and His character and not on the things that are bothering us. When we focus on God's goodness, we don't leave room for worrying.

If you find yourself worrying, stop, pray and give thanks. Prayer and thanksgiving will have you experience God's peace; don't allow worrying to distract you or rob you of God's peace.

Prayer for Today: Heavenly Father, forgive me for worrying. I trust in You and will choose to pray about everything and give thanks in everything to honor You. I will magnify You and not my problems. In Jesus' name, Amen.

Additional Scripture reading: Philippians 4:4-9 and Matthew 6:25

Not Without You

The same God

And this same God who takes care of me will supply all your needs from his glorious riches, which have been given to us in Christ Jesus. (Philippians 4:19 NLT)

In this passage of Scripture, Paul told the Philippians that he had all that he needed because of the gifts they sent to him. They gave to Paul out of their lack and Paul said their sacrifice was acceptable and pleasing to God. When we give to others in their time of need, we are giving to the Lord. The Lord blesses us when we give to others. When we take care of others, the Lord will supply our needs.

God has not changed; this is the truth that we must hold on to. The God of Abraham, Isaac and Jacob; the God of Jesus Christ; the God who took care of us last year is one and the same. His character has not changed. He is faithful and will always be faithful. His love for us is unconditional and He promises to never leave nor forsake us. The God who took care of Paul is the same God who takes care of us.

Your problems are no match for God. If He has taken care of you before, He will do it again; so have faith that, by grace, He will supply all of your needs according to His riches in glory.

Prayer for Today: Heavenly Father, thank You for being faithful. Thank You for not changing. I am thankful that I can trust in Your character and have faith that all my needs are taken care of. In Jesus' name, Amen.

Additional Scripture reading: Philippians 4:10-19

Not Without You

Right living pleases God

The Lord is more pleased when we do what is right and just than when we offer him sacrifices. (Proverbs 21:3 NLT)

More than anything, the Lord desires to have an intimate relationship with us. Evidence of an intimate relationship with the Lord is living according to His word. God is pleased when we obey His word and love His people. Although the Lord takes pleasure in our offerings, He takes more pleasure in our obedience to Him.

If we refer to Proverbs 21:2 NLT, "People may be right in their own eyes, but the Lord examines their heart," we will understand that God searches our hearts and knows when our offerings and sacrifices are in vain, with impure hearts and without repentance. God wants us to turn to Him, repent, and live according to His word. We can make a show for others with our deeds, but God sees our hearts.

Be sure that your heart is pure and that you are living right in God's sight. Don't be fooled into thinking that you can bribe God by giving offerings and not offering yourself.

Prayer for Today: Heavenly Father, thank You for loving me. Help me to draw closer to You and live a life that is pleasing in Your sight. In Jesus' name, Amen.

Additional Scripture reading: Proverbs 21

Know better, Do better

Don't excuse yourself by saying, "Look, we didn't know." For God understands all hearts, and he sees you. He who guards your soul knows you knew. He will repay all people as their actions deserve. (Proverbs 24:12 NLT)

When we are caught or feeling guilty about doing something wrong, the easy way out is to say we didn't know that it was wrong or that we didn't intend to do it. We must understand that although we may say that, God knows our hearts and knows all truth. We can lie to ourselves and think this will help us escape the consequences, but we cannot lie to the Lord.

You may have heard the saying, "When you know better, you should do better." When we receive knowledge, we should apply it; that is using wisdom and what God desires from us. God gives us wisdom and we are foolish if we don't use it.

If we desire a closer relationship to God, we cannot lie to Him; He knows our hearts anyway. No relationship can be healthy, fruitful or progressive if it lacks honesty and transparency. We must learn to trust God with the good, bad and ugly. He knows us and has a prescription to help us become more like Him. We must accept it by faith.

Prayer for Today: Heavenly Father, thank You for the wisdom that You've given me. Let me not deceive myself when I do wrong but to confess my sins and turn away from them. Thank You for Your word that cleanses and helps me become who You desire me to be when I apply it to my life. In Jesus' name, Amen.

Additional Scripture reading: Proverbs 24:1-16 and James 4:17

Not Without You

No time for celebration

Don't rejoice when your enemies fall; don't be happy when they stumble. (Proverbs 24:17 NLT)

What does the Bible teach us about our enemies?

- Don't get revenge; God will repay them for their wrong and;
- Don't rejoice when the Lord repays them.

So what exactly are we to do? Our human nature would like to do just what the word of God tells us not to do: Get even and enjoy it. However, since we are led by the Spirit, we are supposed to do what the Spirit says: Pray for them and love them anyway.

What does this look like? When we see them hurting, offer to help. Showing kindness to them will rattle them more than vengeance ever will. When we see them fall, offer to help pick them up. This is very difficult and takes a lot of spiritual maturity but this is just what the Lord wants from us. He wants us to be His hands here on earth.

We have to become better and not allow our desires for our enemies to get the best of us. We must step back and allow God to do His work in their lives and not take pleasure in it. In the following verse, we are warned that if we do rejoice in their misfortune, the Lord will be displeased with us and turn His anger away from them. Then we lose anyway. So let's submit to the Word of God and learn from what it teaches us about how to deal with our enemies.

Prayer for Today: Heavenly Father, thank You for Your word. Thank You for the wisdom and knowledge that it gives. Even when it is difficult, help me to live by it so that I may please You. In Jesus' name, Amen.

Additional Scripture reading: Proverbs 24:17-34

Self-discipline

A person without self-control is like a city with broken-down walls. (Proverbs 25:28 NLT)

Self-control is the ability to exercise constraint or to have willpower. A person who has self-control has wisdom and knows when to say no. He is able to resist the temptation to engage in excess. If someone aggravates him, he has enough wisdom and strength to not let it get to him. He chooses the high road. A person who lacks self-discipline is the opposite. He does not use wisdom and does not have control over his spirit. When he faces temptation to engage in excess, whether it is food or drink, he loses all control. He gives in to greed. If he is aggravated or pushed to anger, he allows his anger to get the best of him, leaving him vulnerable and susceptible to attacks of the enemy.

When we lack willpower, we leave ourselves exposed and become easy targets for the enemy. The enemy knows our weaknesses and the areas in which we lack discipline. He seeks to capitalize on these things in an attempt to destroy our spirits. We don't have to live in weakness; we can overcome the inability to have self-control. How? Practice. It is a gradual process, but we have to take small steps each day in saying no to whatever it is that we lack willpower to refuse: an extra cookie or drink, cigarette, that thing that eats up all of our time, or allowing life's aggravations to get the best of us.

God wants us to live victoriously through Him. He wants us to have self-control. We can do all things through His mighty power at work within our lives.

Prayer for Today: Heavenly Father, thank You for wisdom. Help me to apply it to every area of my life. In Jesus' name, Amen.

Additional Scripture reading: Proverbs 25

Day 300

~Day of Reflection~

Peace

Read: Colossians 3:15; Psalm 85:8; Philippians 4:7; John 14:27

Meditate: God's peace is far beyond our understanding. There are times when we experience peace when we would ordinarily be *losing our minds*. Recall moments when God has blessed you with His peace.

Apply: Are you experiencing the peace of God today? Give your worries and cares to Him in prayer. Choose not to let anything rob you of your peace.

Sin and sickness

As a dog returns to its vomit, so a fool repeats his foolishness. (Proverbs 26:11 NLT)

When we repent of our sins and the Lord forgives us and sets us free from those sins, we are supposed to get rid of them. We are not supposed to hold on to them and dabble in them every now and again. What happens when we become sick because of something we ate? We vomit to cleanse ourselves of it. Vomit is the body's way of rejecting it. Spiritually, vomiting sin is the spirit's way of rejecting it. When we return to our sin, it is like returning to vomit. Isn't that gross?

We live like dogs when we return to our sin because dogs return to their vomit and lick it up. We desire to do the will of God; therefore, we have to completely turn away from that which made us sick in the first place and turn to the one who can make us whole.

When you think of returning to your sin, think of it as returning to vomit. Think about why you left it in the first place, why it made you sick, what God desires of you, where you're trying to go and why going back to that sin is only going to hinder you. Meditate on this and allow it to motivate you to move forward in God and not backward in sin.

Prayer for Today: Heavenly Father, thank You for the reminder that my sin is like vomit, disgusting. Let me be mindful of the purity and progress that I find in You and seek wholeness to live a life acceptable to You. In Jesus' name, Amen.

Additional Scripture reading: Proverbs 26

Pride and Praise

Let someone else praise you, not your own mouth– a stranger, not your own lips. (Proverbs 27:2 NLT)

Singing your own praises is annoying and comes off as someone full of pride. No one wants to hear someone constantly talk about themselves and all of the great things they've done. When we do good things, we must do them to the glory of God and not for bragging rights, not in competition with someone else and not so that others can give us a pat on the back.

The word of God tells us to let someone else praise us for our good deeds. We must let our light shine before men so that others may see our good works and glorify our Father in heaven. If what we are doing is so great, others will give honor to us anyway. We must remain pure in heart and in deeds. It is wise to be humble because we learn in Proverbs 16:18 that pride goes before destruction. We ruin ourselves when we are prideful.

Prayer for Today: Heavenly Father, teach me humility. Let me be wise in all that I do and not become prideful. Help me remember that all that I do must be done as if I'm doing it to You, and all glory and praise is Yours. In Jesus' name, Amen.

Additional Scripture reading: Proverbs 27:1-22; Proverbs 16:18 and Colossians 3:23

Who will you glorify?

To reject the law is to praise the wicked; to obey the law is to fight them. (Proverbs 28:4 NLT)

When we profess to follow the Lord, we ought to do what His word tells us to do. When we reject His word by doing the opposite of what it says, we are giving praise to the enemy. Our actions demonstrate what and who we believe – when we go against God's word, we're saying with our actions that we give praise to Satan. We certainly don't want to honor the enemy, but that is exactly what we do when we live the way Satan wants us to live. We have to remember that when we reject God's word by being disobedient, we are accepting the ways of the enemy.

When we are obedient to God's word, we are fighting against the ways of the enemy. The only way to fight against the enemy is through the word of God. We learn that our battle is not against flesh and blood but against rulers of dark places; our battle is in the spirit. We give the enemy rule over our spirit when we disobey God, because in turn we are pleasing the enemy. We have to fight the enemy by rejecting him and everything that he stands for.

As you go about your day, remember that a choice to disobey God's word is a choice to give glory to the enemy.

Prayer for Today: Heavenly Father, thank You for Your holy word. Today, I choose to glorify You by being obedient to Your word. In Jesus' name, Amen.

Additional Scripture reading: Proverbs 28 and Ephesians 6:12

Pleasures from God

So I decided there is nothing better than to enjoy food and drink and to find satisfaction in my work. Then I realized that these pleasures are from the hand of God. (Ecclesiastes 2:24 NLT)

Far too often, we find that many of us do not enjoy what we do for a living. We dread getting up each day to go to a job that we hate or a career that we find unfulfilling. If the questions, "What would you do if money wasn't a factor or what would you do if you could start all over again?" were posed to individuals who feel this way, they would likely give the answer of something totally opposite of what they were currently doing. The issue is that we become complacent or driven by money, prestige and material things instead of doing what we have been called to do.

We have all been created with a purpose with different passions and desires. God made each of us unique to accomplish His purpose and part of that is doing what we were created to do. We shouldn't allow the fact that we've been doing something far too long to keep us from becoming what we were destined to become. Depending on where we are in life, the change can be more difficult to make, but we must remember that change doesn't happen overnight. If we are not getting any satisfaction out of our work, we probably aren't on the right track, because true satisfaction comes from doing the will of God. Only when we align ourselves with His will, will we enjoy our work.

No matter where you are in life today, begin taking steps to align yourself with what you have been called to do. You will find much joy and satisfaction when you are living according to God's will.

Prayer for Today: Heavenly Father, thank You for creating me for Your purpose. Even now, give me courage to become who You have created me to be so that I may find joy and satisfaction in my work. In Jesus' name, Amen.

Additional Scripture reading: Ecclesiastes 2:18-26 and 3:22

Seasons

For everything there is a season, a time for every activity under heaven. (Ecclesiastes 3:1 NLT)

As children of God, we often wonder when God is going to bless us with the desires of our hearts or when we're going to receive His promises here on earth. We are impatient people; we want life to move along quickly so that we can buy a house, get married, have children, get the promotion, start our business, expand our ministry, and the list goes on.

Nothing happens all at once and in today's Scripture, we are reminded that there is a season for everything. In knowing this, we must learn to enjoy the season that we're in, because the next season is coming. Just like we have winter, summer, spring and fall, the seasons change in our spiritual lives as well. So if things are not how you want them to be now, remember that your situation is temporary and things will eventually get better.

In your waiting, get closer to your Creator because that is what He wants most from you. Find comfort in His presence that in due season, you will experience all that He has promised.

Prayer for Today: Heavenly Father, thank You for Your word. I trust and believe that my waiting isn't in vain and that I will soon reap my harvest if I do not give up. In Jesus' name, Amen.

Additional Scripture reading: Ecclesiastes 3

Be motivated by the Lord

Then I observed that most people are motivated to success because they envy their neighbors. But this, too, is meaningless – like chasing the wind. (Ecclesiastes 4:4 NLT)

It is destructive to the mind and spirit to covet what others have; it is even more destructive to allow this envy to motivate us to try to achieve what others have achieved. God made each of us unique and the dreams that we should be chasing are the dreams that He has given to each of us. We all have a different road to travel and the Lord is not going to give you the desires to walk along a path destined for another person.

Since the Lord has a plan and purpose for each of us, we should desire the will of God for our lives. It is sin to be jealous of what another person has; besides, we will never know their story and what it took for them to obtain what they have obtained. We shouldn't put our efforts into "keeping up with the Joneses." None of us should be trying to keep up with anyone but the Lord. Our motivation should not come from the desire to have what someone else has but from the desire to do the will of God.

Along the path that God has predestined for you are the rewards stored up for you when you align yourself with His will for your life and not His will for your neighbors' lives.

Prayer for Today: Heavenly Father, thank You for the plans that You have for *me*. Let me never become jealous of another person's success but let me remain focused on Your will and successes for me. In Jesus' name, Amen.

Additional Scripture reading: Ecclesiastes 4:1-6

~Day of Reflection~

God is waiting

Read: Isaiah 30:18-20

Meditate: Is there something that you have yet to take to the Lord? What is the Lord waiting on you to come to Him about?

Apply: Write a prayer releasing this *something* to God so that He may shower you with His love and compassion.

Not Without You

Two is better than one

Two people are better off than one, for they can help each other succeed. (Ecclesiastes 4:9 NLT)

When we set off to accomplish all that God would have us to do, it is helpful to have someone in our corner; someone to pray with us, provide assistance when needed, encourage us, advise us and support us. Although sometimes we may want or have to go through it alone, we are much better off when we have someone beside us who believes in the vision that God has given us as much as we do. In turn, we should also be supportive of them and believe in God's vision for their life as well. We have to become to others what we want them to be to us.

Not only is it a good thing to have someone beside us, it is even better to have God at the center. God gave us the plan so He is the best to provide guidance along the way. Even if we don't have anyone else, we must always include the Lord in all that we do because without Him, we wouldn't have purpose.

As you move closer to your destiny, find someone who is faithful and supportive to be in your corner but most importantly, know that the Lord is there. Don't forget to invite Him in.

Prayer for Today: Heavenly Father, thank You for your goodness and mercy. Thank You for provision; You know who and what I need in my life so I am thankful to You for putting the right people in place to help me succeed. In Jesus' name, Amen.

Additional Scripture reading: Ecclesiastes 4:7-12

No perfect conditions

Farmers who wait for perfect weather never plant. If they watch every cloud, they never harvest. (Ecclesiastes 11:4 NLT)

"If we wait for perfect conditions, we will never get anything done." This quote, based off today's Scripture, blessed me the first time I read it. Many times in life, we procrastinate; and we have reasons that we procrastinate. The reasons are always along the lines of something not being right in our lives. The truth is that there will always be something in our way to keep us from taking the first step (and continue stepping) towards our goals.

We have to be mindful that there will always be something that is not quite right: finances, family, time, etc. However, we cannot let this distract us. We have to use this knowledge as motivation to be creative in finding moments to get started when we feel like there is no time. We may have to stay up an hour later each night or remove a TV show from our list of things to do. We have to get our families on board to support our vision so that they will encourage us to get started. God will give us provision, so we must not worry about finances; we just need to begin doing all that we can do to move forward.

The enemy rejoices in our procrastination because that means we are not moving forward in doing what God has called us to do. If the enemy can keep us in a place of thinking that all things need to be in line before we leap, then we will never leap. The time is now! Each day, do one thing that will move you closer to your destiny, whether it is writing down plans, researching or making a call; you must do something. Your excuse cannot be that you're waiting on everything to be "right" in your life because it never will be.

Prayer for Today: Heavenly Father, thank You for the wisdom to know that things will never be perfect. Help me to take a leap of faith in moving toward the destiny that You have predestined for me regardless of my circumstances. In Jesus' name, Amen. *Additional Scripture reading*: Ecclesiastes 11:1-7

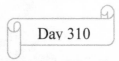

Day 310

Not Without You

Can you see Him?

Then I said, "It's all over! I am doomed, for I am a sinful man. I have filthy lips, and I live among a people with filthy lips. Yet I have seen the King, the Lord of Heaven's Armies. (Isaiah 6:5 NLT)

In this passage of Scripture, Isaiah speaks of how He saw the Lord's glory after King Uzziah died. After seeing the Lord and all of His glory, Isaiah then saw himself for who he really was, a sinner. In verse 1, Isaiah says that he saw *also* the Lord which implies that he also saw someone else.

Sometimes people in our lives can get in the way of us experiencing God like we need to. We often don't recognize it until they are gone; then we see God and recognize our true selves. It is then that the Lord can begin to work in us.

Another great thing to note is that even in Isaiah's sin, the Lord showed Himself to him; note he says that "yet I have seen the King." The Lord is merciful because He doesn't hold our sins against us; He calls us out to be living testimonies and to do His will.

As you go throughout your day, make sure there is nothing in your life preventing you from experiencing the Lord's presence like you need to; if there is, get rid of that thing. It is only in the Lord's presence that we can truly see ourselves for who we are, get cleansed and forgiven and begin to lead the life He has called us to live.

Prayer for Today: Heavenly Father, today I want to see You. I want to experience Your presence and Your power in my life like never before. Please remove anything from my life that hinders me from seeing You. In Jesus' name, Amen.

Additional Scripture reading: Isaiah 6

He is everything

For a child is born to us, a son is given to us. The government will rest on his shoulders. And he will be called: Wonderful Counselor, Mighty God, Everlasting Father, Prince of Peace. (Isaiah 9:6 NLT)

Isaiah was giving a prophecy of Jesus' birth in this Scripture. He foretold of His character and how His people would refer to Him. He is called a Wonderful Counselor because God has given Him wisdom and from Him, we receive wisdom. His wisdom gives us guidance that teaches us to do His will. He is called a Mighty God because He has all power in His hands. He has power and strength above all that; His children can rely on His strength and power to see them through every circumstance.

He is also called Everlasting Father because He is the eternal God. He will always be God even after death. He is called the Prince of Peace because He is a peacemaker. He reconciles us back to the Father; and He also gives us peace beyond our understanding.

Because the Lord is all these things to us and more, we should take the time to get to know Him as such. We should find joy in doing His perfect will because He will give us wisdom; we can rely on His power, presence and strength and He will give us peace throughout it all.

Prayer for Today: Heavenly Father, thank You for all that You are in my life. Thank You for your faithfulness and Your blessings. Help me find joy in Your presence and spend time getting to know You for who You are. In Jesus' name, Amen.

Additional Scripture reading: Isaiah 9:1-7

Knowledge leads to growth

Then the way you live will always honor and please the Lord, and your lives will produce every kind of good fruit. All the while, you will grow as you learn to know God better and better. (Colossians 1:10 NLT)

Our spiritual growth has a direct correlation to how well we know God. We cannot grow if we don't know God, and we won't know God if we don't study His word. Spending time in God's word is essential to spiritual growth. We have to move past simply opening our Bibles during church service; we must dedicate time to God while we're home during the week. If we only spend time in God's word during worship services, we will never grow spiritually or experience God the way that we should.

When we grow spiritually, we also please God by the way we live. As we grow, we begin to live lives that are more pleasing to God because we understand what He requires of us and we desire to do His will. Not only this, spiritual growth produces spiritual fruit: love, joy, peace, kindness, longsuffering.

The Lord desires that we continuously grow in Him; we should not remain the same as we were when we accepted Christ. Take time to grow in the Lord by spending time in His word.

Prayer for Today: Heavenly Father, I want to grow in You. Let me not neglect my time alone in Your presence. Help me to make spending time with You a priority. In Jesus' name, Amen.

Additional Scripture reading: Colossians 1:3-14

Work for the Lord

Work willingly at whatever you do, as though you were working for the Lord rather than for people. (Colossians 3:23 NLT)

This Scripture will change your life if you apply it to all that you do! In whatever we do, whether it is chores at home, interaction with our family and friends, duties at work, serving in ministry, etc., if we apply this Scripture, we will truly live victoriously. Understanding that the Lord is holy and He requires our best is key in application of this Scripture.

When we apply this Scripture, we can give the best of ourselves regardless of how things are going around us because we always recognize who we are working for. Knowing that our servitude is to the Lord and not to anyone else gives us the extra boost that we need throughout the day. We will be able to treat others kindly and love them beyond their understanding because we aren't doing it just for them but for the Lord.

Today, choose to perform each task unto the Lord and watch how you please God and lead a more fulfilling life.

Prayer for Today: Heavenly Father, give me a mindset to do all things as if doing them unto You so that I won't procrastinate, become lazy or become mediocre but instead give my best. Help me to live a life acceptable unto You. In Jesus' name, Amen.

Additional Scripture reading: Colossians 3:18-25

~Day of Reflection~

Prayer

Read: Isaiah 30:19; 1 John 5:14-15; Jeremiah 29:12; Isaiah 65:24

Meditate: Do you have a faithful prayer life?

Apply: What things or activities do you allow to hinder your prayer life? What will you do today to become more faithful to God in prayer?

Allocate time to prayer

Devote yourselves to prayer with an alert mind and a thankful heart. (Colossians 4:2 NLT)

In today's Scripture, Paul encourages us to do three things:

- Devote ourselves to prayer.
- Make sure our minds are focused while we're praying.
- Pray with hearts filled with thanksgiving.

As we press to grow stronger in our relationship with God, it is important that we set aside time to pray and to pray about everything. Prayer is our line of communication with God and we know that no relationship can thrive without effective communication.

In order to have effective communication, we must remove any distractions during prayer time: televisions, phones, people, etc. We have to recognize that this time alone in God's presence is significant and essential to our growth. This is when we give God praise, cast our cares upon Him, present our requests to Him and listen to His voice. This is our time to block out the cares of the world and give ourselves to the Lord.

We should also approach prayer with thankfulness. We should always be thankful to God because of who He is, what He has done and what He will do. Being thankful sets the atmosphere for prayer and shifts the focus from ourselves to the Lord.

Prayer for Today: Heavenly Father, I come to You with a heart filled with praise and thanksgiving. I want to thank You for Your power at work in my life. Let me not miss spending my time alone with You to recharge and receive all that You have for me. In Jesus' name, Amen.

Additional Scripture reading: Colossians 4:2-6

Not Without You

Purposed to please

For we speak as messengers approved by God to be entrusted with the Good News. Our purpose is to please God, not people. He alone examines the motives of our hearts. (1 Thessalonians 2:4 NLT)

Some of us are people pleasers. We want to be liked by everyone; we want to fit in; so we do what we can to please others. When asked to take on a task, even if our schedules are already overloaded, we say yes because we are afraid of people not liking us.

People pleasers tend to be *nice*. They often want to say or do something contrary to what they're actually doing, but since their focus is on pleasing others, they do what they think others want them to do. People pleasers generally aren't happy because they can't be themselves.

We have to realize that we will never be able to please everyone and there will be people who won't like us. That is okay because the only one we should be aiming to please is the Lord. As Paul says in today's Scripture, "Our purpose is to please God, not people."

We need to get in alignment with our purpose and begin to do what pleases the Lord. What pleases the Lord will not always please people, and as children of God who are seeking to become all that we were created to be, we have to be okay with that. God has a much higher calling for our lives than to be worried about who likes us.

Prayer for Today: Heavenly Father, thank You for Your life-changing holy word. I am thankful that I only have to live to please You. Help me to remain mindful of that and keep You as the center of my life. In Jesus' name, Amen.

Additional Scripture reading: 1 Thessalonians 2:1-16

Thanksgiving in all things

Be thankful in all circumstances, for this is God's will for you who belong to Christ Jesus. (1 Thessalonians 5:18 NLT)

In today's Scripture, Paul is encouraging the children of God to be thankful *in the midst* of all circumstances and not *for* all circumstances. There is a huge difference in being thankful *in* all circumstances as opposed to being thankful *for* all circumstances and as children of God, we must differentiate between the two. The Lord doesn't want us to be thankful for terrible things that happen to us but we can be thankful in them.

To be thankful *in* all situations is to understand that we have hope in Christ and this hope produces thanksgiving in us because we know that we are victorious. This is also pleasing to God because He commands us to give thanks in all things. To be thankful *for* all circumstances would be as if we are ignoring that evil exists and pretend that things are always going well, and we know that to be untrue.

We can be thankful *in* all things because we know that God is faithful and that even bad situations are temporary. We can be thankful because we know that things can always be worse than they are; and we can be thankful in all things because we know that God has our best interest at heart and He is in control of everything.

Prayer for Today: Heavenly Father, thank You for Your power and presence in my life. Thank You for providing such comfort in that I can be thankful *in* all things because of who You are in my life. In Jesus' name, Amen.

Additional Scripture reading: 1 Thessalonians 5:12-22

Not Without You

Prayers of the righteous

I urge you, first of all, to pray for all people. Ask God to help them; intercede on their behalf, and give thanks for them. (1 Timothy 2:1 NLT)

As children of God, we should be constantly interceding for others through prayer. If we just take a look at all of the evil things going on in the world, we should be driven to pray even more. We obviously need to see more of God's presence and power here on earth. However, we must do what the Lord has called us to do – pray!

Before we intercede on behalf of others, we must first make sure that we are doing all that we should do, living a life acceptable to the Lord. As the Scripture says, "Prayers of the righteous avail much." We must have clean hands and a pure heart when we go before the Lord on behalf of others. We want the Lord to hear and answer our prayers, so we must go before Him with reverence, praising Him and giving thanks.

We ought to always have an attitude of prayer: prayer for our leaders, the body of Christ, the unsaved, our families and friends and ourselves. We must remember that prayer is serious and that we have to make sure we are on one accord with God before we petition Him on behalf of others.

Prayer for Today: Heavenly Father, thank You for the opportunity and privilege to come to You in prayer. I ask that You forgive me of my sins and purify my heart. I want to be right with You so that my prayers will be received and answered, because Your word says that the prayers of the righteous availeth much. Make me right with You. In Jesus' name, Amen.

Additional Scripture reading: 1 Timothy 2 and James 5:16

Spiritual training

Physical training is good, but training for godliness is much better, promising benefits in this life and in the life to come. (1 Timothy 4:8 NLT)

We exercise because we want to live healthier, stronger and longer lives. However, obtaining the benefits of physical activity does not happen overnight. We have to train ourselves to workout and eat well. Just as we must train ourselves to reap the benefits of physical exercise, we must also train ourselves so that we may reap the benefits of spiritual exercise.

When we train for godliness, we reap benefits similar to those of physical training, but for the spirit. If we want to be healthier and stronger spiritually, we have to work at it. It doesn't happen miraculously or through prayer. We have to be intentional when it comes to living a life that is pleasing to God. We have to make choices that honor God and our relationship with Him; because there is always the opportunity to do things that will spiritually drain and weaken us.

Strive to live a godly life just as you would strive to maintain your physical health. There may be times when you will fall off track, but you can't let that discourage you. You have to pick yourself up and get back in the race. Remember that the prize is not given to the swift but to him who endures to the end. Build your spiritual endurance by waking up each day and choosing to live a godly life. Falling doesn't mean it's over; it's just an opportunity to start again.

Prayer for Today: Heavenly Father, strengthen me so that I may continuously strive to live a godly life. I need You even more when I fall to help me get back up and try again. Thank You for Your patience, forgiveness, mercy and faithfulness. In Jesus' name, Amen.

Additional Scripture reading: 1 Timothy 4:6-10

Not Without You

Age is not synonymous with spiritual maturity

Don't let anyone think less of you because you are young. Be an example to all believers in what you say, in the way you live, in your love, your faith, and your purity. (1 Timothy 4:12 NLT)

Age does not always determine one's level of spiritual maturity or faith and responsibility bestowed upon them. Young adults can be examples to anyone: older, younger or peers. When one has been chosen by God to declare His word to His people, the life of that person should be encouragement to those whom they teach and to those outside the body of Christ.

Sometimes younger Christians can be so modest and humble that they miss a moment to glorify God in words or deeds because they are in the company of someone older and who they perceive to be more spiritually mature.

Don't let your company change your character. Remain firm in your faith and in your calling. The Lord can use you at any time, so don't flick your light on and off, hiding behind your age or other limitations; always be a willing vessel by making yourself available to Him. Always allow your light to shine because you never know who needs to see it to be encouraged by it.

Prayer for Today: Heavenly Father, please give me courage and boldness to let Your light shine through me at all times, regardless of who I'm with. I want to be a vessel for You to speak encouragement and life to Your people. Let me not be intimidated or fearful, because You have given me the spirit of power, love and a sound mind. In Jesus' name, Amen.

Additional Scripture reading: 1 Timothy 4:11-16

~Day of Reflection~

Knowing and choosing what's right

Read: Isaiah 42:18-25

Meditate: Recall a situation where you knew the right thing to do and chose to do the opposite. Why did you refuse to act on what was right?

Apply: What will you commit to doing differently in the future?

Fear isn't of God

This is why I remind you to fan into flames the spiritual gift God gave you when I laid my hands on you. For God has not given us a spirit of fear and timidity, but of power, love, and self-discipline. (2 Timothy 1:6-7 NLT)

We should preserve and protect the gifts that God has given us because we walk in true destiny and purpose when we use them correctly. We should never be afraid to use our gifts because fear immobilizes us. We have to remember that as children of God, we don't have to be afraid because the Lord has given us power to overcome any of Satan's obstacles. When the Lord placed the gifts in us, He also gave us what we needed to use the gifts: strength, boldness and courage. We just have to tap into it.

Consider the gifts that God has given you. Are you using them? If you have trouble identifying your gifts, seek the Lord and consider your passion. The Lord will reveal them to you because He rewards those who diligently seek Him. Just have faith.

Prayer for Today: Heavenly Father, thank You for the gifts that You've given me. Help me to use them according to Your will. Cast out any inkling of fear and replace it with Your power. In Jesus' name, Amen.

Additional Scripture reading: 2 Timothy 1:3-14

Scripture prepares us

God uses it to prepare and equip his people to do every good work. *(2 Timothy 3:17 NLT)*

Scripture can be likened unto a user manual. Think about it. When you purchase something, you read (or should read) the manual to learn how to clean it, operate it and troubleshoot it. The word of God gives instruction regarding how we can be cleaned, how we should navigate through life and what to do when things go wrong.

Scripture 1) equips us for God's work, 2) teaches us what is wrong in our lives and how to correct it, 3) teaches us what is true, and 4) is inspired by God. Scripture teaches us what God requires of us and we should use it as life's instruction manual.

Have you been reading your manual? Whatever issues you are facing, the answer is within the word of God. The word of God doesn't speak specifically regarding all issues, but if you study it enough, you will be able to apply God's principles to all areas of your life.

Prayer for Today: Heavenly Father, thank You for leaving me with instructions in order that I may navigate through this life in a way that honors You. Help me create time in my schedule each day so that I can spend it getting to know Your thoughts. In Jesus' name, Amen.

Additional Scripture reading: 2 Timothy 3:10-17

Not Without You

Listen, receive and apply the word

So we must listen very carefully to the truth we have heard, or we may drift away from it. (Hebrews 2:1 NLT)

When we receive the word of God, whether through our pastors or through self-study, it is important that we keep it in our hearts, meditate on it and do what it says. When we apply the word of God to our lives through daily practice, we remain in fellowship with God and His truth. When we simply listen to the word of God without doing anything with it, we lose it or as the Scripture says, drift away from it.

Since we desire to live godly lives and experience all of the blessings He has in store for us, we have to do more than simply listen to the word of God. We must listen carefully by taking heed to it. Consider a college student who listens to lectures but never studies, writes papers on the subject matter or does what's required of him; most of what he learned in the lecture is lost because he did nothing with the information he received. In the same way, we will never grow in godly wisdom if we don't apply the word of God to our lives.

God wants us to draw closer to Him, not drift away; so we must apply His word of truth to our lives in order that we may retain it and develop a closer relationship with Him.

Prayer for Today: Heavenly Father, thank You for Your word of truth. Let it not depart from my heart. Teach me to apply Your word to my life so that I may be who I ought to be in You. In Jesus' name, Amen.

Additional Scripture reading: Hebrews 2:1-3 and James 1:22-25

God always confirms His word

And God confirmed the message by giving signs and wonders and various miracles and gifts of the Holy Spirit whenever he chose. (Hebrews 2:4 NLT)

I have learned throughout my spiritual journey that God always confirms His word. Any message that He gives to us will always be confirmed in one way or another. In today's Scripture, we learn four ways that the Lord confirms His message: signs, wonders, miracles and gifts of the Holy Spirit.

Signs are a string of events that lead to the same result or answer. Wonders are those "Wow!" moments. Miracles are extraordinary things done by God. Gifts of the Holy Spirit are spiritual gifts that God has given to each of us. Throughout the Bible, there are many examples of signs, wonders and miracles so that we would believe in God's mighty power.

God still confirms His message to us today through signs, wonders, miracles and gifts of the Holy Spirit. He hasn't changed. That message that you keep hearing over and over again is confirmation of something that the Lord is calling you to do that you haven't acted upon yet. Pay attention to God's confirmations, because they all lead you to what He wants you to do.

Prayer for Today: Heavenly Father, thank You for confirming Your word to me. Give me wisdom so that I will not miss what You are calling me to do, and then give me courage to do it. In Jesus' name, Amen.

Additional Scripture reading: Exodus 3 and 4

Not Without You

Jesus went through it too

Since he himself has gone through suffering and testing, he is able to help us when we are being tested. (Hebrews 2:18 NLT)

One of the reasons it should be easy for us to put our trust and hope in Jesus is that He understands all that we go through. He understands because He encountered many tests and trials; the enemy tempted Him and He was persecuted and beaten far more than we ever will be.

Since we know all that He went through while here on this earth, we should find comfort in His arms because He can identify with our heartaches, troubles and pain. Although there are people who are able to help us who have not gone through the same situations, it is always much better to be in the company of someone who knows exactly what we're going through because they have gone through it themselves. We find comfort in knowing that they made it through their suffering and can advise us based on experience.

So when we are being tested and tempted, we can look to the Lord. He will give guidance, strength and comfort because He knows all that we need and what it will take to overcome. We can trust in Him and His way because He is already on the other side of our difficulty. Have faith in His plan and process for victory.

Prayer for Today: Heavenly Father, I am thankful that I can look to You in times of temptation, tests and troubles. Thank You for lifting me when I need You to and showing me the way when I need Your guidance. In Jesus' name, Amen.

Additional Scripture reading: Hebrews 2 and Hebrews 4:14-16

Not Without You

Grow up in God

You have been believers so long now that you ought to be teaching others. Instead, you need someone to teach you again the basic things about God's word. You are like babies who need milk and cannot eat solid food. (Hebrews 5:12 NLT)

At some point in our spiritual walk, we must mature. We have to get to a place where we are teaching and encouraging others and not simply receiving the word of God. We remain spiritually immature, like babies, when we do not study and learn the word of God. In order to progress spiritually, it is an absolute must that we spend time in God's word. It is not and should not be optional. We must crave the word of God and His presence and be uneasy when we miss our time with Him.

Those who are spiritually immature don't know God's word and therefore cannot apply it to their lives. This is an issue when we've been believers for five, ten, fifteen years. We should not be in the same place today as we were five years ago. We should not be struggling with the same sins and issues. We must grow up to experience God like we were destined to do so.

We should regularly assess our spiritual progress. As the years continue on, we should never be in the same place as we were the year before. We have to take control of our progression by learning more and more about the Lord we serve each day. Our greatest desire should be to know more about Him.

Prayer for Today: Heavenly Father, thank You for the reminder to check myself. Help me not to become complacent in my relationship with You but to always seek to reach new levels. In Jesus' name, Amen.

Additional Scripture reading: Hebrews 5:11- 6:3

~Day of Reflection~

Fasting

Read: Isaiah 58

Meditate: Recall the last time you fasted: purpose and results. Did the fast bring about a change in you? Did you grow closer to God?

Apply: Before you begin your next fast, remember the type of fasting that the Lord requires and seek to please Him with your fasting.

Spiritually dull

Then you will not become spiritually dull and indifferent. Instead, you will follow the example of those who are going to inherit God's promises because of their faith and endurance. (Hebrews 6:10-12 NLT)

The Lord's greatest command is that we love Him and love others. When we do not love we become spiritually dull; we are useless because the foundation of our faith is love. We don't add any value to the kingdom of God or practice our faith when we don't love others.

Our lack of love for others hinders our relationship with God. We show our faith in God and our love for God by loving God's people. When we express love to others, our relationship with God is strengthened because of our obedience.

In order to walk in love, we must hold the characteristics of love dear to our heart. We must be patient, kind and unselfish. Our love has to be tangible; we can no longer simply pray for our brothers and sisters but must take action. Love moves us to action! We have to remember that we are God's vessels and we must allow His love to flow through us and to His people.

Prayer for Today: Heavenly Father, thank You for Your love that flows through me. Let me not hold it back but love others as you have called me to love. Let me always be reminded of Your love for me so that I may express that love to others. In Jesus' name, Amen.

Additional Scripture reading: Hebrews 6:4-12

Not Without You

Prepare your heart

And since we have a great High Priest who rules over God's house, let us go right into the presence of God with sincere hearts fully trusting him. For our guilty consciences have been sprinkled with Christ's blood to make us clean, and our bodies have been washed with pure water. (Hebrews 10:21-22 NLT)

As children of God, when we enter into His presence, we must do so with faith, pure hurts and clear minds. We have to remember that the Lord is holy and that he requires us to recognize Him as such. Whether it is entering into His presence by prayer or worship, we must first make sure that we have prepared ourselves.

How do we prepare? Clear our hearts and minds of everything that isn't pleasing to Him by becoming Christ-focused. We have to check bad attitudes, unclean hands, impure hearts and all manner of sin at the door. We should replace those things with that which pleases the Lord. The reality is that we want our praises and prayers to be pleasing and received by God; we don't want anything to get in the way of that, including ourselves.

We have been made righteous by the shedding of Christ's blood for our sins but there is a right way and a wrong way to enter into His presence. Remember that the Lord is holy and that you should always revere and respect His name.

Prayer for Today: Heavenly Father, You are so holy and perfect. Help me to be mindful of who You are and let me always honor Your name and Your presence. In Jesus' name, Amen.

Additional Scripture reading: Hebrews 10:19-25

Respect the Lord

Just think how much worse the punishment will be for those who have trampled on the Son of God, an d have treated the blood of the covenant, which made us holy, as if it were common and unholy, and have insulted and disdained the Holy Spirit who brings God's mercy to us. (Hebrews 10:29 NLT)

Accepting Christ as our savior means that we recognize and admit that we are sinners and that we seek and accept God's forgiveness of our sins. Once we accept Christ, we are not supposed to turn around and continue living life the same way before we received Him. When we live like we do not know God, by deliberately sinning, we are insulting Him. Christ died for our sins so when we continue in sin, it is as if we are nailing Him to the cross over and over again.

Non-Christians often don't respect Christianity because Christians don't respect Christianity. We continue to live how we want to live; neither do we stand up for what is right, yet we don't understand why nonbelievers don't want to become followers of Jesus Christ. When people don't see a change in us, they don't see the reason for needing God. We have to allow God to change us so that people can see the difference in the lives of those who serve God.

As you go throughout your day, choose to sin less and walk faithfully in the ways of our Lord.

Prayer for Today: Heavenly Father, thank You for Your holy word that changes, challenges and corrects me. Teach me to apply Your word to my daily life so that You may be glorified and so others may see Your work in me and draw closer to You. In Jesus' name, Amen.

Additional Scripture reading: Hebrews 10:26-39

Not Without You

Trust the Creator

The earth is the Lord's, and everything in it. The world and all its people belong to him. (Psalm 24:1 NLT)

So often in life, we put our trust in many different things. We worry constantly over our finances, our future, our relationships, our jobs, etc. During times of worry, we very seldom stop to think about our Creator. Just like He created us, He created everything else in this world.

Worrying does not and will not change anything. So today and any other day, when worry creeps up on you, began to pray. We must pray without ceasing. Talk to your Creator about your problem(s). Go to your quiet place. Pray. Listen. Pray. He will listen and answer you. Be diligent and steadfast in your prayers. Seek the Lord with all of your heart. Once you're finished praying, do not start to worry, instead Praise God! Praising God shifts your mind, thoughts and heart on Him and off your problem(s).

In good times and bad times, be careful not to neglect your Creator! Trust your life to the One Who Created You.

Prayer for Today: Heavenly Father, I am so thankful that all things belong to You. I don't have to worry about anything but put my trust in You because You are the Creator. I am grateful for Your sovereignty. In Jesus' name, Amen.

Additional Scripture reading: Psalm 24

Get up and write

Earlier, during the first year of King Belshazzar's reign in Babylon, Daniel had a dream and saw visions as he lay in his bed. He wrote down the dream, and this is what he saw. (Daniel 7:1 NLT)

I can appreciate what Daniel did when God gave him visions; he wrote them down. I believe that dreams are one of the ways that God speaks to us; this is how we receive many visions. When I was in grad school, whenever I would have a dream or any kind of thought while I lay in bed, I would get up and write it down. I think it's very important that we get up and write them down because if we don't, we'll lose them. How many times have you dreamed about something, knew it was important, woke up the next morning and could not remember it?

Writing the dream down will allow us to envision in the conscious state what God is trying to say to us. Sometimes the dreams may be very clear and we know exactly what God is saying. Other times, we need to pray about it more.

Even if you think (or know) you will remember it when you wake up, write it down anyway. Write it as a reminder to yourself of how God spoke to you and gave you insight. The next time you need God to speak to you, you will have a reminder that He has done it before and that He will do it again. (It may not be in the same way) He is faithful!

Prayer for Today: Heavenly Father, thank You for dreams and vision. Thank You for choosing me to carry out part of Your holy plan. I am excited about all that You are going to do and I ask that You continue to guide me along this journey. In Jesus' name, Amen.

Additional Scripture reading: Daniel 7

Faith is

Faith is the confidence that what we hope for will actually happen; it gives us assurance about things we cannot see. (Hebrews 11:1 NLT)

Our faith in God and His promises for us is what drives us to live in a way that pleases Him. Faith empowers us because it gives us something to look forward to even when it seems like things are hopeless. Faith is the foundation of our relationship with God because we can't see Him but we believe by faith that He exists and His promises are true.

Throughout this chapter, we read about the faith of God's people beginning with Abraham. Some of these people with great faith did not receive their promise; they died believing in the receipt of God's promises. Instead, their descendants received God's promises because of their faith.

We may not always receive what we believe God for in our timing but we should not allow that to lessen our faith. If you have been pleasing God with your life, believing for His promises and have yet to receive what you have been hoping for, don't give up. Hold on to His promises because they are true and the Lord rewards those who earnestly seek Him; it brings Him joy and strengthens us when we have unwavering faith.

Don't give up hope because without it, there is nothing left.

Prayer for Today: Heavenly Father, thank You for all of Your promises. Help me to remain faithful and confident in Your truths regardless of what I can see. I will remain confident in what I cannot see and believe that all things are working together for my good and Your glory. In Jesus' name, Amen.

Additional Scripture reading: Hebrews 11

Not Without You

~Day of Reflection~

Hunger

Read: Proverbs 16:26

Meditate: What do you hunger and thirst after?

Apply: Your desires motivate you to keep going. Write down your goals and a prayer asking God to keep you focused and encouraged.

Divine discipline

No discipline is enjoyable while it is happening - it's painful! But afterward there will be a peaceful harvest of right living for those who are trained in this way. (Hebrews 12:11 NLT)

Parents discipline their children to instill values in them, teach them right from wrong, and to help them develop good character. Children are disciplined when they disobey their parents and decide to do what they think is right or simply choose what is more pleasurable.

The Lord is our spiritual parent and will also discipline us when we choose a path different from the one He has predestined for us. Our disobedience warrants discipline. The Lord disciplines us because He loves us and wants the best for us - His will. Just as earthly parents discipline their children to get them back on track, so does the Lord.

We must remember that divine discipline is a consequence for our disobedience and must not allow it to discourage us. We should take it in stride and note that God loves us, is looking out for us and desires that discipline will put us back on the right path. Divine discipline is supposed to produce holy living.

When the Lord puts you in time-out, delays a treat or spiritually spanks you, remember that it is for your spiritual growth; allow it to redirect you to where you should be.

Prayer for Today: Heavenly Father, thank You for divine discipline. Help me to remember that it is for my spiritual development so that I can become who You want me to be. In Jesus' name, Amen.

Additional Scripture reading: Hebrews 12:1-13

Divided Loyalties

A double minded man is unstable in all his ways. (James 1:8 KJV)

Earlier in the scripture text, the word of God says if we need wisdom, God will give it to us if we ask Him. When we go before God in prayer, seeking wisdom and guidance, we must enter into His presence with unwavering faith. Prayer requires belief, patience and expectancy. We cannot go to God making requests and not believe that He has the ability or will to grant them.

When we pray, our faith must be in God alone, trusting that He hears us and will grant our request. The granting of wisdom by request is an explicit promise in this passage of scripture; so when we ask for it, we must be ready to receive and willing to apply wisdom in our particular situation. We have to choose God and the wisdom that He so generously gives.

We become double-minded when we waver between God's wisdom and worldly wisdom because they are not the same. Fixing our hearts and minds on the Lord's ways is what will sustain us. When we began to doubt and bounce back and forth between God and the world, we become double-minded not only in our spiritual life, but in all that we do.

Prayer for Today: Heavenly Father, thank You for the wisdom that You so richly give when I ask. Thank You for guiding me along the path that You have predestined for me. Guide my heart so that I may daily choose Your wisdom and Your way. In Jesus' name, Amen.

Additional Scripture reading: James 1:2-8

Listeners and Doers

But don't just listen to God's word. You must do what it says. Otherwise, you are only fooling yourselves. (James 1:22 NLT)

In order to develop a character and lifestyle that brings honor to God, we must allow His word to direct us. We have to decide to live according to His word but we cannot do this if we don't know what it says. So many of us attend weekly services but fail to live a life that is pleasing to God because we only listen to God's word. We don't retain it so we don't put it into practice.

We must get to a place in our relationship with God where we long for His presence, desire to please Him and choose His ways. Obedience and love are two of God's most important requirements for His children. We honor God when we obey His holy word. It is then that we will begin to experience the abundant life that He has promised His children.

Obedience yields blessings. The word of God tells us that God will bless us for doing what His word says. We often want the blessings of God but we don't want to abide by His word. This isn't the way things work and our disobedience is cause for many delayed blessings. As children of God, we must wholeheartedly devote ourselves to Him and choose to follow His word without exception. Choose to move from only listening to the word of God to learning and living it.

Prayer for Today: Heavenly Father, I give praise to Your holy name. Help me to receive, accept, learn and apply Your word to my life in all circumstances. Help me to show my love for You by being obedient. In Jesus' name, Amen.

Additional Scripture reading: James 1:19-27

Be merciful

There will be no mercy for those who have not shown mercy to others. But if you have been merciful, God will be merciful when he judges you. (James 2:13 NLT)

Just moments before sitting down to study God's word, I was slightly upset with my husband. He had just done something that often bothers me and honestly, I was thinking of ways that he should suffer for his mistake. As I flipped open my bible, I prayed and asked God to give me a message that I could carry with me today. I didn't want God to speak to me regarding my thoughts towards my husband; I was looking for something else. However, God is amazing. He knew that I needed to be checked for my current thought process and then I read today's scripture.

We all make mistakes so we should be willing to show others mercy just as the Lord shows us mercy. God shows us mercy when He does not give us what we deserve. He shows compassion for us and continues to give us chance after chance and I had to remember this when it came to my husband's mistake. I decided not to hold it against him; I chose to help him see why his behavior in that particular situation was an issue. Because of the conviction I felt after meditating on God's word, we avoided what could have been a very unpleasant circumstance.

As we strive to live in a way that pleases God, we have to remember to meditate on His word, choose His ways and extend to others the kind of love, forgiveness and compassion that He shows us. When we do this for others, God will do it for us.

Prayer for Today: Heavenly Father, thank You for Your Holy Spirit that knows my heart and just what I need from You. Let me be forever mindful of Your kindness towards me so that I won't be hesitant to show it to others. In Jesus' name, Amen.

Additional Scripture reading: James 2:1-13

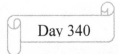

Not Without You

Faith in action

Just as the body is dead without breath, so also faith is dead without good works. (James 2:26 NLT)

We have to back up our faith with good deeds. It is not enough to believe in God; we have to show our belief in God by what we do for others. There are many opportunities to gift ourselves to others but we have to be willing and available to do so. We don't have to become a part of a great movement to be a blessing to someone else; we just need to give to those in need when it's in our power to do so.

People do not share their troubles with us so that we can only pray for them; we have to be moved to action. We may not be able to help in that moment but maybe we know someone who can or can direct them to resources. We have to remember that God works through believers and to fully live out our faith, we must allow Him to use us.

Believers are useless to the kingdom of God if they have no works to support their faith. Imagine what the world would be like if none of us were willing to be vessels for the Lord. It would be much worse than it is currently. Now imagine what the world would be like if all believers put their faith in action. It is then that we would be able to see so much more of God's power and what He can do through us. Let's purpose in our hearts to continuously combine our faith and good deeds; then watch God move!

Prayer for Today: Heavenly Father, thank You for the wisdom and strength that You have planted within me. I want to be an asset to Your kingdom. Help me to always put my faith in action to allow Your power to work through me. In Jesus' name, Amen.

Additional Scripture reading: James 2:14-26

Not Without You

A tongue that honors Him

In the same way, the tongue is a small thing that makes grand speeches. But a tiny spark can set a great forest on fire. (James 3:5 NLT)

A zipper. Steering wheel. Bit. Belt buckle. Shoe lace. Door knob. Toilet handle. What does each of these things have in common? They are all needed to make some larger object function properly. It is amazing how one small part can be so significant and cause so much trouble when not operating as it should.

Our tongues are small, yet significant, as well. When not properly trained or contained, our tongues will cause a lot of trouble for us and dishonor God. We bring shame to the Lord's name when we use profane language, gossip and say evil things about others. Speaking ill of others also ruins relationships. As children of God, we should desire to bring honor to the Lord's name; therefore, we have to be mindful of what we allow to come out of our mouths. The same mouth that we use to praise God is the same mouth we use to tear down others. We learn in today's scripture text that this should not be. God is not pleased.

In order to please God with our speech, we begin by doing two things: Choose to speak things that honor God and study God's word. We have to make a decision to glorify the Lord with our mouths. We also have to study God's word because what we allow into our hearts is what will come out of our mouths. We cannot expect to honor the Lord with what we speak if we don't fill ourselves with more of Him.

Prayer for Today: Heavenly Father, I praise You with all that's within me. Forgive me for the times I used my mouth to dishonor Your holy name. As I commit to pleasing you with my words, fill me with more of You. In Jesus' name, Amen.

Additional Scripture reading: James 3:1-12

~Day of Reflection~

Taming the tongue

Read: James 3

Meditate: Recall a specific moment when you allowed your words to hurt or tear down someone else. What was the outcome? What did you do to rectify the situation?

Apply: Identify situations that often cause you to say things that are not pleasing to God. Write down things that you can (and will) do to help you prepare for these situations in an effort to tame your tongue.

Not Without You

What do you want?

You want what you don't have, so you scheme and kill to get it. You are jealous of what others have, but you can't get it, so you fight and wage war to take it away from them. Yet you don't have what you want because you don't ask God for it. (James 4:2 NLT)

For some reason, things appear more desirable when we don't have them. Think *greener grass on the other side*. We often desire the relationships, careers, vehicles, salaries, homes, families and ministries of others when we haven't worked for them. Issues arise when we will do anything other than work in an attempt to obtain them. We allow jealousy to consume us and become obsessed with what our neighbors have, therefore giving the enemy room to come in and sew discord.

The word of God says that we don't have what we want because we do not ask God for it. When we do ask for it, our hearts aren't pure. We must commit our hearts and our ways to Him, and then God will give us the desires of our hearts because our desires will be in alignment with His will. They will not be self-serving.

We shouldn't desire stuff because someone else has it or simply because it will bring us pleasure; we should want what God has for us. If you desire something and have not received it, examine your heart. Think about why you want it. Is it because your neighbor has it? Do you want it because you have surrendered yourself to God, lived by His word and believed it to be His will? Are your motives pure? Will it honor God?

Prayer for Today: Heavenly Father, thank You for reminding me that I need to ask You for what I want. Help me to see my heart as You see it to determine if my motives are pure. I only desire Your will and the gifts that You desire to give me. In Jesus' name, Amen.

Additional Scripture reading: James 4:1-6

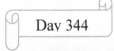

Day 344

Power prayers

The effectual fervent prayer of a righteous man availeth much. (James 5:16b KJV)

When the Scripture speaks of a righteous man, it does not mean a person who does no wrong. We all have sinned. The Scripture refers to a person who has a pure heart and does not hide sin in his heart. Consider Psalm 66:18 which states, *"If I had not confessed the sin in my heart, the Lord would not have listened."* When we go before God in prayer, or ask someone else to pray for us, it is important to have pure hearts and a clear mind.

When we seek God in prayer the right way, our prayers have the power to move God to act on our behalf. That's what we want –answered prayers. We pray because we desire God's healing, presence, wisdom, blessings, forgiveness, strength, guidance, deliverance, peace, mercy, grace, etc. Purity, honesty and faith yield results.

I encourage you to stop sending up prayers that do not get God's attention. Remember that He is holy and that there is a certain way to go before His throne of grace – with a pure heart and right spirit. Turn away from sin and choose the ways of the Lord; God honors the prayers of the righteous.

Prayer for Today: Heavenly Father, I honor You today. Forgive me for my sins and remove anything from me that hinders my prayers. Help me to be mindful of Your holiness. I want my prayers to have enough power to receive that which I seek from You. In Jesus' name, Amen.

Additional Scripture reading: James 5:13-18

Great expectation

All praise to God, the Father of our Lord Jesus Christ. It is by his great mercy that we have been born again, because God raised Jesus Christ from the dead. Now we live with great expectation. (1Peter 1:3 NLT)

God raising Jesus from the dead gives us hope. We have faith in the power of God because of this great work. We know that nothing is impossible with God and we can trust in His power. We can live with a spirit of expectancy because we know what God is capable of doing. Since He resurrected the dead, surely He can do great things in our lives as well.

Anticipate the move of God in your life. No matter what your struggles or concerns are today, remember that the Lord God is much greater in power. His grace and mercy are more than sufficient. He is able to do more than you can ever ask or think, just don't be afraid to trust in Him. Put your faith in Him and His character. Because of all that He has done before, you can rest assured that your anticipation of His move in your life will not be in vain.

Lean on God's unchanging hand. He is the same God today as He was when He raised Jesus from the dead. He can exercise the same power in your life but you have to trust and turn your life over to Him. Live a life filled with expectancy of all that He will and can do for and through you.

Prayer for Today: Heavenly Father, I choose to live in expectancy to see Your mighty power in my life. I know that You haven't changed and I walk in faith believing in Your authority. Let me not allow life's troubles to cause me to doubt You. In Jesus' name, Amen.

Additional Scripture reading: 1 Peter 1:3-5

Faith builders

So be truly glad. There is wonderful joy ahead, even though you have to endure many trials for a little while. (1Peter 1:6 NLT)

Experiencing troubles aren't always the result or consequence of us doing something wrong; troubles are a part of life. These trials come to test and strengthen our faith. The bible says that our faith is tested as fire tests and purifies gold. When fire purifies gold, the gold is more pure and refined than before. Likewise, our trials make us better than we were before we were tested.

Don't become discouraged by trials because they are an opportunity to show your faith. It is also a chance for you to learn more about your strengths and weaknesses. Weaknesses will continue to be tested until strengthened; strengths can be used to encourage others.

As you go throughout your day, remember that troubles come to reveal that your faith is genuine. Choose to learn from your trials and allow them to build up your faith. God will continue to allow trials to perfect your faith until He returns. All things really do work together for your good when you love the Lord and are called according to His purpose, so look at trials as *faith builders*.

Prayer for Today: Heavenly Father, thank You for the faith builders that come my way. Help me to see them as a chance to honor You and show what I truly believe. Sometimes my trials are really difficult but I trust that You will give me enough strength and wisdom to get through them. In Jesus' name, Amen.

Additional Scripture reading: 1 Peter 1:6-12

Don't slip

So you must live as God's obedient children. Don't slip back into your old ways of living to satisfy your own desires. You didn't know any better then. (1 Peter 1:14 NLT)

As children of God, we are called to live obedient and holy lives. We are supposed to abandon our old ways of living and live in a way that pleases God. We please God when we love one another and obey His holy word. The bible encourages us not to return to our old ways but the issue is that many of us never gave up our old ways.

It is impossible to please God and continue living in sin. We will not experience God like we should if we choose to only please Him on Sundays or special holidays. We have to become Christians who seek to please Him at all times; that means giving up our own desires because they are often in conflict with what God desires.

Keep in mind that God is holy and because He chose us, we must be holy as well (v. 15). Make the decision today to commit to living a life that is pleasing and acceptable to God. Because you know how God requires you to live, you are now held accountable for doing what is right.

Prayer for Today: Heavenly Father, thank You for Your word that reminds me of who You have called me to be in You. Help me not to return to my sinful ways but to stay committed to living a life that brings honor to You. In Jesus' name, Amen.

Additional Scripture reading: 1 Peter 1:13-25

Rejection and disobedience

They stumble because they do not obey God's word, and so they meet the fate that was planned for them. (1 Peter 2:8b NLT)

We reject God when we are not obedient to His word; when we are not obedient, we stumble. As long as we choose not to adhere to God's holy word, we will continue to stumble. We often make excuses and attempt to choose which Scriptures we want to obey but God is not pleased. If there were Scriptures that He didn't intend for us to abide by, His word would say so.

Being obedient to God's word is not always going to feel good or please our flesh but that is not the intent. We obey God to honor Him and live in a way that pleases Him. We are His creation, so we must do what we were created to do. We often want to be obedient when it is convenient for us or when we want God to answer our prayers. If we can choose to be obedient then, we can choose to follow Him at all times.

As you go through your day, remember that you are faced with a choice. Obedience is a decision. We know the results of disobedience and that is our fate when we choose it: pain. Today I encourage you to choose to show others the goodness of the Lord by living as an obedient child of God.

Prayer for Today: Heavenly Father, I praise You. I know the consequences of my sin so let me be reminded of that when I am faced with a choice to obey you or my selfish desires. I truly want to please You. In Jesus' name, Amen.

Additional Scripture reading: 1 Peter 2:4-12 and 1 Peter 4:1-11

~Day of Reflection~

Holy compliance

Read: 1 John 5:3-5; Matthew 7:21 and John 14:23

Meditate: What areas do you have difficulty obeying God? Why?

Apply: What will you do to change your heart and thoughts toward these areas? Write a prayer asking God to help you turn over these things to Him in order that you may strengthen your commitment to God's word.

Not Without You

Productive and useful

The more you grow like this, the more productive and useful you will be in your knowledge of our Lord Jesus Christ. (2 Peter 1:8 NLT)

We become assets to the kingdom of God when our faith is accompanied by love, knowledge and good works. It takes a mature Christian to put his faith in action and live in a way that pleases God. God has given many promises to those who live a godly life. In the preceding scriptures, we are told to respond to God's promises by:

- Being morally excellent
- Getting knowledge
- Having self-control
- Having patient endurance
- Being Godly
- Having affection for one another
- Loving everyone

First, we must uphold high ethical principles and be people of integrity, doing the right things at all times, even when no one is around. Then we must add knowledge of God to our moral excellence. We need to develop control over our thoughts and actions; by His divine power, God has given us everything we need to do this. We have the power of God at work within us. We must add to this strength and godliness, in that we must model the character of God. Last, but certainly not least, is love; one of the greatest commandments is to love one another. We must be intentional when it comes to loving one another and treating others the way God desires. When we have all of these things, including love, we are most useful to the kingdom of God; it is then that we become the vessels that God wants us to be, bringing glory to His name and growing in faith.

Prayer for Today: Heavenly Father, thank You for equipping me with Your divine power. Help me to remember that You have already given me all that I need to become more like You and live a life of purpose. I want to be useful to Your kingdom. In Jesus' name, Amen.

Additional Scripture reading: 2 Peter 1:3-11

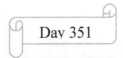

Day 351

Not Without You

Follow the instructions given to you

He cried out to the man of God from Judah, "This is what the Lord says: You have defied the word of the Lord and have disobeyed the command the Lord your God gave you. (1 Kings 13:21 NLT)

In 1 Kings 13, the Lord sent a man of God from Judah to Bethel to speak of the Lord's disapproval of Jeroboam and his policies. The Lord gave the man of God specific instructions of what to do while there – not to eat or drink. An old prophet approached him and requested that he come to eat and drink with him. At first, he obeyed God, telling the old prophet that he was instructed by God not to eat or drink in that place. However, he changed his mind after the old prophet announced that he was a prophet, and an angel gave him a command from the Lord to bring the man of God home to eat and drink. After hearing this, the man of God conceded and went with him to eat and drink (*exactly what the Lord instructed him not to do*).

After the man of God was given explicit instructions from God regarding what not to do in Bethel, he changed his mind and did those things just because someone else said they received a message from God regarding him. He seemed pretty sure of himself before but what was it that made him change his mind? Was it because of who the old prophet announced himself to be?

When you receive instructions from God to do or not do something, be careful not to waver because someone else (regardless of who they are) comes to you and tells you about some message that God gave to them for you. You're ultimately responsible for the decisions that you make especially when you've already been given specific instructions (when you know better). Seek the Lord for yourself by spending time learning His voice and His holy word.

Prayer for Today: Heavenly Father, thank You for Your holy word. Help me to hold fast to Your direction and discern when things are not of You. I know that if it doesn't align with Your word, it doesn't align with You. I trust in Your guidance. In Jesus' name, Amen.

Additional Scripture reading: 1 Kings 13

Cover-up

"When the period of mourning was over, David sent for her and brought her to the palace, and she became one of his wives. Then she gave birth to a son. But the Lord was displeased with what David had done." (2 Samuel 11:27 NLT)

2 Samuel 11 discusses David's sin of sleeping with and impregnating Bathsheba (another man's wife). David attempted to cover up his sin by sending for her husband (who was away at war) so that he could come home and sleep with her. When that didn't work, David arranged for his murder. In addition to that, he brought her into the palace and married her after her husband's death. (This was David's attempt to make it right)

Have you ever tried to cover up your sin by trying to make it right? Although many of us may not have done exactly what David did, we may have times in our lives where we tried to *fix* our wrong. The truth is that we cannot fix our sin. We must simply confess our sin and turn away from it. We cannot be deceived into thinking that we can fix our sin or that we won't reap the consequences of our actions.

Choose to give your sin to God. Allow Him to cleanse, forgive and make you whole. Don't attempt fixing things yourself because many times, you will make them worse. Confess it. Release it. Turn away from it. Move forward.

Prayer for Today: Heavenly Father, forgive me for the times I attempted to cover up my sin without repentance. Today, I choose to repent, accept Your forgiveness and live in a way that pleases You. In Jesus' name, Amen.

Additional Scripture reading: 2 Samuel 11

Not Without You

God will bring you back

But God does not just sweep life away; instead, he devises ways to bring us back when we have been separated from him. (2 Samuel 14:14b)

Sometimes we find ourselves in strange places, not knowing how we got there. When we make a series of wrong choices or choices outside of God's will for our lives, we will definitely end up in places we shouldn't be.

God's desire for us is to love Him and His people and walk according to the purpose that He has set before us. When we do not spend time in His presence praying and listening to Him or studying His Word, we end up "lost."

Even though we won't always do what God wants us to do when He wants us to do it, the great news is that within His wonderful plan for our lives, He has meticulously arranged for us to find our way back to Him. So every time something *bad* happens in your life, don't give credit to Satan. God could be using that situation to bring you back into His loving arms because He desires closeness with you.

Prayer for Today: Heavenly Father, thank You for loving me enough to bring me back to You. Thank You for being merciful and not giving up on me. In Jesus' name, Amen.

Additional Scripture reading: 2 Samuel 14

Getting dressed

Therefore put on the full armor of God, so that when the day of evil comes, you may be able to stand your ground, and after you have done everything, to stand. Stand firm then, with the belt of truth buckled around your waist, with the breastplate of righteousness in place, and with your feet fitted with the readiness that comes from the gospel of peace. In addition to all this, take up the shield of faith, with which you can extinguish all the flaming arrows of the evil one. Take the helmet of salvation and the sword of the Spirit, which is the word of God. (Ephesians 6:13-17 NIV)

My three year old daughter is absolutely obsessed by anything princess-related! Disney movies, dolls and dresses. In fact, she associates any type of dress with being a princess. Whenever I wear a dress, she questions me as to whether I'm a queen or princess. Whenever she wears a dress or a nightgown, she identifies herself as a princess. When she wears a dress, her attitude changes; she feels prettier and she acts differently, prancing around the house, twirling around in her dress. Even the phrase "getting dressed" is different to her. To her it means to *put on a dress* and not *put on clothes* as it does to the rest of us. See the obsession?

My question for you today is "what are you *wearing*?" Are you putting on the full armor of God? When you wear the full armor of God, is your attitude different? Do you feel strengthened? Are you more confident? You are an ambassador of Christ and what you "wear" should be representative of this fact. Take care not to neglect dressing your spirit man. What you're wearing spiritually is very important as it will impact your attitude and your entire day. So take care to dress like God's royal child by putting on the full armor of God each day.

Prayer for Today: Heavenly Father, thank You for the armor that You have provided for me. Let me not neglect *getting dressed* so that I may be able to stand firm in my faith. In Jesus' name, Amen.

Additional Scripture reading: Ephesians 6:10-20

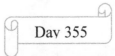

Day 355

Not Without You

No more bubbles

Blessed are those who find wisdom, those who gain understanding. (Proverbs 4:13 NIV)

My toddler loves bubble baths. Mommy does too! When I'm taking a bubble bath, I cannot get her out of the bathroom. She soaks up her clothes because she is too busy reaching over into my tub full of bubbles, attempting to blow them into my face. Once, we had a "bubble fight" and I blew bubbles into her eyes. I wiped the bubbles off with a dry towel and we continued to play. Apparently she enjoyed it because she started rubbing bubbles into her own eyes (*on purpose*)! I, of course, insisted that she stop but she would rub bubbles in her eyes and then say, "Ouch mommy, it's itching." She continued to do this many times until I sent her out of the room to do something else.

Most of her shenanigans cause me to say something to her that reminds me of how we are with God. In this particular instance, I thought about how we as Christians, continue to put *bubbles* in our eyes even when we know that it will cause some level of discomfort. We often know what the outcome will be when we do things like overeat (gluttony), procrastinate, lie, hold grudges, etc. but we continue to do them anyway. Why do we keep putting these *bubbles* in our eyes? Why do we continue to do things that will pull us away from God? Why do we not spend time reading our Bibles, studying or praying?

Whatever your answers are to those questions, I pray that you recognize them for what they are: excuses and ploys of the enemy to keep you from moving forward. As you go about your day, refuse to put *bubbles* in your eyes. Walk in wisdom and in the path that God has created for you.

Prayer for Today: Heavenly Father, thank You for Your faithfulness. Help me to use knowledge and wisdom not to continue doing things that I know are damaging to myself and my relationship with You. In Jesus' name, Amen.

Additional Scripture reading: Proverbs 4

~Day of Reflection~

A light for your path

Read: Psalm 119:105-112

Meditate: What issues have been troubling you lately? Have you searched God's word regarding them?

Apply: God desires that we seek Him in all things. The word of God should be the first place you turn in times of trouble. The word gives guidance and lights the way. Search the scriptures to see what the word of God says about your issues and be sure to do what God commands. Write the issue down. Write down what the scriptures say. Journal what happens after you begin to follow God.

Not Without You

The Lord requires more of you

He has shown you, O mortal, what is good. And what does the Lord require of you? To act justly and to love mercy and to walk humbly with your God. (Micah 6:8 NIV)

The Holy Spirit speaks to me a lot when I'm dealing with my children. I'm often reminded of how much more God loves me and is so much more patient with me when I'm not acting the way that I should.

If you have children, you know how most two-year olds are. Stubborn! There are many times when I try to get my child to do something and she really doesn't cooperate. One particular day, I think I may have been asking her to pick something up off the floor. She continued to be stubborn with her usual *no's* and *I did it already*. After ignoring my instructions, she asked for a snack and to watch Disney Jr. I reminded her: "You cannot continue to be disobedient and expect to get what you ask for all the time!" Immediately, it was as if I heard the Lord repeating those exact same words to me! However, He reminded me of His faithfulness and mercy to me even when I don't deserve it.

Oftentimes, we are not being the person whom God has called us to be, yet we continue to ask Him to bless us and do all of these things for us. Although God sometimes grants our requests when we haven't done what we're supposed to do, our scripture today reminds us of what God requires. God wants our obedience; so let's remember to check ourselves to make sure that we are doing all that God has called us to do. As you go about your day, seek to be obedient. Think about how faithful and kind the Lord is to you even when you do not deserve it.

Prayer for Today: Heavenly Father, thank You for Your faithfulness and kindness even when I am unfaithful. Teach me to act justly, love mercy and walk humbly. In Jesus' name, Amen.

Additional Scripture reading: Micah 6

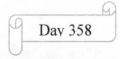

Day 358

Not Without You

How much longer will you waver?

Then Elijah stood in front of them and said, "How much longer will you waver, hobbling between two opinions? If the Lord is God, follow him! But if Baal is God, then follow him!" But the people were completely silent. (1 Kings 18:21 NLT)

There are obviously many different distractions the enemy uses to get us off course. However, it is up to us to remain steadfast and faithful to what God has called us to do and who He has called us to be.

In the text, Elijah was challenging the people of Israel to follow the Lord because at that time, many of them were following another god (Baal). If you continue reading throughout this chapter, you will note how the followers of Baal were doing all sorts of silly things to themselves to invoke a response from Baal to set fire to the altar. They shouted unto Baal from morning until noon and cut themselves with knives and swords until blood gushed out. Guess what? Nothing happened. Silence from Baal.

Elijah goes on to prove that the Lord is God, the only true and living God. He had them drench the altar with water, prayed to the Lord and the Lord set fire to the altar. This was done solely to prove that the Lord is God.

You may not be serving Baal but you may have some other thing(s) in your life that you elevate to the position of a little god. Dismiss it! You cannot serve it (them) and the Lord! James 1:8 reminds us that "a double minded man is unstable in all His ways." I challenge you today to choose the Lord, spend time getting to know His ways and live the life you have been destined to live.

Prayer for Today: Heavenly Father, thank You for all that You are in my life. I choose to serve only You. If there are things in my life that I have elevated to the position that only You should have, please show me that I may remove them. In Jesus' name, Amen.

Additional Scripture reading: 1 Kings 18:1-40

Not Without You

But with power

The Spirit of God, who raised Jesus from the dead, lives in you. And just as God raised Christ Jesus from the dead, he will give life to your mortal bodies by this same Spirit living within you. (Romans 8:11 NLT)

I have watched the movie, "*The Lion King*" at least 365 times. When my baby sister was about 2, she wanted to watch it every day and we did. Now that I am an adult with my own children, I have watched it a few times with them as well. "*The Lion King*" is a very powerful movie with quite a few life lessons in it.

As a young cub, Simba was excited to become king! In fact, he sang about it and talked about it quite a bit. It was his destiny. He was born to become the next king and he knew this. As life happened and he grew older, Simba lost sight of who he was and who he was destined to be. He started to live as though he had no purpose because of something terrible that happened and discouraged him.

When Simba's new found friends, Timon and Pumbaa eventually learned that Simba was supposed to be king, their attitudes changed. Pumbaa started graveling at Simba's feet and Timon said, "Wait, he's not the king! Are you?" Simba then commented that he was going to be but that was a long time ago. He told them that they didn't have to treat him differently because he was still the same person. Timon said, "Yes, but with *power*!" I love that part of the movie! It reminds me of us as God's children. When we accept Christ as our savior, we are still the same people but with the *power* of the Holy Spirit on the inside of us. Don't take this lightly; you were created for purpose. Do not allow past circumstances to discourage you. If you have, it is time to reclaim the power that you have been given by the Holy Spirit.

Prayer for Today: Heavenly Father, thank You for the power that You have given me through Your Holy Spirit. Help me not to lose sight of it and to always walk in Your strength and mighty power. In Jesus' name, Amen.

Additional Scripture reading: Romans 8

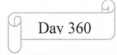

Day 360

All things

I can do all things through Christ who strengthens me. (Philippians 4:13 NKJV)

What dreams or visions have God placed in your heart? What have you done to prepare yourself? What have you done to see them come to pass? There are several truths about the dreams/visions that God gives to you:

- He chose you to see it to fruition.
- He has already equipped you to accomplish it.
- It is for His glory.
- He knows that you can do it.

What can you do to beat procrastination, fear and doubt? First, you must know that these are all tactics of the enemy. He seeks to kill, steal and destroy your spirit. He does not want you to live out God's will by doing what God has called you to do. He will do anything to stop you. Secondly, develop a written plan to hold yourself accountable and stay on track. Begin by setting goals and working on seeing your vision come to pass one step at a time. Sacrifice time in front of the television or some other time stealer to work on your goals.

Keep yourself motivated by not giving the enemy room to work. Remember that you are doing it for God's glory and you can do *all* of the things that you were destined to do. You can do all things through Christ because He is the one who gives you strength.

Prayer for Today: Heavenly Father, thank You for the visions that You've given me. Help me stay focused and commit to doing Your will. I desire to live a life that is pleasing to You. Order my steps and lead me in the paths of righteousness so that I may bring glory to Your name. In Jesus' name, Amen.

Additional Scripture reading: Philippians 4

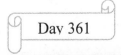
Day 361

The Money manager

She goes to inspect a field and buys it; with her earnings she plants a vineyard. (Proverbs 31:16 NLT)

Today's scripture reference tells us that the *Proverbs 31 Woman* is a woman who manages her finances well! She is an accountant, investor and entrepreneur wrapped into one! Verse 16 indicates that she researches a purchase before actually making that purchase. She doesn't buy things on a whim. She knows the status of her finances and does not put herself in a bind to make purchases (accountant- keeping track of her money). She makes sure that the purchase will be beneficial to her household. She reinvests her money so that she will get the most out of it (investor and entrepreneur).

This woman isn't lazy. She works hard and makes her money work for her. Verse 18 tells us that she makes sure that her dealings are profitable. (entrepreneur). She doesn't waste her time or money on things that won't add value to her or her household.

Her husband has entrusted her to manage the money; her family's wellbeing depends on the way she manages the finances. Therefore, she makes smart decisions when it comes to money. In the same way, I think we should be more mindful our spending. We don't have to spend our paychecks before we get them or buy something just because "*it's on sale.*" It is important that we learn to tithe, save and pay our bills first. We need to account for every dollar. We need to hold ourselves accountable to get ahead.

Take a serious look at your finances and the way you have managed your money. Create a financial plan and assess how well it works quarterly. For Proverbs 27:23 says that we should know the condition of our flock. Know the condition of your finances.

Prayer for Today: Heavenly Father, help me to manage the resources that You've given me. Thank You for Your blessings. In Jesus' name, Amen.

Additional Scripture reading: Proverbs 27:23 and Proverbs 31:16-18

Not Without You

An enriching wife

Her husband can trust her, and she will greatly enrich his life. She brings him good, not harm, all the days of her life. (Proverbs 31:11-12 NLT)

As women who seek to become all God has called us to be in every area of our lives, we must also seek to be the women God has called us to be for our husbands. We must be trustworthy and add value to his life. For a husband to trust in his wife, she must be honest and truthful. She must be naked before him –transparent – hiding nothing. I believe that when a husband knows that his wife is transparent, it produces trust because she has nothing to hide. We must add value to his life by contributing to the relationship and supporting him in prayer and deed.

As a *Proverbs 31 woman*, a wife must look for ways to be good to her husband. I believe that her relationship with the Lord will help manifest this scripture in her life. Sometimes, a wife has to look beyond her husband and remember the Lord and His love for her – remember God's faithfulness and sovereignty. Truthfully, no wife is going to want to be nice when she is upset or there's an unresolved issue. Face it; we're imperfect people who serve a perfect God. We become who God has called us to be in our marriages by doing everything as unto the Lord. It is then that a *wife does her husband good and not harm* all the days of her life.

Prayer for Today: Heavenly Father, thank You for reminding me that even in my marriage, if I work to please You, I will enrich my husband's life. Help me to be mindful that I should do all things as unto You. In Jesus' name, Amen.

Additional Scripture reading: Proverbs 31:10-12 and Ephesians 5:21-33

Not Without You

The Potter and the clay

"O Israel, can I not do to you as this potter has done to his clay? As the clay is in the potter's hand, so are you in my hand." (Jeremiah 18:6 NLT)

Our lives are in God's hands. As a potter does to clay, the Lord does with us. He uses different situations to mold and shape us into who He desires us to be. Oftentimes, we don't look for, neither do we learn the lesson that God is trying to teach us through our circumstances. When we fail to take heed to the message the Lord is sending, the Lord starts the molding process all over again.

Through His molding and shaping, God wants us to become valuable and useful to the Kingdom of God. When we don't turn out as we should, the Lord allows things to happen in our lives to reshape us into His image. This is a continuous process. The Lord will continue starting over until we become the fruitful and willing vessels that we were destined to be. Therefore, do not become discouraged by constantly being in the Potter's hands; the Lord is shaping you for spiritual success.

Prayer for Today: Heavenly Father, thank You for loving me enough to spend time reshaping me into Your image. Give me wisdom so that I may understand what You're teaching me during my time of reshaping. Thank You for all that You're doing in my life to help me become more like You. In Jesus' name, Amen.

Additional Scripture reading: Jeremiah 18:1-10; Isaiah 64:8; Romans 9:21

~Day of Reflection~

Make me over

Read: Jeremiah 18:6

Meditate: Think of an area in your life that God needs to make over so that you will look more like Him.

Apply: Commit this are to God for the next 365 days. Write a prayer and a plan in an effort to become more like God in this area. Journal your progress.

Acknowledgments

To my Lord and Savior, Jesus Christ, for choosing me to be His vessel. Thank you for loving me beyond measure and choosing me for such a task. May this book bring your name glory.

My loving and supportive husband, Eddie R. Frazier, Jr. I wouldn't be able to do this if you weren't such a great partner. I love you.

My babies, Eden and Ethan. Mommy loves the two of you so very much. At the time of this update, Emilyn has been added to our family. Mommy loves you equally as much!

My mom, dad, stepdad and sisters. Thank you for your support throughout everything that I seek to accomplish. Your love and support mean everything to me.

My *amazing* circle of friends. I always thank God for placing you all in my life. Thank you for loving me just as I am. I am certain that I could not ask for a better set of friends. I love each of you so much.

My Living Word Fellowship, Higher Dimension Church Family and every supporter of *The Life Your Spirit Craves,* thank you for the encouragement.

Afterword

I pray that this past year has been one of the most amazing years of your life as you took time to be intentional about seeking God. I hope that you will hold on to all the lessons you've learned throughout the year and continue to strive to be all that God has created you to be. Remember that your spiritual journey doesn't end here; it lasts a lifetime. Continue to grow and seek God in all things. Spend the next 365 days strengthening your relationship with God and those you love. May the Lord bless you beyond measure and continue to shine His light through you. Choose to be a willing vessel for God and extend to others the same love and mercy that He extends to you.

About the Author

Natasha was raised in Greenville, MS where she was spiritually nurtured under the leadership of Pastor Larry Benford, The Living Word Fellowship Church. Natasha currently resides in the Houston Metro area with her husband and children. Her family attends Parkway Fellowship Church under the leadership of Pastor Mike McGown. At Parkway Fellowship, Natasha serves as a small group leader for elementary children.

For more information about the author, please visit

www.natashafrazier.com.